New Theology No. 2

New Theology No. 2

Edited by

Martin E. Marty
and Dean G. Peerman

The Macmillan Company, New York
Collier-Macmillan Limited, London

Second Printing 1966

Library of Congress catalog card no: 64-3132
The Macmillan Company, New York
Collier-Macmillan Canada, Ltd., Toronto, Ontario
Printed in the United States of America

Contents

Introduction   7

I: THE PROBLEM OF GOD AND THE GODLESS

Christianity Without Religion   17
    C. B. Armstrong

The Theology of True Secularity   28
    William O. Fennell

A New Linguistic Madness   39
    Langdon B. Gilkey

"Non-metaphysical" Christian Philosophy
and Linguistic Philosophy   50
    James W. Woelfel

Whither the Doctrine of God Now?   62
    David Jenkins

II: NATURE AND LAW

Naturalism, Historicism, and Christian Ethics:
Toward a Christian Doctrine of Natural Law   77
    Douglas Sturm

Autonomy and Reason in Judaism   97
    Alexander Carlebach

The Natural Law Teaching of the
Eastern Orthodox Church   122
    Stanley S. Harakas

Teilhard de Chardin: A Philosophy of
Procession   134
    E. R. Baltazar

III: THE CHURCHES IN RELATION

Judaism and Christianity: Then and Now   153
Krister Stendahl

The Significance of the Ecumenical Councils   165
William Nicholls

Ecclesiology and Roman Catholic Renewal   183
George A. Lindbeck

IV: BIBLICAL TRENDS

A Survey of Recent Gospel Research   201
Harvey K. Mc Arthur

Rudolf Bultmann and Post-Bultmann
Tendencies   222
P. Joseph Cahill, S.J.

V: EXTENSION OF THEOLOGY

A New Trio Arises in Europe   257
John B. Cobb, Jr.

The Form of the Church in the
Modern Diaspora   264
M. Richard Shaull

Through Dooms of Love   288
William Stringfellow

Christ and the Christ Figure
in American Fiction   297
Robert Detweiler

New Theology No. 2

New Theology No. 2 is a self-contained book. After this paragraph no further reference will be made to its predecessor. The numeral in the title reminds us, however, that there *was* a predecessor—a small green paperback which brought together fifteen articles we felt to be representative of the variety and richness of recent theological thought. Our introduction to it ended: "*New Theology No. 1*: the numeral is also part of the title. Time will tell whether there will be succeeding installments. . . . In the bewildering variety that is represented in the modern academy and the modern church, theologians go about their task. And we, for two, are curious about what is new in their achievements."

Time has told and a succeeding installment is here. We are not alone in our curiosity about new achievements in theology, nor have we been disappointed in our search for significant articles published during the past year and a half.

I

In recent decades professional theologians have often been accused of not wanting to talk about what everyone else wanted to talk about. Not only did they seem to remove themselves from the concrete concerns of the man on the street who—or so they believed—seldom thought theologically; they also avoided confrontation with those few topics which came up when people *did* think theologically. On any campus, in any parish, at any laymen's gathering, and even in many a seminary classroom, basic questions like these would recur: What is faith? Is there a God? How do we relate the manifest evil of the world to a God who purportedly is good? If God exists, why does he hide? With a whole cluster of similar questions these represent, in the average person's mind, "the problem of God."

Though supposedly in the business of talking about God, the theologians, rather than illuminating the "God problem," tended to evade it, to miss opportunities, to content themselves with talk about theological method or with refinement of side issues. Happily, however, the situation has changed—as those who have looked into theological journals in recent months can testify. Today more and more theologians are returning to the problem of God or, to be more precise, to the problem of the godless man. Anyone indexing recent theological literature is sure to be impressed by the sudden and dramatic return of this question to the tables of contents of the more influential journals.

Renewed interest in the doctrine of God has come not so much from those who are ever about to correct any imbalance in doctrine as from those who feel constrained to address themselves to a new and widespread experiential understanding. From common observation, from contact with modern philosophy, but most of all from "post-modern" literature and theater, we have come to recognize a new kind of godless man. Atheistic existentialism in literature has often sided with positivistic philosophies which by intention rule out "God-talk." And students of culture have observed a "practical atheism" which makes it difficult to determine from people's actions whether or not they believe God exists.

Once again the nineteenth century proclamations about the death or silence of God are being voiced—and are meeting with wide if less impassioned acceptance. In the universities some Christians have been talking in terms of "doing theology in the absence of God." To the outsider this sounds like non-sense—and it may turn out to be just that. But such talk constitutes an honest attempt to deal with the age-old problem of God in a new and alien cultural setting. We shall not here detail the controversy which rages in theological circles between the "God-talk" and the "non-God-talk" thinkers. The articles of Part I of the anthology speak for themselves.

Presenting a concise summary of recent discussions based on the controversy is C. B. Armstrong, who takes issue with the more radical of recent antireligious statements by religionists, e.g., those of Anglican Bishop John A. T. Robinson in his brief but celebrated book *Honest to God*. William O. Fennell's article is typical of many which see opportunities for specifically Christian witness in a world no longer cluttered with mere "religion," in a secular world where Jesus Christ is at home. Perhaps the book that has provoked most theological debate during this time is Paul van Buren's *The Secular Meaning of the Gospel*. None of van Buren's readers has been neutral. Some see in his effort to verify Christian language by means of philosophical tools a genuine purification and liberation; others view it as "Christological atheism." In this volume's sole book review Langdon B. Gilkey pays his compliments to van Buren but takes a decisive stand against him. James W. Woelfel carries matters much further, contending that, despite the difficulties, Christians must adhere to some sort of "metaphysical" and religious background in their theologizing—or in their believing! Finally, Daniel Jenkins in cogent language brings us up to date on the question of the doctrine of God and lays groundwork for a "Post-Copernican Natural Theology"—which brings us to Part Two, "Nature and Law."

II

No event inside the churches has been more discussed in recent decades than the ecumenical movement, and one of the most significant consequences of that movement is the fact that writers in different fields of religious thought have begun to work together or to occupy themselves with common subjects. Occasionally such a subject will be chosen by a committee or a foundation. More often, contemporary events or an inherent logic in theology itself presses a question onto the mind of the churches and their thinkers. This is true of the topic dealt with in the essays of Part Two: nature, the natural, and law.

After being neglected for almost a half-century, the question of whether some sort of natural law integral to the universe and resident in the heart of men might be related to the divine revelation of law and grace has suddenly come to the fore once again. This century's theological revival began with

a vigorous rejection of the idea of natural law, or at least of
the idea of a simple connection between it and revelation.
When Swiss theologian Emil Brunner made much of such a
point of contact his colleague Karl Barth responded in a pamphlet whose title, to say the least, gave away the plot. "Nein"
he thundered, and his "No" was picked up in Europe and
America, not because men were intimidated but because they
agreed.

Of what use was a natural law if men argued constantly
about its contents? How could one locate it with confidence?
Who were its custodians? Was it not too malleable, too adapt-
able, too manipulatable? If natural law is uniform, why did
some but not all Christians claim that "artificial" birth control
is contrary to it? Why do natural law theories appear in the
Stoics, then in medieval Catholicism, and again in certain
forms of the Enlightenment? How have men managed to get
along between these episodes? Why does the Bible not have
more and clearer references to it? Such questions suggest a
number of reasons why theologians have often been skeptical
of the entire concept of natural law.

Karl T. Schmidt's work titled *Rediscovering the Natural in
Protestant Theology* typifies the renewed concern with natural
law now being manifested in the theological tradition hitherto
most skeptical of it. There are many possible answers to questions such as those posed above, and one should not expect an
unambiguous assent to the validity of the category of "the
natural" from Protestants and others who have been uneasy
with it. However, our duty is to be conscientious reporters of
tendencies. In perusing more than 200 theological journals
we were impressed by the frequency with which articles
devoted to "the natural" appeared.

The new interest in natural law can be accounted for on
several grounds. The "revelationists" may have been over-
emphatic and strident; a natural reaction sets in as with the
swing of a pendulum. But scholars are not likely to devote
time and energy to an idea without believing in its validity
and without being prepared to defend the substance of their
findings. Christian scholars have been motivated to look for
ways of speaking about the natural in a time when the church
is seeking to relate to a secular world. They seek positive re-

lations, and they do not find a bridge in the gospel of Jesus Christ because it is by nature unique, distinctive, particular. In the history of thought, however, law and natural law have provided bridges. Also, Christians are seeking positive relations with other religions in our crowded and interdependent world, but in such a way that their own treasure will not be dissipated. Here again, common inquiry about law and nature seems the most likely bridge.

Discussion of ethics has intensified during the past eighteen months. Countless articles on the "new morality" have appeared. Many people in the Western world are impatient with injunctions stemming from the Christian revelation. Yet they are in search of moral sanctions and patently want to be "good." How do Christians speak intelligibly to such people? Is there any validity in the idea of a meaningful bond between nature and law? Topics such as the Roman Catholic teaching on nature and birth control have become matters of worldwide debate, even in political arenas. The subject of nature and law is being re-explored for practical reasons.

The four articles of Part Two constitute an ecumenical discussion of the subject. Douglas Sturm delineates the current debate on natural law within Protestantism. An Irish rabbi, the only Jewish representative in this book largely devoted to Christian theology, discusses the problem of divine law and human law. While he uses categories associated with the work of the Protestant theologian Paul Tillich, his historical treatment is distinctively Jewish. The Greek Orthodox article is chiefly a historical survey. The Roman Catholic article may seem to depart slightly from the broader topic because it deals with the "process" thought of Teilhard de Chardin (by far the most discussed Catholic thinker in the periodicals we surveyed). Actually the article is very much *a propos*: it suggests that Teilhard and the Bible in their subjective approach offer more hope today for a "natural" category than does the traditional Aristotelian objective approach.

III

Parallel to the ecumenical movement within Christendom, an interest in improved Jewish-Christian relations has arisen. Krister Stendahl of Harvard University starts off the "Church in Relation" section with an argument for Jewish-Christian dialogue based on what is particular in each, rather than on superficial adherence to an already existent Judeo-Christian tradition.

The religious event most widely publicized during this period was the Second Vatican Council of the Roman Catholic Church. Though theologians and their journals are slower paced than newspapers, a number of essays reflecting on that event have already appeared. The Vatican Council has occasioned interest in earlier ecumenical councils; William Nicholls argues for a recovered interest in their deposit and legacy. George A. Lindbeck, a Lutheran observer at Vatican II, eschews ordinary reportage to reflect on the possible permanent meanings of the council for a Catholic doctrine of the church.

IV

No extensive rationale for articles on the Bible and on biblical scholarship is necessary. Christian theology does not go far or rise high without reference to its source and norm in sacred scripture. The biblical renewal has benefited from and contributed to the ecumenical awakening; authentic exchange is taking place between Protestant and Roman Catholic biblical scholars. A Protestant scholar here surveys five basic issues in Gospel research; a Roman Catholic biblical theologian provides a valuable résumé of work done in the tradition of the century's most noted biblical scholar, Rudolf Bultmann. Father Cahill's article is more heavily footnoted than are most in our choices for *New Theology*; we excuse the typographical barrier to our readers with the explanation that the bibliographical references are of considerable utility.

V

The final section is the most varied. First comes a short introduction to three rising German thinkers, written by an American. Next is an analysis by Richard Schaull of forms of church life; it is representative of present-day theologians' concern with history, sociology, and daily life in relation to the church's mission. The remaining two articles might be termed "extensions of theology." William Stringfellow, who has been at the center of the religious involvement in the racial revolution, provides a passionate discussion of the meaning of the cross and of suffering in relation to that revolution. Another layman, Robert Detweiler, is one of the growing number of Christians who see theological significance in modern literature. He also focuses on the figure and meaning of Jesus Christ. Neither Stringfellow nor Detweiler writes formal theology, yet both provide salient examples of how theology can be relevant to other realms of action and thought.

Men talk of God and grace, of nature and law, of Christ and church. "Doing theology" is difficult in the best of times and under the best of circumstances. It is most difficult in times when theology has been relegated to the edge of university disciplines and when even Christians have trouble speaking of a present and living God. A sign of his presence might be the creativity and courage of the many men and women who seem not to be daunted by the difficulty but who are producing theology of originality and freshness.

We thank the various authors and editors for permitting their materials to be reprinted.

The addresses of the journals from which the essays were taken have been provided in each instance; we heartily commend these journals to those readers of this book who wish to pursue further their taste for "new theology."

M.E.M. and D.G.P.

I

The Problem of God
and the Godless

Christianity Without Religion

C. B. Armstrong

A paperback book with the catchy title *Honest to God* has
been the most discussed—as well as best selling—theological
work in English in the past several years. Its author, Anglican
Bishop John A. T. Robinson, synthesized the positions of Paul
Tillich, Rudolf Bultmann and Dietrich Bonhoeffer to develop
a view of Christianity which is not dependent upon "religion." The bishop's somewhat dramatic and unconventional
use of the word "religion" implies man's religious sense, his
conscience, his piety, his reliance on a specific metaphysic.
Robinson's book was one of many evidences that Christian
theologians often wish to leave behind man's religiousness and
to proclaim a Christianity that will be a viable option in a
secular world. Canon C. B. Armstrong, Principal of Worcester
Ordination College in England, provides a summary of the
argument and states his own position over against it. His article is taken from the April-June 1964 issue of *The Church
Quarterly Review*.*

        CHRISTIANITY WITHOUT Religion is not a move-
ment. It is a catch-phrase which sums up a number of floating
ideas: these crystallized themselves in the mind of Bonhoeffer,
found theological confirmation in Tillich, and were popular-
ized by *Honest to God*. The basic idea is that humanity is
passing out of the religious stage of development, in which
God is conceived as a transcendent Person and his dealings
with mankind are mythologically represented in the official
salvation-scheme of the Christian religion and worship, and is
evolving into a post-religious phase in which God is recognized to be the supreme spiritual reality, and his dealings (if
we can say "his") with mankind are by motions from within
and inspirations from without, mainly from the life which was

---

* Holy Trinity Church, Marylebone Road, London N.W. 1.

manifested to the world in Christ. This wider view is thought to transcend the distinction of sacred and secular, and to remove the barrier between the Church and the World, as St. Paul removed that between Jew and Gentile.

This basic idea has been recurrent, to varying degrees, in previous religious thinking. The Gnostics saw God as the supreme and unknowable and beyond, and saw Jesus as his emissary to the darkened world. Those illuminated by the knowledge which he imparted during his temporary or phantasmal sojourn here, were the pneumatici or spiritual, who really understood the divine economy, as contrasted with ordinary believers, the psychici, or one might say the merely religious. The parallel with the pneumatici of to-day is very close—public and traditional religion is a second-best. In the Nag-Hammadi MS. known as the Gospel of Truth and ascribed with probability to Valentinus, we find the process of conversion or awakening described as a return from an alienated existence to our true ontological condition, to the deep, total, and permanent reality of our ego; from the domain of the cosmos, the temporal and phenomenal world to the aeon, the eternal and non-temporal. (Cf. Prof. H. C. Puech in Cross's *Jung Codex*, p. 33.) No existentialist could have put it better.

Montanism took up the theme, namely an attempt to revert to primitive fervour in the face of a growing institutionalism and secularization of the Church. Harnack regarded the metaphysical aspects of Christian theology as an intrusion from Greek sources and stressed the moral side of Christianity, *especially the claims of human brotherhood*, to the exclusion of doctrine—a tendency noticeable in *Honest to God*. In the Mystics generally, especially perhaps Eckhart and Suso, we find a similar depreciation of, or transcendence of, conventional religion. Mysticism may be Christian but it is not necessarily religious. In W. T. Stace's careful study *Mysticism and Philosophy* we find a conclusion that mysticism cannot be considered essentially as a religious phenomenon: but that "if religion is taken as referring to feeling rather than to a creed" there is no reason why mystical experience should not occur without beliefs, as a sense of what is noble, transcendent, and peace-bringing. Christianity without religion is far from a mystical attitude, but its conception of God brings such theology as it has into a mystical or pantheistic category.

The movement in its emphasis on the post-religious age finds its prototype and some similarity of ideas in Auguste Comte. Comte was also overwhelmingly impressed by the scientific humanism of his day; his reaction was to find in it a new *religion of humanity*. He, however, also felt that the religious phase of human development was a back number. But he put the transition from the theocratic phase of human history, expressed in religions, much further back: it died, he thought, when the metaphysics of the Greek philosophers took over: then the bankruptcy of the great system-makers was succeeded by the positive stage, in which the sciences, crowned by sociology, became dominant. Comte ended by founding a religion of humanity in which the worship of a Great Being is linked with veneration of human benefactors, and the dominant spirit is to be love, without any religious beliefs or institutions. Another close parallel.

The reaction against orthodox beliefs and religious practices received an immense impulse from Kierkegaard. His polemic against orthodox Christianity as he knew it is a polemic against religion as in our phrase "Christianity without religion." But religion for him is *worldly* institutionalism, and his attack is not against genuine religious practice. The distinction between Christianity and religion really began later with the progeny of Kierkegaard, the existentialists, and it began because, to existentialism, intellectual reasoning and institutional society are modes of escape from the vital realities with which the individual soul is faced. Hence doctrine and ecclesiasticism are suspect as evasions of the solemnity of the Confrontation of the souls with the Thou of the Living God.

The attack on institutional religion has developed from many different directions. From the linguistic philosophers of the twentieth century a twofold assault has stemmed. In the first place they have raised profound doubts as to the possibility of any large-scale metaphysical system such as that of Hegel. Hegel himself had contributed to a depreciation of theology by his views that philosophy alone could understand absolute truths which were mediated to those who could not be philosophers in the myths and symbols of religious dogmata. St Thomas Aquinas had himself spoken of *revelation* similarly as given by God in mercy because of the *debilitas rationis* of the multitude. Hegel patronized religion as the best *popular* adumbration of philosophical truths.

But to logical analysis Hegel himself falls a victim because the terms on which his system-making is based are abstract, unverifiable, and even meaningless. The attack of analysts on system-making carried with it a depreciation of any theological schema: and in the second place verbal analysis raised profound doubts as to the meaningfulness of theological words and statements. Belief in the immortality of the soul, for example, might evaporate under analysis of the precise meaning of immortality and soul, and on the possibility of verification.

Historical criticism of the Bible has staged a different assault on religious beliefs, not only because of historical obscurity, but also because of the difficulty raised by form-criticism of ascertaining how much of the kerygma was due to the first missionaries and how much to their Lord.

The linguistic criticism too has been reinforced from a popular angle by the changes in our own language, and by a demand for formularies of worship expressed in language which can be understood by all the worshippers. Our services are said to be out of touch with the needs and thought of modern man. And upheavals in popular ethical ideas under many influences, such as psychology, the Welfare State, the submergence of the individual, and the *dysteleology of suspense* have caused impatience at the restrictions and supposed narrow severity of Christian ethics. There is a popular wish to throw off the shackles.

But existential thinking is at the real root of Christianity without Religion. The most powerful theologian of our day, Karl Barth, has forced upon us the human situation in face of the word of Almighty God—the impotence of our reasoning, the continual crisis of God's judgement on the Church, on human conduct, and on theologies. The essentials to him are *faith, hearing, and obeying*, and virtually all else is irrelevant. We have no real knowledge of God except what he condescends to give; our ideas of him by analogy and so on are mere projections of our wishes. God is the unknown, the wholly Other; but God speaks.

Clearly this criticism calls religion into question at every point, but it does not discredit religion as in part revealed by God's word, and as a means of its conveyance in proclamation. Brunner, emphasizing the absolute difference between revealed Christianity and other religions, says that if we call them religions we must not call Christianity a religion at all. It is qualitatively different. It is a radio-receiver for the Word.

Barth himself is not an existentialist, but Bultmann is. An extreme critic of the New Testament, the apostle of demythologization, he compensates for the beliefs which he has lost intellectually, by an existential religion of the inner life which sees, for example, salvation as effected, not by the cosmic atonement of the historic Cross but at the moment when the salvation word, given by God through Christ and Cross and Resurrection, impinges on the individual consciousness. History is precisely existential: it is what past events mean to me personally now; for example, the religious observance of obscure saints' days like St Evurtius is virtually meaningless if their memory is not alive and active as is that of St Francis. What is vital from the past is gathered into the existential consciousness of the present: the rest is dead. The Cross and Resurrection are said to be outside the obscurity of history.

Nygren's idea of motif-research, and his finding the fundamental motif of Christianity in *agape* has also been a factor in the new presentation of Christianity; but the main impulse to Christianity without Religion has come from Bonhoeffer and Tillich, as is abundantly evident in *Honest to God*.

Bonhoeffer died before his thought had fully developed, and some of his most pregnant work was conceived in a Nazi prison. His main ideas are: a protest against what he calls "cheap grace" as purveyed by institutional religions of doctrines, rites, and institutions, and for "costly grace" by which Christ remakes the natural manhood into the new man; costly not only by what it cost him, but by its demands of genuine discipleship. The achievement of this, by the working in us of the form of Christ, is the ultimate stage: but here and now we are in the penultimate stage, when we are concerned with and involved in day to day living. Life, as we find it, must be lived in its natural fullness without flight into religiosity, so often escapist. God and our new manhood must be the conscious background of all thought and action, and a life thus lived in sight of the ultimate *will not shrink from full involvement in the penultimate*. The world has come of age, and dispenses with God as a *deus ex machina*, a God when we need him, or theologically a God in the gaps of our knowledge; he is utterly transcendent, but, in Christ, grasps men in the centre of their lives and pervades their living in all aspects. We must communicate our faith in a non-religious way, primarily by living for others. So also in ethics, we cast away the moralization of all life and cease to be dominated by ought and must as though "every human action had a clearly lettered notice attached to it by some divine police authority, a notice which reads either 'permitted' or 'forbidden'." Man need not be continually doing something decisive. This turns the moralist into a dangerous tormentor and tyrant. Ethical decisions are rare, but always concrete and particular. They imply a subordination of the lower to the higher authority in a definite sociological case, "a concrete relation between the giver and receiver of a command." Ultimately they depend on the commandment of God, interpreted as the total claim to man laid by God in Jesus Christ. Either God does not speak at all, or he speaks as definitely as he spoke to Abraham, Jacob, and Moses, and as he speaks in our Lord. It comes to us in the Church, in the family, in labour, and in government: always, however, in concrete personal situations.

Bultmann had discarded the factual and historical revelation in favour of the kerygma, by demythologization. Buri now criticizes him for calling a halt at the kerygma, and advocates a *dekerygmatization* of the Christian message. There is no special act of God. Grace and revelation are *given with existence itself*. Theology becomes merged in philosophy, the only difference being that theology works within the symbolical and mythological framework of Christianity which has the deepest of the great redeemer myths.

Finally Tillich searches for an ontological basis of our faith which must be based on ultimate reality. His test is objectivity. Nothing that is ultimate can be object to our thought. Hence we must discard our objective ideas of God, Heaven, and so on, and *participate in reality rather than think of religious objects*. God is Being itself, and to be sought by *existential consciousness of Being* rather than by theological search for a supreme Object of our worship. To say that God is Being is the only statement which we can make about him. All else is symbolical.

There is here a curious reminiscence of an early Greek philosopher Parmenides who believed the only possible true statement is that, "Being Is": he then realized that life in the world needs a little more than this, and propounded a natural philosophy with the caution that it was all illusory and phenomenal. Tillich is content to accept the mythological language of Christianity as adumbrating ontological relations. So Jesus sacrifices himself on the Cross to become the Christ, the new Being. And the new Being is the power beyond man that heals his existential conflicts and sin. Man is ontologically awakened to God, and no longer estranged from his true unitive self.

The popularization of all this speculation and all these existential insights in *Honest to God* involves a simplification which has startled those who have not been familiar with what theologians have been discussing for some time. The work is impressive because of its sincerity, and it is obviously written by a scholar who has read widely. The theme is, briefly, that the world has become too adult for belief in the conventional theology of the past. The conception of God as a transcendent person "out there" who somehow "has" a world in which he intervenes from time to time as *deus ex machina* to put things right, is, he believes, now intolerable. The God hypothesis, on lines like this, has been crowded out because it is constantly becoming less needed: and the Christian stories are creations of their age and only tenable symbolically. But the consequent inference of Julian Huxley, atheism, is negative, equally unproven, and untrue to the needs and aspirations of humanity.

Bishop Robinson has recourse to a distinction long familiar to philosophers between existence and reality. God is the ultimately real, ground of all being, but does not exist because to exist is to be finite in space and time, to be a part of the universe even though far away outside. There is nothing very alarming in this, except that it startles simple Christians. We are not all so simple as to believe that God is "out there" or so conceited as to think that he is "in here."

The author then goes on to inquire in what ways we are affected by the ultimately real and how he is to be conceived. Here the Existentialists and Tillich come to his aid. At the deepest level of conscious life there is the supreme personal power of love, self-giving love. Christ is the Word of God because his whole life and death was self-giving love; we see God in him by the pure transparence of a manhood immersed in ultimate reality. He is the new man eternally, and in him new manhood can be ours. The Copernican revolution which Christianity now needs in the light of the new adulthood of the world is a turning away from childish mythical belief, from the stories in which Christianity has been expressed, to the reality beneath all true life. This involves seeing all life as encounter with God, realizing all our relations as "in Christ," abolishing a distinction between sacred and secular, between withdrawal and involvement, between prayer and action, because the opposition is transcended in a synthesis, by *all life* becoming *capax dei*, permeable by the ultimate reality of God.

It is because of this new emphasis on God as the ultimately real that the existential experience of awe, holiness, presence, and *agape*, and the life in which they are dominant becomes genuine Christianity: religion in the sense of creeds, ritual, withdrawal, worship of a God out there, pales into a comparative insignificance, useful symbolically, helpful to some, misleading to others, an intellectualization of the existential, an institutionalization of what is universal. The truth lies in the essential nature of God as seen in Christ, self-giving love: its consequential life is lived "for others": its depth makes nonsense of the old rigidities of religious taboos. We are passing from a distinction between the religious and the secular, into a world-embracing Christianity.

The Archbishop of Canterbury raises, with true charity of approach, some objections and criticisms while recognizing the impatience of the Bishop of Woolwich for something more real and general in place of a self-inclosed religious system. But, he asks, does not the conception of God in depth tend to identify God with the world? If the ultimate, whether in depth or height, is still to be real and personal, will not the religious emotions, awe, dependence, adoration, and penitence still be with us and require the old poetic images to express them?

Further, if we merely theologize the New Testament, the Archbishop asks, into a partially Johannine presentation, its historicity and authority are left in the air. Again he thinks that Dr. Robinson forgets God's aspect of Creator, and the withdrawal for the vision of his holiness which is essential for creaturely worship. And finally that although self-effacing love is the root of the matter, we cannot, any more than Jesus Christ did, throw aside the Law, as interpreted by the Church, and embodied institutionally as divine elements in the natural order.

These are gentle but grave criticisms. And indeed many pages of *Honest to God* speak directly to the soul: for from St Augustine onwards there has always been an existential strain in religion, because it is in the deep places of personal consciousness that the heart is "rooted and grounded in love" and moved by the Holy Spirit.

But it seems to me that there are more fundamental objections to the approach of the Bishop of Woolwich to our contemporary situation, and that it is a symptom of the one-sided incompleteness of his views that the practical impact of his book has been so slight. He has swallowed one aspect of contemporary religious thought whole, failed to assimilate it, and then broadcast it to an unphilosophical public already predisposed by science to think that at last the Church sees what nonsense its theology and creeds have been.

Existential thinking is really ontological feeling: it is an attempt to think outwards to the world from the inner reactions of isolated human being. It is deeper than emotionalism. Anger, for example, is a *commotion*, often physically caused: but anxiety, or despair, or the sense of presence, or awe, or what the Germans call "self-naughting" are deep personal reactions to a situation not understood but felt as real.

We *escape*, they say, from these existential insights into subject-object thinking which is the form taken by reason: we *escape* from our true situation, they say, into institutions and functions: we *escape* from these harrowing "hunches" into theological or philosophical abstractions.

This intensely personal and individualistic mode of approach was a reaction against large scale philosophical systems, like Hegel's, which seemed to have no place for the single individual and his problems.

But it ignores rational thinking of the normal kind on which the whole of society and civilization and, indeed, science, has been constructed. It ignores the fact that we men *are not isolated and lonely souls* but essentially social in our whole make-up. It ignores the fact that human society itself is fundamentally institutional. It isolates men into a nightmare of loneliness, and draws from that desperate self-dependence conclusions for normal living in the world.

If we *think* of God at all, as contrasted with feeling God, we *have* to think of him as object, and endeavour to learn what we can of his transcendent nature. The fact that I make God the object of my thought does not degrade him any more than thinking of love degrades love. I know, of course, that he does not *exist* in *space and time*: but there is no logical contradiction in thinking of him as without spatial and temporal attributes, but beyond this dispensation. My own thought of him is like Whitehead's—personal, teleological, reality but, for us, the reality of the future beyond time; the coming King, the lure of the process. There are, however, attributes of God which I believe he has revealed or allowed us to know which demand an objectivization if we are to think of him at all. This idea of a basic reality of self-giving love penetrating life in its wholeness is true, but not the whole truth. In fact it would in practice evaporate into "living a decent life" for most Christians if Bishop Robinson's Copernican revolution were accepted as complete.

There are other attributes of God like truth, wisdom, majesty, holiness, justice, which must have expression and which in human society must be institutionally expressed. Does Dr. Robinson think, with Karl Barth, that the age-long, intricate, devoted, and progressive search for truth by the greatest thinkers is mere vanity; that systems so coherently and bravely worked out have nothing to teach us; that all we need is to be unselfish and loving in our personal contacts? Besides love itself is a *quality of a person*: it is not a quasi-personal quality existing independently in the depth. We have to know Christ before we know what love is; Christ the historical man who died on the Cross, and Christ the invisible King who rose into the future from the dead. And knowing him we have to worship: and worshipping him we have to express his majesty in acts, symbols, and places and words.

Otherwise we sink into a religion of feeling, abandoning rational thought *by which the rest of the world moves to ever fresh triumphs*. We sink into individual God-consciousness, abandoning the social and institutional set-up without which the forces of love and righteousness have no organization or corporate power. As moralists we become antinomians, forgetting that morality, which is by no means exclusively Christian, has always depended on rules and principles, and is fulfilled but not abrogated by the law of love. At a time when the powers of evil seem to demand a concentration of the forces of light—witness the reunion movements—we are asked to dissipate them into a vague *agape* pervading all human actions and relations.

Religion may not always be Christian in the deepest sense, chiefly because we are not at all times capable of the fulness of devotion. But in its lower values it is still most needful. Its discipline of withdrawal, its rhythm of seasons covering each aspect of life as well as recalling each phase of redemption, its heritage of art, music, and inspired writings and formularies, its provision of spiritual opportunities, its witness to the world, and its consecration of so many activities of human service, make institutional Christianity indispensable. Thank God we do not have to live existentially all the time, or think existentially all the time. It may be, it is, very good for us at times to be brought up against the fundamental realities: but God's way with man's weakness has been *mediation*. Love must permeate a truly Christian life: but love as its inspiration, and *not its sole Substance*. As Bonhoeffer rightly says, living in the world is the penultimate stage and not the ultimate.

The Theology of True Secularity

William O. Fennell

Enlarging upon the ideas of a "religionless" and "worldly" Christianity hinted at in the letters Dietrich Bonhoeffer wrote shortly before his execution by the Nazis, William O. Fennell maintains that the long-standing distinction between "sacred" and "secular" is false to the gospel. For as a consequence of God's reconciling work in Jesus Christ "the radical separation between church and world has not simply been transcended, but broken down." Hence there are no longer two opposing realms, a godly and an ungodly, but "only one realm, the created, creaturely, fallen yet unreconciled and renewed realm over which Jesus Christ reigns as Savior and Lord." Dr. Fennell's article first appeared in the July 1964 issue of *Theology Today*.* He is Professor of Systematic Theology and Director of Graduate Studies in Emmanuel College, Victoria University, Toronto. One of the founders of the *Canadian Journal of Theology*, he at present serves as an Associate Editor of that publication (represented elsewhere in this volume in the article by William Nicholls). Dr. Fennell is a contributor to the symposium *The Unity We Seek*, edited by W. S. Morris.

THERE IS a place in theological writing for venturing risk beyond that which ordinarily belongs to all statements of faith. Theological journals exist in part to encourage such ventures wherein the theologian seeks to set forth, not the final results of years of precise scholarship and considered reflection, but something much more tentative and imprecise. He seeks to give some indication of the direction in which his theological thought seems driven to move, inviting his colleagues to a dialogue of critical comment. Such, at least, is the

* P.O. Box 29, Princeton, New Jersey.

self to be itself, provides a true foundation for the secular approach to nature that inheres in the cultural enterprise of modern man.

It is difficult to see how in the last analysis on any "sacramentalist" view of nature, nature could be treated *naturally* by man. The attitude towards the "sacred cow" would seem to be the appropriate attitude for religious man to adopt towards nature generally. If once nature is viewed in principle "religiously," i.e., as the arena wherein the Lord God is generally made manifest, or as the sphere wherein many gods are thought to dwell, the only consistently appropriate attitude towards nature is the religious one that finds in it a sacrament which is profaned by any secular approach or use. But God has not intended every bush to be a burning bush, nor is his incarnation in a human form a particular, perfect instance of what his relationship to nature generally is intended to be. God's manifestations to Israel, through prophetic witness to his presence and deeds, are from the beginning to their end in Jesus Christ radically unique. If this were not so we would profane nature whenever we approached it in a secular fashion, whenever we sought to know it and use it naturally, i.e., in accordance with its own nature, rather than sacramentally as the locus for the manifestation of God.

God, in creating the world, has brought into being another than himself that in the grace of his being for it, it might be itself. Nature exists in separation from God in a power to be separate which constantly derives from his original and sustaining creative will. God constantly gives to nature its power of independent being. In the unceasing fidelity of his love, God constantly frees nature from himself to be itself. Therefore when man approaches nature scientifically, to predict and control it and press it into the service of human, creaturely ends, he does not thereby engage in the profanation of an essentially religious sphere. It is hard to know how one could ever tend with horticultural care, in order to make it blossom after its own fashion, a bush which is in principle, and therefore ever potentially, a burning bush—a bush intended by the will of its Creator to be the sacramental locus for the appearance of God.

There are other methods of approach to nature than the

scientific one. Nature yields differing kinds of knowledge of itself to man in accordance with the differing methods of approach to it. There are also aesthetic and moral relations to, and knowledge of nature. There is even a transcendent relation that men have called "religious" wherein nature discloses, to those who have the eyes to see, its own mysterious, wondrous, and awesome depths. But it is its own depths that it thus discloses and not the being of God. To the writer's mind this is what the word "heaven" in the creed may be taken symbolically to mean. "I believe in God, the Creator of *heaven* and earth." Heaven as well as earth is a creaturely reality according to the confession of the creed. Can it, then, not be understood to signify that experience of transcendent mystery which men of genius have known and borne witness to? This experience of transcendent mystery is still within the order of man's secular knowledge of the world. It is nature known in terms of its own depth. It is a dimension of the creaturely being that is known and spoken of here.

Of course we must go on to say that the nature which we thus know naturally is not simply that created world upon which God "originally" looked and beheld to be very good. Nature in general, as well as man in particular, is fallen creation. All of creation is subject to the vanity of evil, destruction, and death. But in Jesus Christ the whole of nature participates in God's work of reconciling and renewing grace. For God in Jesus Christ has loved the world in spite of its fallenness. In him God has reconciled the fallen world unto himself and rescued it from its bondage to decay and death. Thus it is that in the Biblical witness to the world's eschatological fulfillment there is, at the end even as at the beginning, a garden. But it is a garden which, according to the picture in the book of The Revelation to John, is freed from unproductivity, decay, and death, and which, according to the vision of first Isaiah, is a habitat of animals that have lost their urge to kill. We cannot attempt here any extensive interpretation of this mythology, but simply state that these myths do bear witness to nature's participation as nature in the New Being of Jesus Christ, in his reconciling work and resurrection life.

II

We turn now from this brief discussion of the Christian attitude toward nature to the question of the Christian attitude toward culture and the creative enterprise of man. Here too it would seem to the writer to be wrong to adopt a "religious attitude" toward culture and find in it what is called a religious purpose and meaning. For the "religious" attitude toward culture is precisely what is meant by *secularism*. It is our thesis that the Christian faith calls man from an idolatrous secularism to a believing secularity. Secularism results from the inevitable tendency on the part of fallen man to make some aspect of his creaturely existence in the world an absolute which serves him in the place of God. Or man himself assumes the status of the absolute and becomes the object of a devotion, hope, and service "religious" in quality and extent. For the church to stand opposed to all such forms of secularism is of course demanded by its faith in the Lord God who is the Creator and Redeemer of man. But the Christian protest against secularism and its idolatry, in the name of the worship and service of the one true God, should lead in the direction not of a religious attitude toward culture but in the direction of a true secularity.

The true secularity which is founded on faith resides precisely in the dethronement of man-made gods through acknowledgement of the one true God revealed in Jesus Christ. In the creation story God set man down in the garden of the world and mandated him to the creative enterprise of taking possession of the earth and subduing it to human purposes. It is of the God self-revealed as Creator and Redeemer that Paul Riceour somewhere speaks: "Our God is a God-Act, a God-Gift, who makes man a creator in his turn in the measure in which he receives and is willing to receive the gift of being free." Even as we said about the realm of nature in general, so now we say about man in particular, God gives and sustains, in his creating grace, freedom to man to be man in the world. Man in himself is not autonomous man, as though his freedom to be man the creator derived from himself. He is theonomous man in that he has his freedom only through and in God. But the freedom which thus originates in and is sustained by God is to be used autonomously. It is given for a human work, and that human work we call culture. Culture no more than nature is to be viewed "sacramentally", as though culture's meaning and purpose were to be found in its transparency to God. All that Christian man does he does in joy and gratitude to God, in an attitude of trust and love and hope toward him. This faith and hope and gratitude is the actualized "image of God" in man, which includes the neighbor in its love. But it is in and from this actualized image of God that there derives man's freedom for the truly human work of culture in the world.

III

Of course, again, the man of whom we speak is not simply the man whom God created and called very good. For man refused his God-given vocation to be free, not by his desiring to be creative in the world, but by refusing to acknowledge in gratitude and answering love God from whom originally and continuously he derived his right and power to be. In pride and unbelief he sought a self-grounded autonomy of freedom, and lost in deep, dark ways his power to be genuinely free. In his sin he lost the knowledge of his Origin and became the victim of false gods. Now his freedom for creativity took the form of a quest for his lost Origin and culture generally became man's attempt at self-redemption. This is the source of the secularism we spoke of awhile ago. Culture becomes the pantheon of religious man's idols. But God acts *against* the religiousness of fallen man and *for* his freedom to be humanly creative within the world. In Jesus Christ God restored to man the lost knowledge of his Origin, dethroned the idols man had worshipped in place of the unknown God, and renewed in man the call to creativity in loving, grateful correspondence with his God.[1] "If the Son shall make you free, you are free indeed." Jesus Christ liberates man for the use of autonomous freedom in the world. Through him the realm of culture becomes a thoroughly dedivinized sphere. It is made the *secular* order by virtue of the fact that he robs it of its *religious* quality and power. Jesus

Christ alone is the man of faith's Absolute. All else, including man's freedom and all that he creates, is relativized in relation to Him. This is the theological ground for, and true meaning of, secularity.

> Because faith frees us from the world, it frees us for the world. Because it does not live on the world, it makes it possible for us to live for the world. Because it puts an end to the misuse of the world, it opens the way to the right use of the world. Because it breaks the domination of the world, it gives domination over it and responsibility for it. And because it drives out the liking and the misliking of the world, it creates room for pure joy in the world.[2]

In the restored calling of man to creative freedom by the forgiving and renewing grace of God in Jesus Christ there is also the promise of God's judging and accepting mercy of all that man creates. In faith, man is made free through the forgiveness of sin and the renewal of his being for a creative life within the world. But in fact, man remains the sinner who is justified by grace. Therefore it cannot but be that all his works in time this side the eschaton will be marred by sin. Even the man of faith remains threatened by idolatry to absolutize himself or some finite achievement in the world. And his so-called "religious" principles, values, or norms are no real challenge to or escape from this idolatry. Indeed, they partake of it. The only cure for this ill is to call man from the idolatrous worship of all false gods or absolutes to the one true Absolute who is Jesus Christ our Lord.

The Christian is one who believes that not only he as man, but also his human work is justified by faith. It is not that his work any more than he will escape a final judgment. For even if, as man of faith, he is freed *from* the quest after his lost humanity through his cultural endeavors, and freed *for* the full expression of his humanity in the joy of a self that has found itself in the Christ, nevertheless he knows that his work still bears upon it the marks not only of a good finitude but also of a baneful sin. But as man of faith he also believes on the basis of the scriptural witness to revelation that in the time of the Kingdom's consummation the nations of the world will bring their glory, the fruits of their cultural and civilizing

labors, and offer them to the King both for his judgment and
his accepting grace (Rev. 21:24-26). Until that time of fulfillment no man can know with any sense of finality what of
his work will win the final approval of God. Yet this he can
believe—that whatever is done in the joy, gratitude, love, and
freedom which are gifted to man in Jesus Christ through the
Holy Spirit cannot fail to find some acceptance.

IV

In conclusion we raise for a very brief discussion the question of the significance of our subject for understanding the
relation between the church and the world. By "church" we
mean the community of the faithful who assemble together to
receive the Word of God in preaching and sacrament, to respond in prayer and praise, and to enjoy that fellowship together which is the communion of the saints. By "world" we
mean all that lies outside the immediate context of this community and its corporate activity.

In Jesus Christ the radical separation between church and
world has not simply been transcended, but broken down.
God was in Christ reconciling the world unto himself, for
God so loved the world. Contrary to much Christian thought
on the matter, faith in Jesus Christ does not, or ought not to
foster in man a *crise de conscience*, a conflict of divided loyalty between churchly existence on the one hand and worldly
existence on the other. If in Jesus Christ the world has been
reconciled to God, then there are no longer two realms, a
godly and an ungodly, standing in irreconcilable enmity toward one another. There is now only one realm, the created,
creaturely, fallen yet reconciled and renewed realm over
which Jesus Christ reigns as Savior and Lord. In recent times
it has been Dietrich Bonhoeffer who through his posthumous
writings has caused many of us to rethink our theological
understanding of the relation between Christ and culture,
between the church and the world.

Sharing in Christ we stand in both the reality of God and
the reality of the world. The reality of Christ comprises the
reality of the world within itself. The world has no reality

of its own independently of the revelation of God in Christ. One is denying the revelation of God in Jesus Christ if one tries to be "Christian" without seeing and recognizing the world in Christ. There are therefore not two spheres, but only one sphere of the realization of Christ, in which the reality of God and the reality of the world are united. Thus the theme of the two spheres which has repeatedly become the dominant theme in the history of the Church, is foreign to the New Testament. The New Testament is concerned solely with the manner in which the reality of Christ assumes reality in the present world, which it has already encompassed, seized and possessed. There are not two spheres, standing side by side, competing with each other and attacking each other's frontiers. If that were so, the frontier dispute would always be the decisive problem of history. But the whole reality of the world is already drawn into Christ and bound together in Him, and the movement of history consists solely in divergence and convergence in relation to this centre.[3]

Of course it must be confessed that although there are no longer two realms, a godly and a godless, standing in unreconciled enmity one to the other there does still remain a distinction between "godly" and "godless" men, i.e., between those who believe in God revealed in Jesus Christ and those who do not so believe. This distinction gave rise to, and continues to give rise to and preserve that community of faith and love for God and man in Jesus Christ which is the church. And this community finds or makes for itself a space in the world for the hearing and the responding to the Word of its life. But since Jesus Christ is the one in whom *the world* is reconciled to God, the community seeks no separate existence for itself as a religious community in radical separation from the world. Rather, like its Lord, and in him, it exists for the sake of the world. It seeks in speech and action and attitude to interpret to the world the foundation in God of its true rather than false worldliness. The church manifests corporately, and in the lives of its individual members, not that love for the world which is enmity to God because it springs from the false and sinful autonomy of unbelief, but that love for the world which springs from God's love for the world as manifest in the Christ.

Thus in Jesus Christ the distinction between churchly existence and worldly existence is relativized. Ultimately—eschatologically—the distinction disappears. And penultimately, though the distinction does indeed remain as a significant distinction, the Christian community must nevertheless always give evidence that it lives in the light of the End in which it believes and for which it hopes. This the Church does, within the context of our present discussion, by manifesting to the world that, in faith, it is possible to engage freely in the secular enterprise of man's cultural existence, not as a human quest for self-redemption but in thankful and joyous celebration of a redemption freely given as God's own self-gift.

NOTES

1. Cf. A. Dumas: "Aussi Barth peut-il écrire cette phrase énigmatique: 'Jesus Christ, est "l'image du Dieu invisible" (Col., 1:15) et par suite le type de l'homme cultivé, puisque orienté vers Dieu et formé par lui.'" Chapter entitled "Théologie et Humanisme" in *Hommage et Reconnaisance*: Cashiers Théologiques de l'Actualité Protestante, Neuchâtel, Delachaux & Niestlé, 1946.

2. Gerhard Ebeling, *The Nature of Faith*: Philadelphia, Muhlenberg, 1961, p. 161.

3. Dietrich Bonhoeffer, *Ethics*: London, S. C. M., 1955, p. 64.

A New Linguistic Madness

Langdon B. Gilkey

One of the most debated of recent books in theology is Paul van Buren's *The Secular Meaning of the Gospel,* in which the author explores the possibility of an empirical Christianity that would dispense with "God-talk" altogether in an effort to be intelligible, meaningful and appropriate to contemporary man. Langdon B. Gilkey, Professor of Historical Theology at the Divinity School of the University of Chicago, finds van Buren's book original, timely, and vastly important. He also finds it irritating. Particularly telling, says Gilkey, are van Buren's strictures against what he sees as existentialist and Whiteheadian distortions of the gospel. However, "he seems to have been quite oblivious of these very criticisms when he launches upon his own interpretation." According to Dr. Gilkey, van Buren too is guilty of distortion in applying present-day standards of validity and meaningfulness to the New Testament and to patristic literature. Dr. Gilkey's review is reprinted by permission of *The Journal of Religion,** in the July 1964 issue of which it initially appeared. His own most recent book is *How the Church Can Minister to the World Without Losing Itself.*

The Secular Meaning of the Gospel. By PAUL M. VAN BUREN. New York: Macmillan Co., 1963. 200 pages. $4.95.

THIS BOOK is good, certainly important, and often, as are most such books, irritating. It is good because it is original—one of the most genuinely creative theological efforts to appear in a couple of decades—and because its main thesis is clearly and powerfully presented. It is important because it addresses itself in a new way to the most crucial contemporary theological problem, namely the nature and extent of Christian language in a secular age. The fact that it is at the same time irritating

* University of Chicago Press, Chicago, Illinois 60637.

may be because it so radically challenges as meaningless and so impossible most of our usual forms of Christian discourse —or it may be because the presentation of this rebellious thesis is neither as careful nor as tight as it might have been. In any case, it is a book which will deservedly be much discussed and argued over and that every student of current directions in theology would be well advised to read and ponder.

The book unites two concerns. First there is the concern, initiated by Bonhoeffer, for an ethical, active, socially relevant Christianity that is totally involved in the life of the world, that, within certain limits, accepts that life and enters into it, and whose purposes and goals are found therefore in an enriched "secular" existence. Second there is the even stronger concern for an "empirical" Christianity (which, incidentally, in disposing of the God Bonhoeffer's religionless Christianity still retained, transforms the meaning of the category "religionless"). That is to say, van Buren urges that Christian discourse must be intelligible and meaningful within the empirical categories of our scientific and technological age and therefore within the closely limited standards of meaningfulness of contemporary linguistic analysis—else it be unable to be a part of the thought and life of modern man. One of the most potent and important theses of the book is this identification between the general secular mentality of our age and its analytic philosophy. For the author the latter is no esoteric game of towered academics but the most direct intellectual expression of our total *Zeitgeist*—so *its* theological implications are weighty indeed for a modern explicator of the gospel. In this identification he is, I believe, right—and thus is his book important.

These two concerns together make up, apparently, what van Buren means by his oft-used but almost totally undefined word "secular": the this-worldly, empirical mood of modern man. The question that animates the book, then, is: Can Christian faith be so conceived as to express and be intelligible to this secular mood, or must being a Christian place the believer in some "religious" realm outside the real world in which he actually lives, forcing his life into a pattern of non-involvement in the world's life and his thoughts into a pattern of repudiation of the world's ways of thinking? Van Buren is clear that, with this choice before us, we can opt only for a secular understanding of the gospel—since being out of touch with the world is obviously a worse fate than being out of touch with historic Christianity (though he tries later to keep diplomatic relations going with both), and since we could not in any case will that repudiation of modernity which "religion" calls for. Thus our task is to interpret Christianity as a secular faith, that is, one that is both worldly and empirical. Then comes the not inconsiderable price tag on this newest theological model: all theological references to God, and so presumably all religious dependence upon him, must be deleted.

Since Christianity is to be understood as a faith without God, it is by the same token not "religion." "Religion," a term which like the word "secular" is crucial for the book but never carefully defined or discussed, is to van Buren the antithesis of his two major secular concerns. Let us note that he means by "religion" not the human *misuse* of the relation to God, as do some other "religionless" Christians, but "religion" is here the term for *any* relation to God, for any relation beyond one's relations to things and persons. Certainly then religion is not empirical in his sense, since it deals with a suprahuman dimension of life beyond empirical verification (as understood by Flew *et al.*); and even more, religion is for the author not involved in ordinary existence, since it is "apart," "separate," not related to the ordinary values of the world. "Either 'being a Christian' is something 'religious' and quite distinct from secular affairs, or Christian faith is a human posture conceivable for a man who is a part of his secular culture" (p. 17). The thought that a man might be both religious and still take an active part in his culture seems not to have dawned on the author. What the source was for this somewhat arbitrary definition of all relation to God as inescapably "separate"—aside possibly from his High Church antagonists—is hard to say. Surely the tradition of liberalism denied this understanding, and, as van Buren well knows, the leaders of recent American theology (the Niebuhrs, Tillich, etc.) have striven mightily to point out the relevance of the religious category to man's ordinary "secular" existence. Van Buren's thesis would have been better founded if in a book for American readers he had tackled this liberal understanding of religion head on rather than assumed that it has never existed. In any case, a "secular" Christianity is not religious on these two grounds: Because of the strict standards of the empirical spirit, it cannot be; and because of modern man's involvement in life, it should not be.

The main purpose and, consequently, the importance of the book, then, is to outline and defend such a secular conception of Christianity. The argument takes two general forms: (1) This interpretation of Christianity is shown to be necessary, since none other is possible for modern man. As van Buren argues at various points along the line, any literalistic, philosophical, biblical, or "mythical" understanding of the gospel that uses the concept of God—whether in literal or sophisticated terms—conflicts with both the empiricism and the this-worldliness of modern man; hence God-language must go. (2) A supplementary effort then shows the fidelity of "secular" Christianity to what the author calls the "logic" and the "intention" of both the biblical gospel and the formative theology of the patristic period. Since for obvious reasons such a faith cannot do much with the doctrines of God, sin, revelation or eschatology, a Christology of some sort is logically the center of such a reconstituted "theology," and so the book revolves almost entirely around this problem. At the beginning a most intriguing modern "Biblical" Christology is presented, which, as van Buren admits, is orthodox enough; but impressive as this "conservative" construct may be to the hopeful reader, at its end its author remarks that "it is still, from the point of view of the theological 'left,' sadly mythological in form, if not in content" (p. 55); and so reluctantly he passes it over.

Van Buren is conscious of the marked similarity between his analysis of the problem of current theology and that of Bultmann and his potent adapter Ogden, and so he spends a goodly amount of time disputing the feasibility of their position. Against their "existentialist" interpretation of the gospel he levels three important criticisms (pp. 69–79): (1) Both continue to make significant use of the word "God," whereas discourse about God is now seen according to the empirical principle (the modified verification criterion) to be meaningless, whether in Bultmann's "analogical" or in Ogden's process-philosophical modes. (2) While the gospel language does speak about man and his needs, nevertheless it also speaks about God and his acts; hence it is false to claim an equivalence between the language of the gospel which speaks of God and the language of existential anthropology that talks only of man. (3) While the gospel language does speak of the believer's decision as important, nevertheless as a form of discourse it also informs us of concrete events in actual history as the basis of these decisions; hence it is false to claim an equivalence between a New Testament discourse about historical events and an existentialist discourse about human decisions.

One cannot but feel the power of these arguments, especially the latter two, against the Bultmannian resolution of the question of meaningful discourse. Here van Buren appeals almost brutally, and often somewhat sarcastically, to the common-sense understanding of the gospel, what it plainly seems actually to have been saying, against a modern existentialist distortion of its evident meaning into something quite different. Strangely he seems to have quite forgotten these very criticisms when he launched upon his own interpretation.

If, then, the existential anthropology of Bultmann united with the Whiteheadian theology of Ogden is unintelligible to the secular mind ("one wonders where the left-wing existentialist theologians have found their 'modern men'" [p. 68]), how can we understand the gospel in a secular way? Clearly a *theo*-logical interpretation is out: No God-figure or surrogate therefore can function in *this* gospel, for all references to anything beyond natural facts and men (e.g., "arcane information about the cosmos" [p. 158]), whether it be of a divine "Person," a metaphysical structure or entity (Whitehead, Hartshorne etc.), or the ground of that structure (Tillich), are meaningless. It is not that God is there for our religion, but not for our theological discourse, as in Bultmann; or that he is not to be used by us but served in the world, as in

Bonhoeffer; it is that he is not there at all, so language and thought about him are meaningless and all relations to him vacant, empty, and unreal. "The empiricist in us finds the heart of the difficulty not in what is said about God, but the very talking about God at all" (p. 84); and "today, we cannot even understand the Nietzschian cry that 'God is dead!,' for if it were so, how could we know? No, the problem now is that the *word* 'God' is dead" (p. 103). In such a secular world where meaningful assertions are either scientific assertions about things, or historical and ethical assertions about people, ours will be a humanistic faith, one that makes no cognitive assertions (i.e., about the way things are, about the character of reality, ultimate or otherwise), but that speaks *only* of men, of the historical dimension within which they live, and of their human problems of valuation, commitment and decision.

In this faith there will therefore be only the following elements: the story of the man Jesus, of his life and his death, and of his extraordinary freedom in himself and availability for others; there will also be the "perspective" (non-cognitive of course—a "blik"—but was this what Hare meant?) on life, its values and commitments which this story can give us; and finally there will be the quite strange (not to say "unearthly"!) "contagion" of Jesus' freedom and perspective, capturing or grasping others over the course of time and out of them forming a community which commits itself to this same freedom and availability. Such a gospel, urging us now to such a freedom from self-concern and a self-surrender in service to others, a freedom that can be "caught" from this "contagious" martyr of the distant past, will be meaningful to the contemporary secular man—or will it?

One wonders where van Buren found *his* "modern man," and also whether he really means his reiterated devotion to the authority of the mind of secularism when it comes to values as opposed to truth. For surely contemporary modern man, committed to the self-oriented values of modern society, would find the self-surrendering, altruistic "perspective" and "freedom" of this ancient martyr as strange, as unintelligible, and as offensive as are the old "myths" in which his story is ordinarily phrased. With van Buren's translation the modern man may find the story of Jesus more credible historically, but can he and will he more easily appropriate its meaning for *himself* and pattern his life after it—if it *really* speaks of the values of Jesus? Unless, of course, this word "contagion" refers to some sort of supra- or extra-human "virus" that grasps or captures us whether we will it or not—and if it does *not* refer to some such "something," what sort of word is "contagion" anyhow, how is it understood and used here, what sort of "analogy" is at work here, how is it testable and so meaningful, etc., etc.? And if the word "contagion" *does* refer to some such power to grasp us, have we not with its use jumped back into the murky unempirical depths of theological meaninglessness and illusion? Finally, if under such "empirical" criticism we have to give up this category of contagion, then one cannot help but ask why all this interest in Jesus and his story; is he not then merely one other interesting and inspiring example of the possibilities of human freedom? It almost seems as if, like many another before him, van Buren has to become theological in order to make intelligible his own relation to the man Jesus.

The remainder of this interesting book was, to this reader, a rather frustrating tour de force. Van Buren has dared to interpret the Christian gospel in about as radically different a way as is imaginable, namely without God. It is, therefore, incumbent upon him to show, in terms of whatever authority for Christianity he recognizes as legitimate, how he can call such an interpretation "Christian"; and it is also useful to show what happens under his interpretation to other associated aspects of historic Christianity, such as ethics, church, and so on. But such an effort would have been vastly different from what he in fact did, namely finding his own version identical with and true to the intentions, the logic and the meaning of classical Christianity—and to this simple-minded reader van Buren's "secular" Christianity, true or false, is a vastly changed article. The extraction of God from the scene is certainly *not* comparable to the pruning of astrology from astronomy (p. 198)! Surely on the face of it such a humanistic gospel is different both as a religious faith and as a system of religious discourse from the way or ways both the New

Testament writers and the early fathers understood Christianity. Further, this new interpretation seems to make at least as much nonsense of many of the usual practices of Christianity as it has of the frequent practice of saying the word "God"—for example, worship, prayer, sacrament, to mention only a few. In such a case, would it not have been better to do as many of the liberals did, and say, "Ours is *not* the religion of Paul or John, nor of patristic Christianity—but we think they were quite wrong!"? But that is not done here. Rather in case after case van Buren seems to say that the *real* meaning of the New Testament and of the early church was to proclaim just such a gospel as his. Although he often admits that both scripture and early church phrased the gospel in "mythical" terms that sound different from his own, nevertheless he insists that the "logic of their language" and the "intention of their gospel" were as his own—he has presented what they were "really" saying. If it was strange that the face of Harnack stared back from the deep well of Jesus-Forschung, it is even stranger when the faces of Wittgenstein and Antony Flew beam at us from the pages of Acts and of Paul, and strangest of all when they keep popping out from behind the pillars in fifth-century Alexandria and Chalcedon!

This becomes then a weird and strange world in which —despite his strong criticism of Bultmann and Ogden for doing *just* this—sentences in scripture and patristics are said to mean something that on the face of it they do not mean at all. Because the New Testament centers, as it certainly does, on Jesus as the revelation of God, the New Testament is "really" not talking about God at all, but is only saying, as we have done, how important Jesus is for us (pp. 136, 138, 141–43, esp. 147–48). And the early church, in speaking at Chalcedon of the humanity as well as of the deity of Christ, is "really" stating only that this man is essential and ultimate for our perspective on life and the world (pp. 159–68). Surely if Bultmann has no right to claim an equivalence between the gospel language and his existentialist anthropology, van Buren cannot claim a "real," "intentional," or "logical" equivalence between the admittedly God-centered language of the New Testament and of the early church with his own

twentieth-century humanistic, naturalistic interpretation! And
if Bultmann cannot legitimately drop out the historical references of Christianity, why can van Buren drop out the
references to God and still state the "meaning" or the "intention" of the scriptural words? Often the author admits this
real difference of language and so, presumably (since, for his
school, language use equals meaning), a difference of meaning
as well between the New Testament, the early church, and this
"secular" Christianity (e.g., pp. 148, 157–58, 160). Then
when this admission is made, the stern authority of empiricism
enters, and this older biblical language, now meaningless, is
pruned off. At that point we are expressing the "intention"
though not the "form" of New Testament language—but one
might suggest that if ontological and theological words are
obscure and unverifiable, surely the meaning of the "intention" of a proposition which is counter to what it seems to say
is an even more elusive semantic *ding an sich!* And again, how
can van Buren prune off from the gospel the divine dimension
on the authority of this modern empirical world view if
Bultmann cannot legitimately prune off the historical dimension on precisely the same authority?

Van Buren thus seems to wish to have his cake and eat it
too, to wish to be a radical innovator, and yet to be "orthodox." On the one hand he uses the authority of scripture to
belabor Bultmann and Company for infidelity to the New
Testament witness, and to claim for his own view the "meaning of their (the New Testament writers) words" (p. 156),
"the logic of the language of the gospel" (pp. 136, 156 n.),
"the real intentions" of the fathers (p. 158 n.), and the support
of almost the entire succeeding panoply of creedal affirmation.
On the other hand, when he presents his own view over against
other interpretations that take the traditional God-language
seriously, then he rejects this biblical and patristic authority
totally and appeals to the entirely different authority of modern
empirical verification.

The first result of this attempt to appeal to two different
sorts of authority, to be orthodox and empirical at once, is
a confusion of the logic of the book. It is never clear on just
what grounds something is being asserted, and the authority

on which an idea is rejected may itself be abandoned a page or so later. One example is the appeal to Barth in van Buren's too brief dismissal of natural theology (p. 98), when surely Barth attacked natural theology on the ground, irrelevant to this "empirical" Christianity, that natural theology dishonored and distorted the God of revelation! The second result is a species of "double-talk" unworthy of a clear-headed semanticist: "to say Jesus is divine, very God of very God" *is* "to say that his perspective is my ultimate" (p. 160); "to say that this hope is 'eschatological' is to say that we would die rather than abandon it" (p. 154). What is van Buren trying to assert here? That the actual historical meaning of Chalcedon is the same as his own meaning? Or that this is what they *should* have meant, all they validly *could* have meant, or what? This confusing pattern of equating apparently different meanings, the one being historically said but the other being what was "really" said (and how are we to know or establish this?) continues throughout the last part of the book and includes almost all the historic, creedal, ecclesiastical, and liturgical formulas of the church.

One can only stare in wonder at such an apparent slurring of contrasting meanings in a work devoted to precision of meaning. Is this process an example of the analysis of "the ordinary use of language"? Is it not rather the distortion of a historical usage in order to commend as really "orthodox" *another* meaning different from that original use? And if there is this distinction between the old usage, and its "real meaning," then what does *that* fact mean for van Buren's formula that "the meaning of language is its use"? Metaphysicians have usually wished to introduce clarity into our thoughts—and hence have eventuated what semanticists like to call their metaphysical madness. Today a semanticist crying for precision of meaning and fidelity to usage seems in this section to have introduced a new form of linguistic madness: "What they mean by these words is not what they say, but what their 'intention' and their 'logic' say." Surely an intention hidden behind what is said is as mysterious and elusive as the old ontological substance! And what *is* this logic of the New Testament and of patristic literature except the use *they* made of their words, a use that included speaking of God as well as of Jesus and mankind? *That* was the logic of their language, if we find that logic by an analysis of their actual historical usage and not by an application to their words of *our* standards of validity and meaningfulness. The logic of their ancient God-centered language is surely not identical to that of a modern naturalistic system which refers nothing to God—for they did in fact speak of God. Thus the "logic" of theological language that van Buren has found in this work is merely the logic of his own contemporary *secular* understanding of the gospel, *not* the logic of the older gospel itself nor of the patristic period. What he says here about a meaningful Christianity for our day may possibly be true—that is another issue—but his authority for that "secular" form of Christianity *must* remain his own contemporary empirical standard and not that of the New Testament and the Councils, else his own argument for it be hopelessly confused and weakened. The liberals admitted the gulf between themselves and the Christian past—and it would be better if he did, too. Perhaps only a semanticist with an Anglican background would reject the use of the word "God" in theological language and then worry about the relation of his thought to Chalcedon!

We have criticized this book at some length because we feel it to be a vastly important and timely book, being the first time a trained theologian "on the inside," so to speak, has taken logical analysis with full seriousness and interpreted Christianity accordingly. Many further questions might be raised about his results, for example, how his view might deal with those issues of life with which man's freedom cannot seem so easily to cope: sin, fate and death, and for which men have historically turned to "God" for help. Let us hope that next time he will defend this faith as a viable view for modern man, in a secular culture that is perhaps not all *that* good, rather than as expressing the "real intentions" of orthodoxy. What must be said, however, is that any inadequacies in the argument of this book are more than made up by the courage and the clarity with which a new, potent, and possibly relevant interpretation of Christianity has been thought out. This is a good and significant book.

"Non-Metaphysical" Christian Philosophy and Linguistic Philosophy

James W. Woelfel

Taking issue with those Christian thinkers who respond to the empiricist critique of metaphysics by attempting to set forth a "nonmetaphysical" philosophical theology, James W. Woelfel suggests that the problems that beset such a response pose serious questions about its fundamental validity. But though he is an advocate of metaphysical theology, Dr. Woelfel contends that it must approach its subject matter "with a humble and chastened outlook" and be willing to make use of the methods of empiricism and linguistic analysis. "The next step for Christian rationalism and metaphysics," he concludes, will "move beyond these analytical movements and incorporate their insights into a more profound synthesis." Mr. Woelfel, a doctoral candidate in theology at Yale University, originally wrote his essay for *Scottish Journal of Theology**; it appeared in March 1964.

IN THE continuing discussion between Christian theology and linguistic philosophy there is a fundamental division of the theological responses which has weighty implications for the whole encounter between the two disciplines. This basic distinction into two types of Christian response is one of those simple categorisations which by their very obviousness are often overlooked. I refer to two kinds of Christian thinkers who deal with linguistic analysis: the "nonmetaphysical" and the "metaphysical." In this article I have

* Oliver and Boyd Ltd., Tweeddale Court, Edinburgh, Scotland.

chosen to discuss certain types of the "non-metaphysical" response.

Whether a Christian theologian deals with Oxford philosophy from a metaphysical or a non-metaphysical perspective is vital to the whole discussion. It is vital to the theologian because linguistic analysis is the latest in a series of philosophical movements beginning with Hume which claim to have undermined metaphysics finally and forever. If the theologian responds in a metaphysical way to the questions asked by the Oxford philosophers, he must justify his appeal to metaphysics over against the critique of metaphysics which lies behind language analysis. If, on the other hand, the theologian replies in a non-metaphysical way, he must demonstrate the epistemological significance of Christian doctrine apart from metaphysical support.

The major contemporary criticisms of theological language come not from language analysis considered independently but from a revitalised logical positivism aided by analytical methods. I call this "new" positivism "linguistic empiricism" or "analytical positivism." Linguistic analysis is fundamentally a method, while positivism is a theory of knowledge. What theology confronts today in men like Antony Flew is a refurbished and broadened positivism sharpened by the methods of linguistic analysis. The verification principle remains for the newer positivist the corner-stone of philosophy.

For this reason I submit that the fundamental discussion for theology is still with positivism. In reading Flew's criticisms of religious language we hear strong echoes of A. J. Ayer's classic manifesto of twenty years ago, *Language, Truth and Logic*. Yet I would also emphasise again that the "new" positivism *is* a *linguistic* one. The exacting methods of linguistic analysis have made positivism more articulate.

Since it is positivism which is the most consciously anti-metaphysical of all philosophies, the wedding of linguistic philosophy's analysis of metaphysical statements and positivism's epistemological critique of metaphysics is a singularly potent union. It serves to heighten the seriousness of the question as to whether a theological response is "metaphysical" or "non-metaphysical."

In the course of my reading in the area of linguistic analysis and its theological implications, I observed that one group of Christian philosophers and theologians have warmly embraced the "non-metaphysical" and even the "anti-metaphysical" stance of positivism, believing that a mortal wound for metaphysics frees theology for its proper task. They would regard traditional theology as the handmaid of metaphysics, restricted by alien categories. With the demise of metaphysics theology can assert its proper concern with the living realities of revelation, faith and history. The Christians in the "non-metaphysical" class do this either (1) by denying the material relevance of philosophy, or (2) by espousing a modified form of linguistic empiricism. I shall discuss the former group of "non-metaphysical" Christians only briefly, focusing attention on the latter group, who seem to be engaged in more genuine discourse with linguistic philosophy.

Of those who deny the material relevance of philosophy to theology, the greatest and most influential is Karl Barth. He and his followers have had a profound effect upon theological attitudes towards philosophy, producing among Protestant theologians generally a suspicion of the philosophical enterprise in so far as it is metaphysical and a concern to express Christian theology solely in biblical terms.

Barth considers philosophy a quite legitimate human enterprise, but maintains that it has nothing material to say to biblical dogmatics. A highly circumscribed, strictly terminological use of philosophy is all Barth will allow.[1] Metaphysics seduces theology into alien categories. Barth's "anti-metaphysical" theology is often called, significantly, "theological positivism."[2]

Another group of Christian thinkers, who are best described as philosophical theologians or Christian philosophers, have taken the other "non-metaphysical" route of adopting themselves a form of linguistic empiricism. Having adopted a philosophical position, these men, unlike Barth, consider philosophy to have a material effect upon theology. Of course, it is the "non-metaphysical" philosophy of analytical positivism. Being philosophers by profession rather than theologians, their approach to Christian theology is likewise the non-Barthian route of philosophical inquiry.

This second type of "non-metaphysical" approach to linguistic philosophy is most prominent in Britain. The discussion is an intra-mural one, carried on within the linguistic philosophy camp between Christians such as Richard Hare and non-Christians such as Antony Flew. The great symbol of this discourse is of course *New Essays in Philosophical Theology*, edited by Flew and Alasdair MacIntyre.[3] The significance of *New Essays* should not be underestimated by thoughtful Christians. It is a monument to the possibility of serious and intelligent discussion between Christian and non-Christian in our day. On a university level, it is part of that "living in the world" which is so vital for the Christian who lives in a "post-Christian" age.

Much of the continuing discussion between Christian and non-Christian linguistic philosophers was given impetus by or is a commentary upon *New Essays*. Hare's now-familiar *blik* argument for the validity of religious language, for example, was, in the essay in which it originally appeared, a very basic and undeveloped notion.[4] It is my opinion, however, that all the Christian responses to linguistic empiricism made by those who have themselves adopted this "non-metaphysical" philosophy can be seen as elaborations of the *blik* concept. The *blik* theory, with its assertion that not only religious beliefs but also all world-views are basic convictions which are beyond the pale of verification or falsification, is an archetype of all the "non-metaphysical" responses.

Hare's language of *blik* is important to the whole problem of religious language. His argument, in one form or another, is under other names a chief device of Christian apologetics. To be able to demonstrate to the sceptic, first, that he has a world-view (a *blik*), and secondly, that his *blik* is no more ultimately verifiable than yours, is a necessary bit of ground-clearing in the apologetic task. But it is *no more* than ground-clearing; that is, its value is largely the negative one of pulling your adversary into the same boat. If pressed as far as Hare takes it, it lays itself open to Antony Flew's devastating suggestion that the religious life becomes "fraudulent, or merely silly."[5] It leaves the sceptic simply shrugging his shoulders and retorting, "So we have different *bliks*. So what?"

Flew's criticism of Hare is applicable, to a greater or lesser degree, to all the philosophically-based "non-metaphysical" Christian responses to analytical positivism. I suggest that this may be an endemic weakness of the "non-metaphysical" approach; namely, that it cannot ultimately avoid Hare's position and hence Flew's criticism. Since the "non-metaphysical" response accepts for the most part the positivist critique of metaphysics, its attempt to grapple with religious statements of a transcendental nature is severely restricted to some such notion as Hare's *blik*.

Thus we find, for example, in such "non-metaphysical" Christian philosophers as T. R. Miles and Alasdair MacIntyre[6] what amounts to a detailed theological defence pursuing its course from a particular *blik*. Miles is the most avowedly positivistic of the "non-metaphysical" Christian thinkers I have read. Having concurred with positivism as to the impossibility of making meaningful statements about any sort of transcendent realm, he proceeds to defend the Christian *blik* as a language of *parable*. Miles's theological position can be stated succinctly: he calls it "silence qualified by parables."[7] The Christian truths philosophically considered are parables accepted by the believer in the face of his inability to know anything about transcendent realities behind his experience and his consequently reverent silence before mystery. Miles observes: "As a technical philosopher it is not for me to say whether this parable is the right one to live by; but as a plain man I am in no doubt that it is."[8]

The "metaphysical" Christian may register a criticism at this point, pointing out the vocational schizophrenia implied in the quotation from Miles. Such a criticism is a serious one and, I think, substantially justified. Miles's rejoinder, however, would probably be that as a philosopher he has been enabled to perform the vitally important task of *clarifying* just what theological language is and what the Christian—what Miles himself—is doing when he uses it. There is also truth in this reply to the critic. Something of the same criticism and the same reply hold true in the case of Alasdair MacIntyre.

Like Hare and Miles, MacIntyre places himself squarely in the "non-metaphysical" philosophical camp. Unlike Miles, however, MacIntyre is more of a "pure" linguistic analyst and less of a positivist. Yet all three view the task of philosophy similarly. For MacIntyre the special task of philosophy is to uncover the seeming contradictions in theological language. He regards this task as a neutral one, with no religious or metaphysical connotations. The contribution of the theological response to the linguistic search for clarification, declares MacIntyre, is to show that theology's contradictions are only *seeming* ones; that in reality they are not contradictions at all.

What is MacIntyre's peculiar elaboration of the Christian *blik*? I call his theological response the language of *authority*. "We accept what Jesus Christ says and does as having an authority that requires our complete submission."[9] God is not approached through rational exploration or argument.[10] The only approach to God is through personal trust. In trust we accept an ultimate authority for our life, an ultimate criterion which by definition is logically impossible to justify. That ultimate criterion is for the Christian the person of Jesus Christ. In supra-rational trust we submit ourselves in obedience to His authority. Thus philosophy and theology operate in different spheres, rational and existential; and it is at theology's overlapping point, the systematising and rationalising of Christ's authority in theological language, rather than at its centre, that philosophy has the task of clarification. The Christian *blik* (like all *bliks*) is beyond rational justification, since it is an ultimate authority claiming the believer's obedience. MacIntyre concludes that "belief cannot argue with unbelief: it can only preach to it."[11] From an unexpected quarter we hear in this sentence a view very reminiscent of Barth.

A philosopher who is something of a transitional figure between a "non-metaphysical" and a "metaphysical" stance, and who is therefore of crucial importance to the present discussion, is Ian Ramsey. Ramsey still stands squarely in the linguistic camp; in fact his analysis of religious language is more technical and thorough than those of the other three philosophers we have considered. On the other hand, and significantly, it seems to be his thorough immersion in linguistic problems which leads him in a metaphysical direction. He stands as a pivotal figure, looking backward towards the "non-metaphysical" responses with confident mastery of the problems of religious language and forward towards a "metaphysical" response with caution and hesitancy.

Ramsey's defence of the Christian *blik* is what I call the language of *oddness*. Religious language, Ramsey states, has to be logically *odd* in order to be appropriate to the oddness of the religious situation. The religious situation is characterised as a "discernment which provokes a commitment."[12] Discernment occurs when a situation is "perceptual and more" than perceptual.[13] It occurs when one's awareness of a situation is not exhausted by empirical designation. When discernment occurs something "clicks" for the discerner and the situation before him takes on a new dimension.

Religious discernment is a peculiar variety of general discernment which stimulates total commitment. Hence religious language is language used to describe this peculiar discernment-situation.

What of the *commitment* which religious discernment arouses? Ramsey is concerned to show that there are many partial, non-religious commitments in life beyond which the committed one does not appeal. They grow out of that something called "discernment" which gives dimension and depth to what are otherwise mere object-situations. Two kinds of partial commitment are (1) "mathematical" or "impersonal" commitment, such as commitment to certain axioms as the *terminus ad quem* of geometry; and (2) "personal" or "quasi-personal" commitment, such as commitment to a loved one. *Religious* commitment partakes of both kinds of partial commitments, because it is "a *total* commitment to the *whole* universe."[14]

Religious situations, then, are empirical situations in which language is used to evoke religious discernment and total commitment to the universe. The words involved in this odd situation of vision-and-response have an odd logic. They fuse the partial discernment-commitments of impersonal and personal situations into a description of a total discernment-commitment. In so doing they acquire an odd sort of finality; they become "key" words, "apex" words, "integrator" words.

Discernment of a religious sort requires object language *and more*, and that is why its language—religious language—is odd. There is a guide in our ordinary linguistic usage, says Ramsey, to this aspect of linguistic oddness in religious terminology: it is the pronoun "I." In order to speak of the full range of what "I" means to each of us, we must begin with observational language but then qualify it in some way to indicate that its meaning is not exhausted by observational language. Similarly with the word "God." "The central problem of theology is how to use, how to qualify, observational language so as to be suitable currency for what in part exceeds it—the situations in which theology is founded."[15] Religion takes word models and appropriately qualifies them in order to evoke the characteristically religious situation.

Ramsey calls his position "logical empiricism." He accepts the charge that logical empiricism renders theology "verbal," almost devoid of metaphysical "entities." The discernment-commitment situation which is the religious one is best described, says Ramsey, not by clinging to "a whole heap of metaphysical furniture," but by the word *worship*.[16] Theology must use the language appropriate to this empirical reality which is empirical and more: the language of oddness.

Tentative moves are made in a metaphysical direction, however, when Ramsey elaborates on the suggestion that the pronoun "I" is the appropriate model for the word "God." He suggests that "solipsism is the logical primitive metaphysics,"[17] and seems to indicate a Cartesian starting-point for a metaphysical theology. The statement "I exist" furnishes the inescapable context for all our linguistic usage, whether "objective" (impersonal) or "subjective" (personal). It is this matrix which is always more than simple description which requires logical oddness and suggests a metaphysical elaboration. Similarly, "God" is the odd matrix, the "contextual presupposition," of the whole universe, including the universe of "I's." This preliminary extending of feelers in the direction of a kind of personal idealism is as far as Ramsey will take his metaphysical interest.

Ramsey's thorough grounding in linguistic analysis and modern empiricism quite rightly restrains him from the unbridled speculation of which much classical metaphysics has been guilty, and indeed from positing *any* sort of metaphysical entities behind the world of experience. He represents in his own philosophical inquiry the impasse of the contemporary philosopher who is metaphysically inclined but who has accepted the empiricist critique of transcendental metaphysics.

Of vital importance in a critical assessment of the "non-metaphysical" Christian philosophers is Ronald Hepburn's brilliant and sympathetic *Christianity and Paradox*.[18] Hepburn considers himself a sceptic with a "naturally religious mind," and his critical study of the major current themes in Christian apologetics, made from the standpoint of linguistic empiricism, reveals an ability unusual for one outside the theological "circle" to understand theological discourse knowledgeably and appreciatively.

For those in the "non-metaphysical" camp of Christian responses to analytical positivism, Hepburn's trenchant criticisms of such modern apologetical devices as the appeals to personal relationship, the fact of Christ, history, morality and the cosmos, are fairly devastating. While his criticisms of each position are by no means without weaknesses of their own, and while each position considered is itself possessed of real strength, the student of theology will do well to examine the weaknesses in contemporary theological language which Hepburn analyses so cogently.

The remarkable thing about *Christianity and Paradox*, however, is that while on the one hand it seems to give aid and comfort to the "non-metaphysical" (or, if you will, the *blik*) Christian of philosophical orientation, it should on the other hand make him terribly uneasy and somewhat embarrassed.

For one who, for example, finds T. R. Miles's version of the Christian *blik* most congenial, Hepburn's last chapter, "Scepticism and the Naturally Religious Mind," is nothing short of astonishing. For here he spells out in detail what he has been intimating throughout the book; namely, that the solution for the religiously-minded sceptic like himself lies in the *language of parable*. The only difference that I can see between Miles's theological position and Hepburn's is that Miles, as a Christian, restricts himself to the Christian "parable," while Hepburn, as a sceptic, feels free to draw not only upon the Christian parable but also upon any other parables which in the course of history have helped man to understand himself. Hepburn as much as says[19] that his position is similar to that of R. B. Braithwaite's *An Empiricist's View of the Nature of Religious Belief*. Miles likewise acknowledges the parallels between his own and Braithwaite's view.[20]

The upshot of this should be clear: Here is a *sceptic*, however religiously sympathetic he may be, whose fundamental attitude towards religious language is almost identical to at least certain types of the "non-metaphysical" *Christian* response. I said earlier that the fact that the "non-metaphysical" responses were basically elaborations of Hare's *blik* theory may be an endemic weakness of this theological approach to linguistic empiricism. If ever a case illustrated it, the one I have just described does. Just wherein do Miles, say, and Hepburn differ, except that the latter has taken the option of selecting from a variety of *bliks* rather than confining himself to one *blik*? Furthermore, Hepburn considers himself a sceptic and not a believer, and yet his view of theological language and its epistemological status is identical to that of Miles. What precisely *does* the "non-metaphysical" Christian have to commend to someone like Hepburn? Indeed, there is the even more acute question as to whether the "non-metaphysical" Christian such as Miles has not completely abandoned any semblance of traditional theology.

For the Barthian or otherwise radically biblical theologian —those "non-metaphysical" Christians who do not believe philosophy to have a material effect on theology—the theological problems posed for the men discussed in this article may seem relatively unimportant or even useless.[21] For those, however, who call themselves both Christians and philosophers, the empiricist critique of metaphysics, coupled with the clarifying methods of linguistic analysis, has raised serious epistemological questions for their theology.

Even those "metaphysical" theologians who continue to press for a fully metaphysical theology in our day are constrained to spend large portions of their theological writings demonstrating to their satisfaction against positivism and linguistic analysis that the metaphysical enterprise is still valid.[22] The chief "metaphysical" options for the theologian today seem to be some form of Thomism, personal idealism, process philosophy, or existentialism. There is much constructive work going on in each camp, and yet it seems to me that there must be even more serious attention given to the epistemological problems which Hume and his empiricist successors have posed.

For those Christians who find that they cannot accept either the Barthian rejection of metaphysics or the various "non-metaphysical" *blik* philosophies, the only direction remaining is a metaphysical one. It seems to me, in that case, that the first task will be to continue Dorothy Emmet's restatement of metaphysics as an "analogical art" rather than as a deductive science. The second task will be the grounding of this enterprise in the firm soil of empirical data. Thirdly, the rigorous methods of linguistic analysis will provide a lucid conceptual and linguistic structure.

I believe that a fruitful possibility for future metaphysical theology is a personal idealism grounded in the solid foundation of Ian Ramsey's linguistic analysis, with the pronoun "I" as the model or analogy for further metaphysical assertion. The case for an idealist metaphysics is far from closed, since it is grounded in that self-consciousness behind which the knower cannot go. Furthermore, it seems to me that personal idealism accords with the biblical understanding of God and man. But these are very tentative suggestions. Christian metaphysical theology must approach its subject-matter with a humble and chastened outlook and with a resolution to be logically analytical and soundly rational.

It has been the aim of this article to point out, first of all, that there is a significant division of Christian responses to linguistic empiricism between the "metaphysical" and the "non-metaphysical." Secondly, I have tried, through a brief presentation of some of the major philosophically-oriented "non-metaphysical" responses, to present what I believe to be their basic assumption and to suggest some problems which are not only unresolved by this assumption but which actually pose serious questions to its fundamental validity. Those of us who feel that Christian theology still has a stake in philosophy cannot rest content with the "non-metaphysical" option of a *blik* theory. The way out of the predicament seems to me to be a metaphysical and rational one. Nevertheless, as I hope this article has made clear, there can be no going behind the insights of empiricism and linguistic analysis. The next step for Christian rationalism and metaphysics will rather move beyond these analytical movements and incorporate their insights into a more profound synthesis.

NOTES

1. Karl Barth, *Church Dogmatics,* I, 1, tr. G. T. Thomson and Harold Knight (Edinburgh, 1956), pp. 141–2.
2. Dietrich Bonhoeffer called it a 'positivism of revelation,' *Letters and Papers from Prison,* tr. R. H. Fuller (London, 1953), p. 148.
3. New York, 1955.
4. ibid., pp. 99–103.
5. ibid., p. 108.
6. I am aware that MacIntyre is no longer a Christian. However, for the purposes of this article I am considering only his Christian writings.
7. T. R. Miles, *Religion and the Scientific Outlook* (London, 1959), p. 162.
8. ibid., pp. 161–2.
9. Alasdair MacIntyre, ed., *Metaphysical Beliefs* (London, 1957), p. 85.
10. MacIntyre's critique of the classical 'proofs' for God's existence is one of the strong points of his little book *Difficulties in Christian Belief* (London, 1959).
11. *Metaphysical Beliefs,* p. 211.
12. Ian T. Ramsey, *Religious Language* (London, 1957), p. 90.
13. ibid., p. 90.
14. ibid., p. 37.
15. ibid., p. 38.
16. ibid., p. 185.
17. Ian T. Ramsey, ed., *Prospect for Metaphysics* (London, 1961), p. 174.
18. Ronald W. Hepburn, *Christianity and Paradox* (London, 1958).
19. ibid., pp. 192–3.
20. Miles, op. cit., p. 165.
21. Karl Barth, *The Humanity of God* (London, 1961), pp. 58–59; here, in brief compass, Barth criticises both linguistic analysis and the Bonhoeffer of *Letters and Papers.*
22. Two recent examples on the British scene are Eric Mascall's *Words and Images* (New York, 1957) from a Thomist perspective; and F. H. Cleobury's *Christian Rationalism and Philosophical Analysis* (London, 1959), which restates the case for personal idealism.

Whither the Doctrine of God Now?

David Jenkins

David Jenkins is convinced that the "beyond theism" program of fellow Anglican John A. T. Robinson, Bishop of Woolwich, is wrongheaded. It attempts, says Dr. Jenkins, to come to terms with "Post-Copernican Man" entirely on his own terms, and in seeking a third way between theism and atheism it is logically destined to end in the latter. Contrary to the bishop's contention, theism is not "mythological"; it is either true or false. "The debate is not about talk but about the way things really are." Nonetheless, theists must face up to the reasons which prompted the search for a third way, must show how theism can be entertained as a live option in today's world. Viewing the challenge of Post-Copernican Man as "a challenge to learn more of God," Dr. Jenkins offers suggestions for a "post-Copernican Natural Theology." Fellow and Chaplain of Queen's College, Oxford, and Bampton Lecturer for 1966, Dr. Jenkins first wrote his essay for *The London Quarterly and Holborn Review** (July 1964 issue).

THIS PAPER does not get nearly far enough. But I do not believe we have yet gone deep enough in diagnosing the situation with regard to the doctrine of God. Until this is done we cannot see anything clearly about where the doctrine of God should go. Hence this paper is intended as a contribution to the future development of the doctrine of God by being an attempt to diagnose the present situation more clearly.

The question has been raised as to whether we are or ought to be in sight of the end of theism. Theism would come to an end if one of two mutually exclusive sets of conditions obtained. The first possibility is that there is no God and that

* 25-35 City Road, London, E.C. 1, England.

everyone comes to realize this. Theism is thus known to be void, ceases to exercise any hold and fades completely away. The second possibility is that the Christian symbol of the Last Day stands for that which will be realized in the eventual experience of all men. In that "event" men would "in the End" see God with an immediacy which is best described as "face to face" and theism would be shattered not because it was voided but because it was fulfilled. The point is that theism does not exist in its own right. It is either totally superstition or a body of belief, understanding and practice which in some form or other is required by the intermediate and interim nature of our situation and our experience. Theism is either mistaken about reality or else properly expectant about reality. In neither case is it completely and straightforwardly descriptive of reality.

Our present debate, however, is immediately occasioned by some who, while intending to remain Christians, wish to deny the continuing validity of some clear and exhaustive distinction between the positions of theism and atheism as just touched on. In raising the question "The end of Theism?," Bishop Robinson clearly did not think he was pointing to either of the possibilities referred to above. Rather he was suggesting that the symbol of a transcendent and personal God which was the essence of theism had indeed now turned out to be superstitious. That is, this symbol not only did not correspond in any understandable or life-enhancing way with reality, but was positively misleading and mythological about reality. Thus, if modern "believers" are to continue to keep hold of those features about reality for which the symbols of theism had once stood and if others are to be helped to come to grips with those aspects it is necessary to recognize the end of theism. We must face the possibility of abandoning the symbols of theism associated with and focussed upon that of the personal and transcendent God and find other ways of talking and organizing our experience. None the less, this is not a programme for atheism. It is aiming at some third thing which would rescue theism from superstition, and atheism from unbelief. Reluctant believers and enthusiastic unbelievers, however, tend to refuse to accept this and hold that the programme does look, logically, like a programme for atheism.

For reasons which will, I hope, appear, I agree with this diagnosis. For theism to come to an end in this world would only leave everyone as atheist. But it will merely encourage everyone to become or remain atheist if theistic believers do not face up to the reasons which prompted that sort of an attempt to find a third way (between theism and atheism) of which Robinson has given us an example. In this connection there are two sets of considerations, the first to do with the climate of thought in which theism is to be entertained as a live option and the second to do with the manner in which a theistic position has in fact been occupied and maintained over a very large range of recent and general Christian thought and practice.

With regard to the climate of thought, I wish to focus on what seems to me to be the crucial point for the development of theology by talking of "Post-Copernican Man." I choose this symbol from Kant's preface to the second edition of his *Critique of Pure Reason* and I do so because I believe that Kant rightly perceived the inwardness and the implications of the revolution in thought which modern man was producing and which was producing modern man.

Kant was concerned "to introduce a complete revolution in the procedure of metaphysics, after the example of the Geometricians and the Natural Philosophers." He proposed "to do just what Copernicus did in attempting to explain the celestial movements. When he found that he could make no progress by assuming that all the heavenly bodies revolved around the spectator he reversed the process and tried the experiment of assuming that the spectator revolved while the stars remained at rest." In this Copernicus was typical of the various experimentalists who had "learned that reason only perceives that which it produces after its own design, that it must not be content to follow, as it were, in the leading-strings of nature but must . . . compel nature to reply to its questions." Kant saw that this revolution in thought about the world (the replacement of the objective knower with his divine gift of reason by the subjective observer with the human capacity for experiment) required a revolution in thought about thought. Men did not gain their knowledge by the pure and *a priori* use of a reason which had the intrinsic capacity of penetrating through the appearances of phenomena to the ultimate realities. It was no longer one's understanding of reality which determined one's articulation and assessment of the observed appearances. Rather one's observation and articulation of the appearances were on the way to becoming that which determined one's understanding of reality.

It is necessary to say "on the way to becoming" when we are at Kant's stage and part in the revolution because, as is well known, Kant himself held that while the speculative reason could not go beyond its own categories and the phenomena, practical reason took one validly into the sphere of reality in which talk about God, Free Will and Goodness was proper, necessary and truthful. Here Kant remains a believer in transcendental reality, to the knowledge of which he held that the practical reason could build a rational bridge.

Post-Copernican Man in his maturity has not allowed Kant's revolution in philosophy to stem the whole revolution and preserve the transcendent realities in the manner Kant himself intended. He has carried through the revolution in thinking about the world and in thinking about thought to the completion of a revolution in the understanding of understanding itself and of knowledge. The result is that the first question which must be faced in any serious and relevant attempt to maintain, develop, re-state or even re-establish a doctrine of God is not "Is there a God?" or "What is meant by 'God'?" but "What is it to know?" For the answer to that question implies and presupposes an answer to the question "What can be known," i.e. "What can, with reasonable confidence, be held to be real?" or, even, "What is real and how is it real?" The spirit in which Post-Copernican Man explicitly or implicitly answers such questions is well reflected, for example, in the definition which Professor D. R. Newth gives (in his contribution to *Science in its Context*, ed. J. Brierley) of science as "the process by which men create knowledge in which they can place a high and often measurable degree of confidence." Knowledge is that which is produced by the use of the experimental method when men "compel nature to reply to . . . questions" (*vide* Kant cit. *supra*). Such knowledge is firm and can be confidently used, although it is never "final" in more than a strictly limited sense. As Heisenberg says (*The Physicist's Conception of Nature*, p. 27f.): "In the exact sciences the word 'final' obviously means that there are always self-contained, mathematically representable, systems of concepts and laws applicable to certain realms of experience, in which realms they are always valid. . . . Obviously, however, we cannot expect these concepts and laws to be suitable for the subsequent description of new realms of experience." A little later he remarks: "The exact sciences also start from the assumption that in the end it will always be possible to understand nature, even in every new field of experience, but that we may make no *a priori* assumptions about the meaning of the word 'understand.'"

Knowledge is a strictly human achievement which is strictly limited and relative, but which is none the less extremely potent within its limits, not least because these limits are precisely known. For Post-Copernican Man knowledge is the articulated understanding of observable and measurable realities so far achieved. There is more to know by the same and developed techniques. As such knowledge is gained it will change our understanding of what has hitherto been known. Truth is relative and it becomes truth as it is discovered, established, put to the test, articulated and used as the basis for further discovery, further relative but relevant truth. You cannot "go beyond" the knowledge you have save by building on what you have got in strict continuity with it. Experience, experiment and techniques for testing by application in understanding and action are the tests of knowledge and thereby of reality.

The symbol "Post-Copernican Man" as representing the attitude to knowledge and reality not very precisely indicated above is, I believe, a more useful representation for our purpose in considering theism than the vaguer "modern man," for the symbolism draws attention to the fact that the crisis for belief is, at its centre, epistemological—to do with knowing and what is knowable. Further, anyone who embodies or expresses the qualities and approach symbolized by Post-Copernican Man has today an unquestioned authority, an authority which is believed to be self-evident. Any other approach will not be heeded unless it can give a very good account of itself in terms which at least overlap those of Post-Copernican Man and which can establish their own claim to relevant meaningfulness. This is why Robinson attempted a version of what I have called the third way. Theism (belief in and talk about a transcendent and personal God) goes beyond the knowable facts. Theism is therefore not knowledge concerned with reality. Once it was symbolism referring mythologically to features of reality but now, on Post-Copernican principles, it is seen to be superstition and must therefore come to an end. The features of reality the symbols of theism used to refer to must be found now more firmly located in "real" reality, i.e. that which is now known and judged to be knowable. Hence the programme to re-express theism in terms of depth, concern, encounter and relationships.

But, understandable as such a programme is, it is not really a programme to replace outmoded symbols. The trouble about symbols is only symptomatic of the real trouble which is that about knowledge and reality. For the programme is an attempt to come to terms with Post-Copernican Man on his terms and these do not envisage the possibility of there being a reality which can only, and must always, be pointed to by symbols. That which is real is that which is known and that which is known is that which has been described. There is always more to know but we shall know this when we are able to describe more. Knowledge and reality remain relative terms. Hence if theism is to become acceptable to Post-Copernican Man it must become atheism, i.e. it must surrender to him, for he has no terms for anything other than relative reality and relative truth. Whatever the symbols of theism stood for, they stood for something that was in logic (and, the theist contends, in reality) different from anything which falls within the logical possibilities of Post-Copernican Man's terms. For the theist, the significance of God's presence, immanence, availability is always derived from his otherness and his absoluteness. This is a matter not of mythology, but of logic. Part of the confusion in *Honest to God* and in much of the current debate is the failure to recognize this. Anyone concerned with the future of the Doctrine of God must face up to the starkness of the clash involved here. Concentrating on symbols can simply disguise the fact that the full development of the approach of Post-Copernican Man to the world is literally godless. Symbolism is certainly a question for the doctrine of God but only after, or at least as part of, the answer to the question as to how a Doctrine of God is to be maintained and commended in a world where the acceptedly authoritative man is godless.

I have spent half of this article seeking to define more clearly what seems to me to be the essential nature of the challenge now presented to theism and to make clear how stark and definite a challenge it is because I am myself sure that the future of theism, the direction for the development of the doctrine of God, is to be found in facing up with accuracy and rigour to the challenge of the situation. This is a theological conclusion derived from my present understanding of the doctrine of God and it is reached as follows.

Any doctrine of God which is in continuity with the theism of the Bible and of Christian tradition must be clear about at least the following. *First*, the word "God" refers to, or, better, names (a) reality who/which is other than the sum total of the realities which constitute the observable (or theoretically observable) universe.

The being named "God" is not simply different *from* other beings or realities. He is different *in* being and reality. That is the logical point indicated by the caution which has to be used in referring to him as *a* being. That is also why he can be referred to only in symbols, analogies, etc. To use the name "God" and to believe that one is using it meaningfully is to assert that the reality of the world is not exhausted by the realities in the world and that symbols of the type "out there," "beyond this," "on another level" or the like (logically like, that is) are inescapable if we are to attempt to do justice to the reality in which we are involved. It is also why the conflict between Post-Copernican Man and the theist is logical with the certainty that one position or other in its ultimate conclusion about the world is false, rather than mythological with the hope that a third way would resolve the conflict. The debate is not about talk but about the way things really are. Thus the radical otherness of God (in a logical, ontological and existential sense) is a theistic axiom.

Secondly, however, the theist in the Biblical and Christian tradition holds that this is no absolute bar to the knowledge of God because God relates himself to the world and to man. The symbols which refer to this relationship are primarily "Creation" and "Revelation." The symbol of Creation stands for the assertion of the fact as a fact that the existence of realities other than God is ultimately dependent upon God. Therefore, it is conceivably in the nature of things that these other realities in their own reality may reflect God or be usable as a means of communication about God or even of God. The symbol of Revelation stands for the assertion of the fact that God so relates himself to the world that he evokes knowledge of himself in, and in connection with, particular persons and events.

Now this belief in, and assertion about, God as reality, who is both other and at the same time related as Creator and Revealer, seems to have been almost completely thrown on the defensive by a full and open confrontation with Post-Copernican Man. In this defensiveness theism is false to its own premises and experience. This brings us to the second set of considerations related to the future of the Doctrine of God—those to do with the manner in which Christian theism has very largely been practised and doctrine of God taught as men have moved into the Post-Copernican era. There has been a widespread failure either to teach sufficiently radically about, or take practical notice of, the fact that theism does not exist in its own right. It has been unconsciously assumed that on the basis of a taken-for-granted authority of the Bible and/or the Church talk about God would remain both meaningful and relevant in its own right. But religious symbols which are taken for granted and left to have force in their own right and by their own weight become idols. The very name of God is only too easily taken in vain and the repeated sin of religious men is to rely on their religion (their concepts and their rules) rather than on the God to whom the symbols pointed and with whom the religion was validly concerned. Symbols are inescapably necessary in theism. But they operate only as stultifying idols unless they are used in a manner which is not self-contained but open. God is radically other. Therefore, the truth about Him or the reality of Him cannot be contained in or be equivalent to any particular set of symbols, symbolic acts or significant encounters. All such may be means of knowing God but are not to be equated with God.

But God is related and present as Creator and Revealer. Hence the Universe is always furnished with potential symbols, and the possibilities of symbolic acts and opportunities for encounter which can kindle and have kindled the knowledge of God. Hence when theism is threatened and much (or even all) of the symbolism seems to be going dead the believer in the God with whom the theistic tradition has to do will look for a renewal of theism. (He knows that, as there is God, theism cannot either fade away or be done without.) This renewal he will look for by seeking a greater openness to God. And *this* he will seek by a greater openness to the real (and not the supposed, muted or turned aside) challenge of the situation. For the God who is other is known in the intermediate and interim manner of theism through His presence and relatedness. And because God is real and is concerned with reality He is not to be found in our illusions about the situation, but He is to be found as we seek to come to the closest grips we can with the objective reality of the situation.

It is here that the true concern of the theist meets up with the maturity of Post-Copernican Man. For Post-Copernican Man is determined to put everything to the test of experience and experiment and to proceed inductively from the knowledge he has to the building up of further knowledge. In fact, he is taking the givenness of what the theist would call the created universe absolutely seriously and in its own right. His ideal is to be open to observed and verified facts and thereby to dispel illusion and unclarity and to work in the light thus gained. This ideal represents an absolute commitment to pursuing the truth of the matter which is wholly proper to the givenness of a created universe, the data of which demand the respect which rejects all *a priori* treatment. The theist who believes that "created" is a proper adjective to apply to the Universe must not and cannot go back on this achievement of Post-Copernican Man in which he is more mature than theists have generally shown themselves to be.

What the theist knows is that there is also God to be known and that ultimately it is this knowledge which is both primary (God is the proper context of everything) and ultimate (God is the proper fulfillment of everything). He cannot, however, blame Post-Copernican Man for refusing to allow that he (the theist) has anything that can be called knowledge about "God" if he neither behaves as if he has knowledge (i.e., does not approach given reality on the basis of a real—because competent and practical—understanding of something real) nor can give any reasonably plausible account of the source or bearing of his knowledge. The questions which Post-Copernican Man puts to the theist are "How do you know God?" and "How would you suggest to me that 'knowledge of God' is knowledge?" These questions require answers based on experience (How was the body of knowledge built up and how is it passed on?) and related to possibilities of experimental living.

In facing this challenge of the situation, I would suggest, we are required to work our way towards a Post-Copernican Natural Theology, an account of revealed truth which is always sensitive to origins on the one hand and practical relevance on the other, and the development of a spiritual discipline and discipleship which is clearly an experimental attempt to make sense of our modern life in the light of our theistic understanding and to make sense of our theistic understanding in the light of our modern life. In other words, there is no way forward in the doctrine of God save on the broadest of fronts and by combining a number of enterprises.

It may be thought that on my usage "Post-Copernican Natural Theology" is a contradiction in terms, but I do not believe this is so. As a theist, I maintain the view that the universe is rightly characterized as "created." The experimental and inductive approach of Post-Copernican Man is the mature approach to the givenness of the created universe. If the theistic approach is in accord with the reality of things, then careful, sensitive and prolonged investigation of the methods, results and presuppositions of the Post-Copernican approach must yield material for a natural theology. It must be possible to find material to make a case for the "theistic hypothesis," although it will never be possible to establish it finally. (This is where the other two aspects of the enterprise mentioned above come in.)

Among the areas for search may be included: epistemology itself (Logical Positivism is by no means as complete or satisfactory as some of its first proponents supposed or as some *avant-garde* but possibly behind the times theologians now suppose. Also pure existentialism may perhaps without much difficulty be shown to lead to "the Absurd"); freedom and morality (particularly the former where it may fairly speedily become evident that man cannot be established or maintained as human on strictly Post-Copernican principles. But in either field the insight of Kant—that here lies a bridge to the transcendent—needs to be vigorously explored); psychology and sociology. (The more we know about individual and group features which affect and produce persons and personality, the more we may be able to see features in which self-contained descriptive and reductionist accounts of what personality is or what persons may be or may become are self-evidently unsatisfactory and incomplete). There is also the need to investigate and re-assess those ranges of human experience which Post-Copernican Man tries to undervalue or ignore in relation to knowledge and which have their revenge in producing a modern literature which is largely pessimistic, uncertain and unclear in contrast to Post-Copernican Man's certainty, clarity and optimism. But this again must be investigated in its own right and not be prostituted and distorted by being prematurely forced into ready-made theological categories (re guilt, sin and the like). The natural theology must be built up from what is observed in the natural as it is given to us.

But this search for a Post-Copernican Natural Theology would never be undertaken nor would it have any hope of success if it were not the case that there existed a reliable tradition of revealed knowledge of God and a constant community of current experience recognizably continuous with the experience of those who were the means of producing the tradition. God is to be known in and through the realities of the situation, but God is not the same thing as the situation, the otherness remains a reality. Natural Theology can aim at showing that there is a possibility of God in the situation. But to look for a possibility of God one must have some idea of what "God" could mean and this comes from a sensitive and lively confrontation with the tradition in which one begins to separate the symbols from the logic, and the mythology from the experience. It is to this end that the tradition, whether in the Bible or in doctrinal formulations or in the worshipping and praying practice of Christians, is to be studied and sifted with particular regard to origins (the situations which gave rise to the Tradition) and relevance (the way situations were held to be affected by that which was formulated into Tradition). (Here particular attention will have to be given to the data of and about the historical Jesus. I would venture the prophecy that more can reasonably be known in this field than the present prevailing fashions in exegesis will allow, overwhelmed as they are by a probably unsound existentialist epistemology. There may well be sufficient facts of a "hard" [by Post-Copernican standards] sort about Jesus to go quite a long way in legitimately raising the question as to whether the reality of the world is contained in and exhausted by the realities in the world.)

But that which convinces the theist that there is a God and that the challenge of Post-Copernican Man is a challenge to learn more of God and not a summons to fight a rearguard action on God's (doubtful) behalf are the occasions, whether individual or corporate, whether vivid or faintly and evasively remembered, when the challenge of the situation and the givenness of the Tradition are kindled into an awareness which makes practical, comforting and illuminating sense of both, by giving what must be described as the knowledge of a Presence and a Power. Hence it is that no doctrine of God can go forward unless it is clearly related to a spiritual discipline and discipleship which is experiential and experimental in relation both to the Tradition and to the current situation.

Thus the future of the development of the doctrine of God

must lie in sustained attempts to give an account of the ways in which confrontation of the situation, exploration of the Tradition and personal discipleship yield knowledge of God and what the content and bearing of this knowledge is. Such attempts must emerge from and be backed up by a Christian community which is plainly living experimentally and openly. The challenge of Post-Copernican Man has decisively reminded us that Christian theology and Christian living must be conducted together.

II

Nature and Law

Ethical reflection is a constitutive dimen-

Naturalism, Historicism, and Christian Ethics: Toward a Christian Doctrine of Natural Law

Douglas Sturm

Following an examination of the hypothesis that affirms a radical differentiation between the idea of natural (moral) law and Christian faith, Douglas Sturm presents an alternative position which holds that a form of natural law is a "necessary implicate" of Christian faith. It is Sturm's thesis that "Christianity does indeed 'take history seriously,' but does so by means of its apprehension of that permanent character or pattern of reality by virtue of which there is a single universe or world within which change (thus history) is possible and natural." Dr. Sturm's paper, from the January 1964 issue of *The Journal of Religion,** was originally presented at the January 1963 meeting of the American Society for Christian Social Ethics. An Assistant Professor in the Department of Religion at Bucknell University, Dr. Sturm has recently engaged in a study of law at the Law School of Harvard University under a fellowship from the American Council of Learned Societies.

ETHICAL REFLECTION is a constitutive dimension of the Christian theological enterprise. That is, if "the task of theology is that of the adequate conceptual statement in a given historical situation of the existential understanding of God, the world, and man, which is given in and with faith in the kerygma or proclamation of the Christian church,"[1] and

* University of Chicago Press, Chicago, Illinois 60637.

if, as seems evident, any existential understanding of God, the world, and man is of ethical import, then the theological task is incomplete without consideration of "the ground and goal, the motives and norms, the means and the consequences of right action."[2] This consideration may well involve the theological ethicist in comparative analyses in order to demonstrate by contrast or lack of contrast in what respect(s) his understanding of ethics is congruent with or divergent from other ethical alternatives, Christian and/or non-Christian.

As a result of such a comparative analysis, some theological ethicists have in recent decades been led to draw a severe line of differentiation between Christian ethics and the tradition of natural (moral) law theory in any and all of its forms. Thus Jacques Ellul sees

> a striking contradiction between [the concept of] natural law and what is revealed in scriptures regarding law and called divine law by us, for want of a better term. The doctrine of natural law as a Christian doctrine is thus ruled out at every point.[3]

And William Stringfellow, applauding vigorously, affirms "an original opposition between natural law and Christian faith," for the notion of natural law

> rests upon the idea of the good as the aim of human life. But the Gospel does not rest at all on this concept, but upon the event of Jesus Christ and Christ is not some concept but the Person in whom Christians know the living God.[4]

It is the purpose of this essay to examine this hypothesis of radical differentiation between the idea of natural (moral) law and Christian faith, first, by a presentation of its basis and, second, by the presentation of an alternative position. In the latter part of the paper it will be argued that, contrary to the position expressed above, there is a form of natural law that is a necessary implicate of Christian faith.

Here we shall take the term "law" (in the sense of moral law) to mean "any kind of rule or canon, whereby actions are framed"[5] or "a rule and measure of acts, whereby man is induced to act or restrained from acting."[6] By "natural" is meant that which is inborn or is of an inherent quality. Thus the natural is to be differentiated from the artificial or from that which is man-made. Consequently a natural (moral) law is a canon or rule of action which in some sense inheres in or is constitutive of any situation within which action takes place.

I. Foundation of the Opposition Between Natural Law and Christian Ethics

The fundamental difficulty that leads Christian ethicists to reject the doctrine of natural law is found in the judgment that natural law seems to suppose, that is, inherently to involve, a theory of reality that is radically alien to the Hebraic-Christian apprehension of the nature of reality. Specifically, the doctrine of natural law implies a naturalistic view of reality whereas the Hebraic-Christian view is historical. To clarify the exact character of this conceived opposition we shall describe more precisely the meaning of the terms "naturalism" and "historicism" as they relate to the problem at hand.

A. NATURALISM AND CLASSICAL ANTIQUITY

It is a truism that the Western natural-law tradition finds its roots in classical antiquity.[7] To be sure, the doctrine of natural law varies in content as differing "climates of opinion" prevail, altering the character of the mists that becloud men's eyes[8] and/or as differing modes of economic production and distribution "create" varying ideological superstructures;[9] nonetheless the ancients seem to have retained their position as having "stolen" (or, more accurately, formulated or at least prefigured) men's best ideas, and this is true of the development of natural-law doctrine as well. The term "naturalism" is here used to designate that fundamental view of reality that is characteristic of classical antiquity.

The "Greek mind," if one may be permitted such a generalization in an age of hardheaded empiricism,[10] viewed the world as governed in a unified and universal fashion by "definite and comprehensible laws."[11] In art, in literature, in philosophy, in education, the Greeks sought a "clear perception of the permanent rules which underlie all events and changes in nature and in human life."[12] It must be made clear that the laws or rules of the universe were viewed in the dominant Greek tradition not mechanistically, but organically. According to this organic perspective, each aspect of the world was considered a part of a living whole. It is in this sense that "the idea of the cosmos is one of the outstanding contributions of Greek philosophy."[13] Yet at the same time, each object was itself seen as possessing the quality of wholeness. On either the macrocosmic or the microcosmic level, to see the "whole" of the thing is to see its "idea"; and its "idea" is its nature. Thus

> to the Greek, it has been said, the natural apple was not the wild one from which our cultivated apple has been grown, but rather the golden apple of the Hesperides. The "natural" object was that which expressed most completely the idea of the thing. It was the perfect object.[14]

The nature of a thing is its internal and essential principle of motion and rest, its definitive form constituting its resident potentiality which is fulfilled only as actualized.[15] On this basis one can speak intelligibly of the "innate tendency" in all "productions of nature" "in the direction of the best conditions of which they are capable."[16] An object's innate tendency constitutes the law of its being. Thus the Greeks were members of the "school of immanence" with respect to their doctrine of law.[17] From this perspective reality as a whole is basically and inherently orderly, regular, uniform, systematic. "Any glorification of change was an idea foreign to the Greeks. They . . . held the static and the immutable higher than that which fluctuates."[18] This understanding of a permanent and inherent lawful order that is constitutive of things, underlying all movement and all change, is a constant theme "from Thales to Plotinus"; "it informs not only Greek metaphysics and cosmology, but also ethics; and it is the most powerful single factor in determining the Greek view of man."[19]

It should be observed at this point that the Greeks were above all concerned with man.

Their anthropomorphic gods; their concentration on the problem of depicting the human form in sculpture and even in painting; the logical sequence by which their philosophy moved from the problem of the cosmos to the problem of man, in which it culminated with Socrates, Plato, and Aristotle; their poetry, whose inexhaustible theme . . . is man, his destiny, and his gods; and finally their state which cannot be understood unless viewed as the force which shaped man and man's life—all these are separate rays from one great light. They are the expressions of an anthropocentric attitude to life . . . which pervades everything felt, made or thought by the Greeks. Other nations made gods, kings, spirits; the Greeks alone made men.[20]

And the Greeks made men by the process of education, that is, by educing toward fulfilment or maturation the resident potentialities of human nature. Education and, in fact, the whole social-political order are conceived as instruments of ethical realization, means of molding the human character in conformity with the inherent laws of *humanitas*.[21] It is intelligible within this view to say that "man's basic and prime duty is to become (in fact, actually, fully, completely) what he is (in idea, potentially, germinally, essentially)" or that "the supreme principle of oughtness is simply this: Become your essential being."[22]

However, whether the appeal is to the soul of man (Aristotle) or to the soul of the universe (Zeno), the final court of judgment in matters of moral behavior is the inherent nature of things, the permanent, eternal, immutable "rightness" that characterizes the cosmos in its innermost essence. Immorality is disease, abnormality a distortion of the natural inclinations of the organism.

This capsule depiction of the "Greek mind" involves, of course, a reckless neglect of the definitive differences in metaphysical and ethical theory and in the concomitant use of the term "natural law" in the history of Greek life and thought.[23] Nonetheless, it may suffice to demonstrate in a manner not wholly inaccurate the general understanding of reality within which the notion of natural (moral) law (i.e., a canon or rule

82 DOUGLAS STURM

of action which inheres in or is constitutive of any situation within which action takes place) is intelligible. It is an understanding of reality that is naturalistic, humanistic, immanentalistic—and non-historical. On each of these points, the Christian ethicists referred to above demur.

B. HISTORICISM AND CHRISTIAN FAITH

The demurral results from a second truism, namely, that Christianity, as well as its Hebraic prologue, is a historical religion and involves a historical view of reality. The historicism that is characteristic of Christianity is of dual meaning. First, Christianity is founded upon a given historical event.

> The God of the Bible is revealed not so much in the permanent structures of life through which history flows as in the "mighty acts," the peculiar events of history which point beyond themselves to the ultimate ground and the mystery and meaning which give significance to our existence.[24]

What A. J. Heschel writes of Judaism in this respect[25] is equally true, *mutatis mutandis*, of Christianity. Judaism, he argues, is a "religion of time"; the God of Israel is not discovered in the facts of nature, but manifest in the events of history; since God is a living God, he is not merely at our disposal but speaks when he wills to speak. Thus "the root of Jewish faith is . . . not a comprehension of abstract principles but an inner *attachment to sacred events*," a "commitment to revelation."[26] In the case of the Israelites, the event constitutive of their existence is the revelation of God on Mt. Sinai and the covenant there consummated between Yahweh and the people. In the case of the Christians, the definitive movement is the event of the revelation of God in Jesus Christ. Indeed this special revelation is conceived to be the historical event par excellence, for history, by definition, tends toward the unique, the non-repetitive, the *einmalig*, and

> revelation means the unique historical event which, *by its very nature*, must either take place once or not at all. And it is *only* revelation in this Christian sense which contains this element of absolute and never-recurring actuality.[27]

In this sense it has been said that of religions, Christianity is the "only one that takes history seriously."[28]

The holiness of the scriptures of the Hebraic-Christian tradition derives from the fact that these documents constitute the immediate testimony to this particular and unique sacred event. It is the task of Christian thought, relying on the witness of scripture "to state the significance and implications of these historical facts [the life, character, teaching, and death of Jesus Christ, and, above all, his resurrection] for our ultimate philosophy or attitude towards life."[29] This is to say that the Christian view of reality is based primarily, if not exclusively, upon the revelatory event wherein the Word of God is declared in Jesus Christ. Christian theology is thus kerygmatic; it is centered in the proclamation of what God has done; it articulates and interprets the "good news" of salvation made possible by divine grace. The destiny of man is understood anew as a result of God's action on man's behalf. Further, it is in relation to what God has done in the event of revelation that the Christian community arrives at its understanding of "right action." Ethics, that is to say, is a subsidiary, yet an integral aspect, of theology. The didache of primitive Christianity (the instruction in the "ethical principles and obligations of the Christian life") is based upon and is the practical implication of the *kerygma*.[30] This relationship between the proclaimed act of God and the practical act of the Christian is, indeed, one of "conformation" (Bonhoeffer), for

> the Christian life is here understood as a reenactment from below on the part of men of the shape of the revelatory drama of God's holy will in Jesus Christ. . . . *This same shape of grace*, in its re-capitulation within the life of the believer and the faithful community is the nuclear matrix which grounds and unfolds as the Christian life.[31]

The "divine imperative" (Brunner) is thus the implicate of the divine indicative. That is, the "shape of God's deed" in the particular and unique historical event of Christ constitutes the foundation of that rule or measure of human action which is typically Christian.

At this point is to be understood the second (and related) meaning of historicism in Christianity. History, as indicated

above, tends toward the unique and the non-repetitive. Each
historical moment has its own (relatively) singular character;
it presents man with a novel configuration of possibilities, is
composed of a complex of demands that has never confronted
man before in exactly the same form. The commitment of the
Christian is ever to heed the Word of God and ever to conform to the will of God. But the will of God is both known
and unknown.

> It is known in Christ who is the incarnate concretion of
> God's ultimate and relentless will-to-restoration; and it re-
> mains unknown in the fact that the actual service of this
> will is presented to the believer not as a general program
> given in advance but as an everlasting and fluctuant obli-
> gation to the neighbor in the midst of history and life.[32]

The divine imperative is not, in the Christian view, derived
from an apprehension of the essential nature of man. Rather
the demands of God "arise quite simply from the crisis of decision in which man stands before God."[33] The utterances of
Jesus in the Sermon on the Mount are not general principles
definitive of the category of *humanitas*, but of an "occasional
character," momentary concretizations of the revelation of
God in Christ as that revelation confronts differing historical
situations.[34] The Christian ethic is an ethic of obedience, duty,
decision—but the particular *content* of the ethic is variable,
contingent upon the moment of action. In this sense, the
Christian life is a life of "openness to the future";[35] it is a life
that is "open to forms and occasions of obedience that the
emerging and unpredictable facts of man's involvement in social change constantly present to him for obedience."[36]

It appears that Jacques Ellul may be an advocate of virtually the same thesis when he asserts that the "problem of the
content of the divine law" is a matter for an investigation that

> proceed(s) from God's revelation as it has been recorded
> in time, and received and understood today by men who
> in turn live in time . . . we can grasp revelation only in
> one particular form and express it in one form for our
> own time.[37]

Thus Christianity is a historical religion both in the sense that it originates in a certain complex event that constitutes the normative element in the Christian community in all of its subsequent phases and development and in the sense that it views God's imperative Word as being addressed anew to each novel moment of human history.

Given this statement of the nature of Christianity, the contrast and clash with the Greek view are strikingly evident. Whereas the Greek view of reality is naturalistic, anthropocentric, and humanistic, emphasizing the immanence of the laws of man's moral nature and the permanence of the human type, the Christian view of reality is historicistic, theocentric, emphasizing the historically revealed will of God as the source of man's duty and the variability and uniqueness of the situation and demands of human action. The Greek ethic is an ethic of self-realization; the Christian ethic is an ethic of obedience. It is on the basis of this contrast that the argument of the incompatibility of the doctrine of natural law and Christian faith rests.

II. Foundation of the Congruence Between Natural Law and Christian Faith

However, the pattern of relationship between the notion of natural law and the ethical import of Christian faith assumes a different cast when a more adequate account is taken of the complete structure of the Christian understanding of reality. There are three basic propositions that constitute this structure, each proposition possessing (at least) a dual reference—to God and to man. First, God is creator; the anthropological correlate of this proposition is that man is created by God specifically in God's own image. Secondly, God is judge; the anthropological correlate of this statement is that man is a sinner, in whom therefore the image of God is deformed. Thirdly, God is redeemer; the anthropological correlate of this equation is that God initiates and effects a transformation of man thereby accomplishing a restoral of the image of God.[38] The same triadic structure is evident in the doctrine of the Christ. Christ is the Word (Logos) of God through whom all things were made, the origin and "location" of the normative character or intentionality of creation. Christ is therefore also the judge of creation, before whom all creatures are evaluated in relation to the divine intent. Christ is finally the one who reconstructs or reforms creation, fulfilling the divine purpose in creation.

Within the structure of this doctrine, a number of characteristic judgments about the ethical meaning of the doctrine of Christ are properly understood:

> In Christ, therefore, man is confronted with that Word, Wisdom, or Law which is the law of his creation, the same which was partially disclosed to Israel in the Torah, and is known in some measure to all mankind, through conscience and reason, as the Law of Nature.[39] For the answer to the question "What is good?" the Christian looks at God's revelation in Jesus Christ. Christ is the restoration of the true image of man, because he is the incarnation of the love which is the meaning of our existence.[40] The idea that Christ is the "essential" man, the perfect norm of human character is expressed scripturally in the Pauline phrase that Christ is the "second Adam." . . . The actual phrase is used sparingly. But the whole New Testament consistently regards Christ as the final norm of human character. The Johannine prologue regards Christ as the historical manifestation of the divine *logos* which is the pattern of the whole creation.[41]

> Hence, the imitation of Christ [which is here presented as one of the typical features of the primitive Christian ethic], being the imitation of God himself so far as God can be a model to His creatures, becomes a mode of absolute ethics.[42]

It is also within the context of this structure that the historicity of Christianity receives its appropriate interpretation. In relation to the first meaning of historicity, the event of the revelation of God in Jesus Christ does *not* mean that "when Christ came the attitude of God to men altered, or His purpose for them took a new direction, or even His character changed for the better." Rather with the coming of Christ there was an effective disclosure in action of what the attitude, and purpose, and character of God always was, always is, and always will be. [Thus] the God of our redemption is the same as the God of our creation. [And, therefore] the law of the new covenant, which is correlative with the act of God in Christ, is aboriginal. It is the law of our creation, and its field of application is as wide as the creation itself.[43]

It is an implication of this position that "the decision for or against Christ is made by people who do not even know his name."[44] Thus while it is proper within the Christian understanding of the nature of things to emphasize the necessity of the revelation in Christ of the law (the rule or canon of action) that applies to the human creature, the "hidden Christ" that "operates in history" must not be overlooked.[45] To assert this doctrine of the "hidden Christ" that confronts man with the law of his being at every decisive moment of his existence is not to overlook the radically sinful condition of man, for

it is at least conceivable that what makes authentic existence everywhere factually possible is not that man is not completely fallen, but that, in spite of his fallenness, he is everlastingly the object of God's love, which is omnipresently efficacious as a redemptive possibility.[46]

Thus the historic event of Jesus as the Christ, which constitutes the origin and the normative foundation of the Christian community, is an efficacious manifestation of what always has been, is, and shall be the case, namely, that man "discovers," or is confronted at each moment with, the law of his being in an encounter with the living God, who is his creator, judge, and redeemer. In this sense, the historicity of Christianity in no way conflicts with the notion of natural (moral) law, at least in its formal character. Indeed, in this sense, the notion of natural law (i.e., a canon or rule of action that inheres in or is constitutive of any situation within which action takes place) is an essential implication of Christian faith. This is not to say that the "law of man's being" is known or is operative independent of the revelation of God; rather it is to say that the law is "grounded in the claim of God which is his

Word, that is to say, in the universal confrontation of all men by the self-revealed God."[47]

However, even if it is the case that the originating historical event of the Christian community is nothing more (though nothing less!) than an efficacious and decisive manifestation of the omnipresently operative grace of God, calling men toward the actualization of the divine purpose of creation, there is the second (and related) sense in which historicism is integral to Christian faith; and it is in relation to this sense that the notion of natural (moral) law is also often eschewed by Christian ethicists. Each historical moment is conceived to possess its own singular character; there is an ever changing, mutable, transformative character to the course of historical events; consequently (it is said) each instant of moral decision confronts each man with a novel complex of possibilities and demands. The content of the faithful man's ethical obligation is held thus to be ever fluctuant, taking account of the peculiarity of the circumstances of action. On the other hand, natural (moral) law seems to present itself as possessing the characteristics of permanence, immutability, universality, constancy,[48] for it presumes to present a rule or canon of action that is the same for all men at all times and in all places. There is a tendency in a moral law that is founded in the common nature of the human species or in the nature of the cosmos to "leave out of account the variability of human desires and sensitivities in different times and climes,"[49] or to consider such variability unnatural, or of a lesser order of reality than the static and unvarying. Where Christianity "takes history seriously," the tendency is for natural-law theorists to assume a non-historical or transhistorical stance. Stated in this way it would appear that an ethic must *either* conceive moral principles as permanent, immutable, static *or* view men's obligations as changing, mutable, variable. However, it can be argued that there is a third position, according to which the ethic in some sense synthesizes both these alternatives. Indeed, it can be argued that the natural (moral) law that constitutes the primary (if not the exclusive) ethical obligation of Christian faith, while immutable, permanent, and universal, yet is of such a character that it incorporates within itself an imperative insistence upon taking full and proper account of the mutable, the transient, and the particular. To be specific, according to Christian understanding, the natural (moral) law is the law of love.[50] That is, the fundamental rule or canon of action is the twofold commandment: "Thou shalt love the Lord thy God with all thy heart, and with all thy soul, and with all thy mind. This is the first and great commandment. And the second is like unto it, Thou shalt love thy neighbor as thyself."[51] The appropriate form of human action is thus a repetition of the form of divine action. As God loves, so is man meant to love. Love in this instance means the creation of a bond of sympathy, concern, care for the other; it means acting on his behalf and for his benefit; it means concretely meeting his needs; it means the intention or active determination of will that is directed toward the fulfilment of the requirements of his well-being. Love so conceived is both universal in scope and individual in attention. "God is held to love all, not just a few; always, not just at times; in all their being, not with neglect of this or that aspect."[52] Given this love which is expressed supremely by God and is meant to be responsively actualized by man, the resultant form of relationship is "a synthesis of . . . change and permanence, or the one and the many, or order and creative freedom."[53] That is, love, by its very nature, although ever the same, takes full account of the historicity of existence and is the principle of action that itself involves or spontaneously necessitates attention to the particularity of circumstance within which it attains actualization. Thus love, as the supreme rule or canon of human action in human relations, means sympathetic concern and active care for the neighbor—for each neighbor and every neighbor in each particular and peculiar moment of existence and at every particular and peculiar moment of existence.

It might not be inappropriate to observe that this understanding of love as the rule or canon of action aims ultimately toward the actualization of a relationship of mutual care and concern or of mutual love.[54] This is so because if to love is God's nature, and if therefore for man to love is to actualize the image of God in which man is created and so to fulfil the divine intent for mankind, and if to love one's neighbor is actively to intend the fulfilment of his being, then to love another is to desire that the other in turn love as he has been loved. This is to say that the intention of the creative, judging, and redeeming impress of God upon the events of human existence is the formulation of "a community knit together by self-giving love"[55] which in its final form gathers up all the nations into one. In such a community "what flows from each enriches the life of all and each participant in the whole life finds his own good realized through the giving of self to the life of the whole."[56] Thus the love commandment intends or means a "condition of complete harmony between the soul and God, its neighbor and itself."[57]

This natural (moral) law of love, which directs man toward the realization of a universal community of love, is understood within Christian faith to be a universal, permanent, immutable law, and in general structure it is ever the same. But its precise actualization, given its very nature, is variable, as the conditions of human existence vary. In this sense, the natural (moral) law of love is more a "quality and direction of action"[58] than a principle that provides within itself a precise and detailed indication of all that is required of man. Thus the actualization of love will assume

> various typical forms in reference to the *historical climates* or *constellations* through which the development of mankind passes. . . . And it is according to these historical climates, as recognized by a sound philosophy of history, which is here indispensable, that we have to conceive the *concrete historical ideals*, or prospective images of what is to be hoped for in our age: ideals which are neither absolute nor bound to an unrealizable past, but which are *relative*—relative to a given time—and can be proclaimed and pursued as *realizable*.[59]

Consequently in the Christian ethic, the fundamental principle of action is permanent, immutable, static, yet is of such a character that according to it men's obligations are, in the respect indicated, changing, mutable, variable. In other words, Christianity does indeed "take history seriously," but does so by means of its apprehension of that permanent character or pattern of reality by virtue of which there is a single universe or world within which change (thus history) is possible and natural.

It is possible, therefore, by taking adequate account of the complete structure and meaning of the Christian understanding of reality, to conclude that a line of absolute differentiation ought not to be drawn between Christian ethics and the notion of natural (moral) law. Indeed, according to Christian faith, there is a rule or canon of action that is constitutive of every situation within which men act, for

There lives the dearest freshness deep down things;
. . . .
Because the Holy Ghost over the bent
    World broods with warm breast and with ah! bright
        wings.
(Gerard Manley Hopkins, "God's Grandeur")

And this natural law, although possessing the quality of constancy, immutability, and permanence does not ignore and does not depreciate historical particularity and historical process; rather it incorporates within itself an imperative declaration that the uniqueness of the situation of decision and action be heeded and be (in part) determinative of the precise form of the actualization of itself.

It is an implication of the position here presented that while the Greek classical "concept of nature as a closed system, determined by its own exclusive laws"[60] is unacceptable, Christian faith does not imply the opposite—sheer historicism —in its rejection. Rather it involves and implies a principle of reality that takes full and integral account of both order and activity, structure and process, law and freedom. Consequently modern Christian ethical reflection might well benefit from a consideration of classical moral and political philosophy (as in fact it has done in the past!), not repudiating the Greek tradition out of hand, but learning from the tradition while bringing to bear upon it the determinative criterion of its own understanding of the nature of reality and the consequent natural law of human action—the law of love—that is a constitutive part of and is derived from that understanding.

92 DOUGLAS STURM

NOTES

1. Schubert M. Ogden, "The Concern of the Theologian," in *Christianity and Communism,* ed. Merrimon Cunninggim (Dallas: Southern Methodist University Press, 1958), p. 60.

2. James Luther Adams, "Ethics," in *A Handbook of Christian Theology* (New York: Meridian Books, 1958), p. 110.

3. Jacques Ellul, *The Theological Foundation of Law,* trans. Marguerite Wieser (London: SCM Press, 1960), p. 68. See pp. 68 ff. for Ellul's enumeration of the various points of contradiction between divine law and natural law, thus demonstrating the radical incompatibility between the two. The parenthetical addition in the quotation is to account for Ellul's distinction between natural law as a concept and natural law as an event.

4. William Stringfellow, "The Christian Lawyer as a Churchman," *The Christian Scholar,* XL (September, 1957), 229.

5. Richard Hooker, *Of the Laws of Ecclesiastical Polity* (London: J. M. Dent, 1907) p. 154.

6. Thomas Aquinas *Summa theologica* I-II. Q. 90. art. 1; *Introduction to St. Thomas Aquinas* (New York: Modern Library, 1958), p. 610.

7. See, e.g., Reinhold Niebuhr, "The Two Sources of Western Culture," *The Christian Idea of Education,* ed. Edmund Fuller (New Haven, Conn.: Yale University Press, 1957), p. 239; and Ernest Barker, "Translator's Introduction," in Otto Gierke's *Natural Law and the Theory of Society* (Boston: Beacon Press, 1957), p. xxxiv.

8. See chap. i of Carl Becker's *Heavenly City of the Eighteenth-Century Philosophers* (New Haven, Conn.: Yale University Press, 1959).

9. See Friedrich Engels, "Excerpts from *Herr Eugen Dühring's Revolution in Science,*" in *Marx and Engels: Basic Writings on Politics and Philosophy,* ed. Lewis Feuer (Garden City, N. Y.: Doubleday & Co., 1959), pp. 270–80.

10. By way of justification, it might be worthy of observation that the introduction to Werner Jaeger's massive, detailed, and classical study of *Paideia, the Ideals of Greek Culture* (2d ed.; New York: Oxford University Press, 1945), Vol. I, is sprinkled throughout with such terms as "the Greek mind," the "Greek spirit," the "Greek mindset," the "Greek orientation."

11. *Ibid.,* p. xx.

12. *Ibid.,* p. xxi.

13. A. J. Heschel, *God in Search of Man* (New York: Meridian Books, 1959) p. 92.

14. Roscoe Pound, *An Introduction to the Philosophy of Law* (rev. ed.; New Haven, Conn.: Yale University Press, 1959), p. 10.

15. Aristotle *Physics* ii. 1.

16. Aristotle *Ethics* i. 9, trans. J. A. K. Thompson (Baltimore: Penguin Books, 1955).

17. See Alfred North Whitehead, *Adventures of Ideas* (New York: Macmillan Co., 1952), pp. 142–52.

18. Herschel Baker, *The Image of Man: A Study of the Idea of Human Dignity in Classical Antiquity, the Middle Ages, and the Renaissance* (New York: Harper & Bros., 1961), p. 20.

19. *Ibid.*, pp. 3–4.

20. Jaeger, *op. cit.*, p. xxiii.

21. See Werner Jaeger, *Humanism and Theology* (Milwaukee: Marquette University Press, 1943), pp. 20–21. The Ciceronian concept *humanitas* is the Latin equivalent of the Greek *paideia*, according to Jaeger, representing the Greek ideal of man, the ideal pattern of humanity, the true man, the model for each and every individual.

22. Heinrich A. Rommen, *The Natural Law: A Study in Legal and Social History and Philosophy*, trans. Thomas R. Hanley (St. Louis: B. Herder, 1947), p. 178.

23. For a judicious rendering of the development and of the particular differences in the theory of natural law in the Graeco-Roman period, see James Luther Adams, "The Law of Nature in Greco-Roman Thought," *Journal of Religion*, XXV (1945), 97–118. See also Heinrich Rommen, *op. cit.*, Part I, "History of the Idea of Natural Law."

24. Reinhold Niebuhr, *op. cit.*, p. 240.

25. *Op. cit.*, passim.

26. *Ibid.*, p. 213. (Italics in original.)

27. Emil Brunner, *The Mediator*, trans. Olive Wyon (Philadelphia: Westminster Press, 1947), p. 26.

28. G. Ernest Wright and Reginald H. Fuller, *The Book of the Acts of God* (Garden City, N.Y.: Doubleday & Co., 1957), p. 18.

29. Alan Richardson, *Creeds in the Making* (London: SCM Press, 1958), p. 7.

30. C. H. Dodd, *Gospel and Law* (Cambridge: Cambridge University Press, 1951), chap. i.

31. Joseph Sittler, *The Structure of Christian Ethics* (Baton Rouge: Louisiana State University Press, 1958), p. 36.

32. *Ibid.*, p. 73.

33. Rudolf Bultmann, *Jesus and the Word*, trans. Louise P. Smith and Erminie H. Lantero (New York: Charles Scribner's Sons, 1958), p. 87.

34. Joseph Sittler, *op. cit.*, pp. 49–50.

35. Bultmann, *Primitive Christianity*, trans. R. H. Fuller (New York: Meridian Books, 1956), p. 184 and *passim*.

36. Sittler, *op. cit.*, pp. 55–56.

37. Ellul, *op. cit.*, pp. 139–40.

38. See, e.g., Heinz-Horst Schrey, Hans Hermann Walz, and

W. A. Whitehouse, *The Biblical Doctrine of Justice and Law* (London: SCM Press, 1955), pp. 67–72; see also the basic structure of such theological works as John Calvin's *Institutes of the Christian Religion*.

39. C. H. Dodd, *New Testament Studies* (New York: Charles Scribner's Sons, 1952), p. 142.

40. Daniel D. Williams, *God's Grace and Man's Hope* (New York: Harper & Bros., 1949), p. 65.

41. Reinhold Niebuhr, *The Nature and Destiny of Man* (New York: Charles Scribner's Sons, 1951), II, 76–77. See also *The Final Report of the Treysa Conference*, reprinted in Schrey *et al., op. cit.,* pp. 186–97. Section B.I.1. reads in part: "The true and proper man, as God in his creation intended him to be, is Jesus Christ. The Christian has been restored and created anew according to that perfect image of God."

42. C. H. Dodd, *Gospel and Law*, p. 42; see also Schrey *et al., op. cit.,* pp. 102–3.

43. C. H. Dodd, *Gospel and Law*, pp. 78–79.

44. Paul Tillich, *Biblical Religion and the Search for Ultimate Reality* (Chicago: University of Chicago Press, 1955), pp. 45–46. The statement continues: "What is decisive is only whether they act for or against the law of love for which Christ stands. Acting according to it means being received in the unity of fulfilment. Acting against it means being excluded from fulfilment and being cast into the despair of non-being. This is biblical ethics."

45. Reinhold Niebuhr, *Nature and Destiny of Man*, II, 109, n. 6.

46. Schubert Ogden, *Christ without Myth* (New York: Harper & Bros., 1961), p. 121. On pp. 141–44, Ogden presents three lines of evidence to document this position exegetically: (1) with reference to Rom. 1:20–21, Ogden states that "the New Testament never doubts for an instant that before God each individual person is entirely and radically responsible for his final destiny." (2) With reference to I Cor. 15: 24–28, he argues that "the only basis of man's salvation the New Testament knows anything about is the everlasting love of God that is primordially active in the mighty works of creation, preservation, and redemption." (3) With reference to Matt. 25: 31–46, Ogden affirms that "the only final condition for sharing in authentic life that the New Testament lays down is a condition that can be formulated in complete abstraction from the event Jesus of Nazareth and all that it specifically imports."

47. Schrey *et al., op. cit.,* p. 135.

48. See, e.g., James Luther Adams, "The Law of Nature: Some General Considerations," *Journal of Religion*, XXV (1945), 88: "The concept of the Law of Nature involves essentially a consideration of the perennial problem of the One and the Many. This is the problem of discovering something that abides in the midst of change and serves to measure it."

49. *Ibid.*, p. 96.

50. It has been argued that the central or constitutive category of the Christian ethic is not love, but faith. See, e.g., the argument presented by Sittler in his *The Structure of Christian Ethics,* pp. 42–64. There is a sense in which this is correct. If one takes faith to mean "ultimate concern" (Tillich) or "the attitude and action of confidence in, or fidelity to, certain realities as the sources of value and the objects of loyalty" (H. R. Niebuhr) and if, as follows, the specific character of one's faith is the determinant of the specific mode or pattern of one's activity, and if one conceives love to intend or itself to mean a certain specific pattern of activity, then a given form of faith precedes and is the foundation of love. Yet it must be observed that within such a form of faith, love would constitute a *sine qua non* of faith; and in fact, it would constitute the central category so far as an explication of the *ethical* implications and significance of that form of faith is concerned. Further, it is difficult, given these indications of the meaning of faith, to know precisely what the specific difference is, if any, between faith in God and the love of God! It has also been argued that love (agape) constitutes the ultimate Christian ideal, a higher righteousness which is clearly distinguishable from justice. The latter alone is analogous to the natural-law concept of the Greeks and others. See, e.g., Walter Marshall Horton, "Natural Law and International Order," *Christendom,* IV (1944), 2, 20. On the other hand, G. Ernest Wright in *The Biblical Doctrine of Man in Society* (London: SCM Press, 1954), pp. 167–68, indicates that "the all-embracing guide to relative choices and ethical judgments is, of course, the law of neighborly love" and whereas "much has been written in modern times to indicate the difference between, and the relation of, love and justice" the fact of the matter is that "the biblical words for 'righteousness,' 'justice,' or 'judgment' or even 'vengeance' . . . reflect the biblical knowledge of God's nature as the dominant Actor in history. Hence they involve both 'love' and 'justice.' These two conceptions simply cannot be separated because they are united in God." And, of course, Paul Tillich in his *Love, Power, and Justice* (New York: Oxford University Press, 1954) argues that both love and justice possess ontological status and are integrally related such that one cannot speak of love as a higher morality than justice.

51. See, e.g., Augustine *Letters* 189.

52. Charles Hartshorne, *Reality as a Social Process* (Glencoe, Ill.: Free Press, 1953), p. 135.

53. *Ibid.*, p. 136.

54. See Augustine *City of God* xix. 14; *Letters* 138, 9–15.

55. Schrey *et al.*, *op. cit.*, p. 108.

56. D. D. Williams, *op. cit.*, p. 78.

57. Reinhold Niebuhr, *Nature and Destiny of Man,* I, 286.

58. C. H. Dodd, *Gospel and Law,* pp. 71 ff.

59. Jacques Maritain, *Man and the State,* ed. Richard O'Sullivan

(London: Hollis & Carter), pp. 142–43. In this passage from *Man and the State,* Maritain is discussing the pattern of relation between church and state that is appropriate, given the modern historical climate as distinguished from the medieval historical climate; in *True Humanism,* trans. M. R. Adamson (London: Geoffrey Bles, 1954), the same conception is discussed with reference to the basic structure of modern Western civilization as a whole. While the quotation above is taken out of its original context, there is no essential distortion of Maritain's conception. See also John Calvin, *Institutes of the Christian Religion,* IV, xx, 15.

60. Charles Norris Cochrane, *Christianity and Classical Culture* (New York: Oxford University Press, 1957), p. 411.

Autonomy and Reason in Judaism

Alexander Carlebach

The religious problem of autonomy versus heteronomy—reliance upon human reason as opposed to unquestioning submission to the revealed will of God—is a difficult and perennial one. First tracing the various ways the problem has been treated in different periods of Jewish history, Rabbi Alexander Carlebach argues against both the tendency to absolutize the Torah as an imposed system of duties (heteronomy) and the tendency to interpret the Torah solely from a subjective or humanistic standpoint (autonomy). Dr. Carlebach opts for a median way—for a Torah-inspired life that would affirm rather than thwart modern man's hard-won inner freedom. The Fall 1963 issue of *Tradition: A Journal of Orthodox Jewish Thought* * is the original source of Dr. Carlebach's article. He is the rabbi of Belfast, Northern Ireland, and Editor of the *Belfast Jewish Record*.

THE OVERWHELMING stress on Torah as Law, as a normative system of duties imposed on the Jew, has tended to result in an overemphasis on the heteronomous character of Judaism.[1] It is the purpose of this essay to examine this fundamental and perennial problem of religion: autonomy versus heteronomy.

It will be necessary to define the essence and extent of the problem and to recognize its position in relation to cognate themes of religious philosophy. To the Jew who has accepted Torah as the sum total of divine revelation and who believes in such revelation as both possible and necessary and, moreover, as a historical fact, the question of autonomy is first of

* Rabbinical Council of America, Room 1101, 84 Fifth Avenue, New York 11, New York.

all one of *motivation*. Do we perform our duties as men and
Jews solely in blind submission to the will of God, or because
and only insofar as our own human mind and instinct, our
thinking and feeling approve of and harmonize with the demands of Torah and Him Who gave it? The word "blind" in
the first half of the alternative and the phrase "and only
insofar as" in the second indicate that we have stated the
two extreme antitheses within which intermediate and
compromising positions can and should be found. The first
position is, indeed, an extreme of heteronomy pure and simple
—no less heteronomous in character because it can be named
theonomy in view of its origin. From the point of view of
him who performs the command, this "blind" obedience is
indeed the *Kadawer-* (cadaver) or *Hunde-gehorsam* (canine
obedience) of which Geiger wrote and which expression so
much incensed Samson Raphael Hirsch[2] and which is perhaps
not as blasphemous as Hirsch thought. Once the obedience
springs "from the ardent desire of the Jew to understand and
to obey God's declared will and to make it his own" (Dr.
Grunfeld's words in answer to Geiger), one can no longer
speak of a purely heteronomous motive. On the other extreme,
to fulfill Torah and *Mitzvot* only because and inasmuch as
they are approved by our own reason and conscience constitutes a radical rationalism and humanism which is bound to
endanger our *a priori* faith in the general validity and binding
force of revealed religion, of Torah in particular.

Ta'amei ha-Mitzvot

Somewhere between these two polar positions of exclusive
heteronomy or autonomy must be sought others, intermediate
ones, which will try, in different ways and by various degrees,
to compromise between them and to harmonize the motives
of religious and moral conduct. The need to do so has been the
main incentive for the search for *ta'amei ha-mitzvot,* the reasons of the commandments of the Torah. This in turn is only
an aspect, though an important one, of the general problem
posed by the duality of revelation and reason which has been
the dominating theme of Jewish religious philosophy from
Saadia onward. In its most acute form it puts before reason

the necessity to justify why divine revelation was and is necessary in addition to what man's own thinking, methodically or by intuition, may reveal to himself. It is across this bridge of rationalization that the voice of God speaking to man and the inner voice of man's reason and conscience are able to meet; reason, in the widest sense of the word, thus becomes the common denominator of autonomous and heteronomous morality. In a way, revelation is at a disadvantage here, as the reasonableness of our own autonomous moral demands appears to be self-evident and somehow inherent in and synonymous with the attitude and actions required, which is not always the case with the contents of revelation coming, as it were, from the outside. Reason is thus apt to sit in judgment over what has been revealed to us. This disadvantage finds some compensation in that revelation speaks with greater authority and objectivity than that enjoyed by the more subjective and fallible judgments of man. It is, in fact, through this clash of objective authority and autonomous though subjective freedom on the battlefields of reason that the fate of our ethico-religious existence is decided.

While the search for *ta'amei ha-mitzvot* may produce agreement and consonance of moral motivation over a wide area of our Torah-given duties, there remain important sections that resist rationalization, failing to satisfy either our logic and reason or our moral judgment, or are even felt to be antagonistic to them. This, in turn, has resulted in the division and classification of commandments according to the extent of their conformity to the standards of autonomous reason and morality. While it is, of course, possible and perhaps even desirable that our reason and conscience should submit to what is recognized as the command of an over-riding authority and wisdom, there is surely a limit both to the extent and the universality to which such submission can be accepted as possible or legitimate, taking into account the very premises and fundamentals of Torah revelation, let alone those of a purely humanistic, inner-worldly orientation. What we consider possible in this respect, not merely for a particular individual or group, but as generally valid, must have a strong bearing on what is, philosophically and religiously, legitimate and admissible.

Two Sources

The dichotomy between autonomy and heteronomy in the field of Torah life and observance gains particular sharpness where it reveals not merely a diversity in motivation but a difference in value judgment expressing itself either in indifference or in antagonism. We are not thinking here, I repeat, of an extreme philosophical position (such as adopted by Kant) which recognizes the human conscience and its categorical imperative as the only possible source of moral ideas and rules of conduct and which denies both the possibility and the need for a heteronomous revelation. But even for those who accept a duality of sources for human and Jewish religious morality—and they are the vast majority of Jewish teachers and thinkers across the ages—and who conceive of Torah-inspired life as one in which divine revelation embodied in a historical tradition plays a decisive role alongside human reason, feeling, and conscience, the failure of communication or a conflict between these two sources remains an ever present possibility, whether in the realm of thought and theory, or in that of practical performance, generally or in a particular historical or personal situation. This possibility must not be confused with the obvious and unavoidable tension which must exist between moral and religious demands of a normative system of law and the weakness of the flesh and of nerve which too often leave the former unfulfilled. This, in turn, cannot entirely be separated from the material conditions of life which themselves are interwoven with the intellectual climate prevailing at any given moment of history. It cannot be denied that such temporal circumstances have a bearing on the ability and/or willingness of the individual Jew or an entire group of Jews to live up to the eternal standards of Torah life. All the same, the problem has to be viewed on its highest and most general level and with the utmost seriousness as one of the sparking points of religion in general and of Torah Judaism in particular, before it can be viewed against the backdrop of a particular civilization, of the human and Jewish condition at a given point of its progress in history.

In attempting in what follows to sketch our problem as it presented itself and the treatment it received in the main periods of Jewish history, it will become only too evident that one is dealing not only with a crucial question confronting the modern Jew but with a hardy perennial which has to varying degrees exercised Jewish religious thought and thinkers at almost every stage and age.

Theonomy in the Bible

What about the Bible? Here, in this primary source book of divine revelation, we may hope to find, though not in the form of ordered and systematic thought, the raw material for the construction of an integrated religious and philosophical view. Not that the Bible proclaims its message in a religio-historical vacuum, for many an idea and institution in the Torah must be understood against the background of the civilization of contemporary antiquity. However, the idea of absolute obedience and service to the voice of God is certainly paramount in the Pentateuch and in large areas of the prophetic, historical, and wisdom books.

The exhortation, "And now, if you will harken unto my voice" (Exod. 19:5), is an integral part of the programmatic preface to the revelation on Sinai and this is echoed and re-echoed, particularly in Deuteronomy. Already of Abraham it was said, "because he hearkened unto My voice" (Gen. 26:5), and he is generally taken as the exemplar of blind and unconditional obedience to the voice and will of God as shown in the story of the *Akedah* (the sacrificial binding of Isaac). But in spite of the strong heteronomous note, the autonomous one is heard often and unmistakably. That man, created in the image of God (and therefore endowed by Him with a share of His own spirituality), possessed *ab initio* and *a priori* moral sense and freedom can be seen from many of the stories and statutes of the Bible, both before and after Sinai. "The Seven Noachide Laws" are not all explicit and though they were found hermeneutically in Genesis 2:16— here, as elsewhere, "a verse cannot depart from its literal meaning." Cain and Lemech, the generations of the Flood and the Dispersion, Sodom and Gomorrah and many others, individuals or people, are assumed in the Bible to have a sense of right and wrong, even of the proper and acceptable way to worship God, without having vouchsafed an explicit supernatural revelation as was given to Israel on Sinai.

In fact, throughout the Bible basic ethical concepts such as charity, justice, law, purity and impurity, sanctity, abomination, violence and others are assumed to be known and accepted in their ethico-religious connotations. The laws of God are recognizable both by Israel and the nations as righteous statutes and laws (*chukim u'mishpatim tzadikim*), and the Torah is recognized as neither too difficult (intellectually) nor too far (strange) for Israel; it is "in your mouth and in your heart to do it" (Deut. 30:14). And even if "in your mouth" refers, as S. R. Hirsch and D. Hoffmann explain, to the "from mouth-to-mouth" tradition, "in your heart" can only mean that the word of the Torah must find an instantaneous echo and understanding. Where the fear of God is mentioned as the awareness of a general morality, it is not so much the idea that this morality stems from God but that He is its guarantor and will punish those who violate it. Moreover, one cannot say that the Pentateuch contains rules for all possible conditions and problems and that in it all religion and all morality are exhaustively expressed. If that were so, there would have been no need at all for prophetic and other biblical utterances or indeed for the Oral Torah of our sages, all of which is comprised under the term of *Kabbalah* (Tradition).

In the prophetic books, too, the ideas of heteronomy and autonomy find equal expression, the former as in Samuel's words,

> Hath the Lord as great delight in burnt-offerings and
>   sacrifices,
> As in harkening to the voice of the Lord?
> Behold, to obey is better than sacrifice,
> And to harken, than the fat of rams.[3]

Even here the idea of mere obedience is softened by the protest against sacrifices as a possible "bribe" for God. Nor was Saul's disobedience prompted by "humanitarian" considerations, though a passage in *Yoma* 22b imputes these to him. But Micah, in a very similar appreciation of the relative value of sacrifices, whether human or animal, addressing himself to man (not to Israel!) makes his classic proclamation of prophetic morality on what God requires from man: justice, loving-kindness, and modesty. The same train of thought, appealing in the name of God to that innate feeling of right, of kindness and decency in man, as opposed to mere formal, outward, mechanically performed religious acts, can be found in many prophetic passages such as in the 58th chapter of Isaiah, the Yom Kippur *Haftarah*. It would be tempting and worthwhile to examine each book of the Bible from the angle of autonomy versus heteronomy, but what has been said must suffice.

Talmud and Midrash

Turning now to the sages of the Talmud and Midrash, we hope to find with them even more guidance and enlightenment on the problem before us. They were no more systematic philosophers than those who conveyed to us the revelation contained in the Bible, though according to their own particular method and style they treated theological and philosophical questions in a more reflective and dialectic way than the Bible with its greater immediacy and spontaneity. This is due, in no small measure, to the fact that the rabbis were active in a historical setting in which the challenge of foreign ideas and civilizations on Jews and Judaism was more pressing than ever before. Hellenism, Roman institutions, emerging Christianity and other syncretistic oriental faiths and cults, not to mention the internal struggles caused by the Sadducees, the Essenes and other splinter sects, forced the rabbis to formulate Torah views and attitudes and place them before their hearers and disciples. Inevitably the cut and thrust of these grand debates, the confrontation, in particular, with triumphant Hellenic and Hellenistic civilization, exercised a deep influence on these teachers, helped them to clarify their own Torah-based ideas, to reject what ran counter to them and adopt or adapt what appeared true and useful. This applies in particular to the humanistic elements in Hellenism which made man and his reason the measure of all things. This idea dominated the minds of men in the Hellenistic era and penetrated into the Jewish domain as well. The rabbis, therefore, had to deal with this religious challenge. Their freedom of thought and expression was all the greater as every individual teacher was making *his* contribution in accordance with his own character and temperament, his training and experience, and at the same time he was aware of all those others who worked towards the same end. Thus, over the generations, they produced in the dialectic system of *Aggadah*, a kaleidoscopic wealth of views which left no aspect of any possible problem outside their intellectual or religious probe.

Before we examine some of the halakhic or aggadic statements that seem to bear on the problem of theonomy, we ought to recognize to what extent the very activity and method of the sages of Talmud or Midrash shed light on the problem mentioned. Leaving aside those traditions which, as Oral Torah in the narrow sense of the word, have been preserved for us in this literature, the teachings and interpretations resulting from the inexorable intellectual debate to which the rabbis submitted every detail of Torah show that the sovereignty of men's logic was the unspoken but unquestioned *a priori* assumption of all their work. The fact that the traditional hermeneutical rules are considered *Halakhah le-Mosheh mi-Sinai* (Halakhah given to Moses on Sinai)—not all of them being purely logical rules—makes them no less an inherent, autonomous function of the human mind. In other words: Oral Torah, in the wider sense, is the product of the clash and interaction of the written Torah, as well as the rest of Scripture, and other traditional material with the logical mind and the moral sense of our sages. This is perhaps less obvious than it sounds. Is it really self-evident that Torah and *Mitzvot* must be subject to the Law of Contradiction? I submit that it is not, unless, of course, one sees in God-given human reason the arbiter of revelation. And what is true of intellect and logic is true of moral sense and intuitive feeling as well. What is it that entitles the rabbis to raise moral objections to stories and actions described in the Bible, to aspects of its legislation, unless they assumed their right and duty to listen to the voice of their minds and hearts? When they ask, "If a man has sinned, wherein has the animal sinned" (*Yoma* 22b; *Sanhedrin* 54a) or, "How may one do business with one's neighbor's cow?" (*Bava Metzia* 35b) or when they state, for example, "A sinner should not have any profit" (*Ketuvot* 11a), they assume the validity of certain unstated and yet self-evident moral principles to which Torah law and teaching are expected to conform. The rabbis, of course, never doubt that they do conform and they regard it their duty to prove it, despite any *prima facie* difficulties. Suffice it to say that here we have before us the basic, essential mechanism of the Oral Torah and incidentally the justification of autonomous reason, both logical and moral, as being in partnership with the Giver of the Torah in the full revelation, deployment and continuous potency of the Sinaitic message.

There is, of course, no shortage of rabbinic statements asserting the heteronomous, theonomous character of Torah and *Mitzvot*. Man and the Jew in particular stand to God in the relation of either son or servant, implying obedience to His will either out of reverent fear or love, or both. In either case, what man does from these motives is determined solely by being the will and command of God. (We may leave aside for the moment the question whether the ability of man to love and fear God is not in itself the beginning of his autonomy.) Terms as fundamental and ubiquitous as acceptance of the yoke of Heaven (or of *Mitzvot*, or of Torah) show a prevalence of the idea of heteronomy, of obedience to God, the Law-giver, as the dominant religious motive of our conduct. Its most general formulation as a deliberate submission, not to say abdication, of one's own will and reason is found in the midrashic elaboration of Israel's declaration at Sinai: "We shall do and we shall listen;"[4] on the other hand, God was said to have threatened to bury them under the mountains [if they did not accept the Torah]. Perhaps too much should not be made of these homilies; the early act of more or less free acceptance of the Torah is periodically renewed, as stated in the Bible and described by our sages in the words, "they confirmed what they had already accepted."[5] This is quite apart from the rabbis' insistence on the need for a daily renewal by the individual of his submission to the divine yoke.

Two Categories of Mitzvot

In any event, the idea of theonomy in these terms or statements is perhaps less explicit than in the much quoted passage of Rabbi Elazar ben Azaryah:[6] "How do we know that we should not say, 'I have no desire to eat swine's flesh' or 'I have no desire to commit a forbidden sexual act'; on the contrary we should say, 'I have a desire for these forbidden things, but what can I do when my Father in Heaven decreed that they are forbidden to me.' " Maimonides quotes this statement in his Introduction to *Avot* (Chapter 6), but both the examples cited by Rabbi Elazar and by Maimonides are restricted to a particular type of *Mitzvah*. Maimonides[7] identifies them as those commandments of tradition[8] which cannot be explained rationally, as opposed to those commandments which can be derived by reason. These categories were introduced into Jewish philosophy by Saadia, and were anteceded by the division of *Mitzvot* into those which, if they had not been written in the Bible, should by right have been written, and those to which Satan objects.[9] The latter are of course, those which Hirsch[10] has grouped together as statutes (*chukkim*) and although he refuses to regard them as either irrational (Rashi) or esoteric (Maimonides), they are largely those which though capable of rationalization are not postulated by reason. It is difficult to understand why Rabbi Elazar ben Azaryah included illicit sexual relations in this category; they are, in fact, included among the "rational" ordinances in *Yoma* and *Sifra*. Yet, only to this limited group of *Mitzvot* are applied the apodictic declarations: "I am the Lord Who has decreed (the *chukkim*) and therefore you are not permitted to criticize, to change, or to transgress." In any event, the emphasis on heteronomy in the passage quoted is a limited and not a general one.

Metzuveh Ve'oseh

Another much quoted passage emphasizing the heteronomous nature of the *Mitzvot* is Rabbi Chanina's statement[11] that "he who fulfills a commandment because he is commanded to do so is greater than he who fulfills it although he is not commanded to do so" which appears to have been accepted as authoritative.[12] Here we find no restriction as to the type of *Mitzvah*; but on the other hand, no scriptural proof is adduced by or for Rabbi Chanina. The word "greater" is explained in the Gemara as referring to the reward to be expected and not to the intrinsic religious value of the act, though the two are very much connected. Tosafot justifies the greater reward by saying that to conform to a command involves painstaking care and trouble not present with one who performs voluntarily.[13] This, of course, is far removed from the ideological pathos with which Hirsch and his disciples propound the idea of heteronomy. One would have to reconcile or rather dialectically confront Rabbi Chanina's bold assertion with other rabbinic statements which extol the virtue of those who act without being commanded.[14] Perhaps what he wishes to state is a maxim of religious pedagogy, stressing the value of obedience to the will of God, rather than a theological principle. Let us note that such a staunch defender of autonomy as Moritz Lazarus[15] found it perfectly possible to harmonize autonomous religious ethics with the normative tendency (*Gesetzlichkeit*) which is expressed in Rabbi Chanina's dictum.[16]

Balancing of forces

It would appear from the foregoing that our sages, or rather those among them who pronounced on our problem and on those akin to it, adopted a dialectic method not so much to arrive at the truth as to assure the full, continued, and correct observance of *Mitzvot* and to defend the Torah against critics and adversaries from both outside and inside. It was this primarily educational but also apologetic task which was their main object and concern. That the whole Torah and all *Mitzvot* were "all given by the one shepherd from the mouth of the Lord of all Works" was as axiomatic with them as that absolute obedience was demanded. They were equally convinced that God requires nothing from man but what is reasonable and morally right and useful, even if occasionally this was not apparent. By stressing or elucidating the "morality" and rationality of *Mitzvot* they appealed to the human heart and mind whose approval would reinforce obedience and conformity to the will of God. Where there was difficulty, they would fall back as a last resort upon heteronomy (theonomy) as the inescapable normative appeal and motive for performance. From their understanding of Scripture as much as from their rational or instinctive experience they had a high opinion of the place of man in the God-given order of things in which he was "but little less than the angels" by virtue of his spirit, his consciousness, his intellectual and moral freedom and potentialities. Greater even than the Angels of Service, he was capable of becoming God's partner in the work of creation and *was,* in fact, his partner in achieving the purpose of that creation. When man merges his will with that of his Creator (*Avot* 2:4), the problem of heteronomy is effectively solved. But before this happens, the balancing of the two motive forces, which do not always pull in the same direction, is as difficult as it is necessary. Rationalists, both inside and outside the talmudic world, fear that overemphasis on heteronomy is not only intrinsically wrong but tactically dangerous as it might lead to a revolutionary explosion of the human mind. But there are others who fear that by encouraging the human mind to assert its autonomy, it will set itself up as a supreme authority with dire consequences for belief and observance.

This danger became manifest, even within the talmudic period, for those sections of Jewry who lived in the Hellenistic diaspora and were therefore much more exposed to the influence of Greek and Hellenistic thought and civilization. They are best typified by Philo and Josephus. Hellenists believed in the existence of an autonomous natural law[17] before whose tribunal all legislation had to justify itself. And Jewish-Hellenistic writers set their whole pride and employed their considerable gifts in proving that in fact our Torah fulfilled all moral and utilitarian demands of the *jus naturale*. They addressed themselves not only to their fellow Jewish Hellenists, who were very much in need of encouragement in whatever observance was still theirs, but also apologetically and as religious propaganda to a large Gentile public which, as we know, was interested in and attached to Jewish faith and practice. Inevitably the question of the divine origin and authority of Torah and *Mitzvot* became less important than their intrinsic value and philosophical and moral character in the eyes of Greek science. It also led to greater value being attached, at least by the intelligentsia, to obviously ethical laws in preference to purely religious and ceremonial observances. On the other hand, it was just those which gave Judaism its characteristic distinction from other religions and it was they which appealed to the Gentile imagination. While to us today Hellenistic Judaism seems shadowy and diluted compared with its talmudic and medieval counterparts, one must give their due to those who wrestled hard with the problems of keeping Jews loyal to their heritage in a spiritually hostile environment and under adverse conditions. We may have much to learn from an episode and experience in Jewish history, the setting of which has so many parallels with our own.

From Saadia to Abravanel

Jewish philosophy in the Middle Ages is even for us moderns a most important laboratory of ideas. Philosophers from Saadia to Abravanel are distinguished from Philo and other Hellenists in that the former were firmly rooted in the entirety of rabbinic tradition and, on the other hand, were of much greater stature as philosophers and scientists. While Judaism in the age of Hellenism faced the challenge of an all-pervading popular culture, the medieval philosophers dealt chiefly with an intellectual and academic problem: the relationship between reason and revelation. The Middle Ages differed from antiquity in that the demand for a deep, self-searching philosophical examination was addressed by Greco-

Arabic philosophy to a Jewish-Islamic-Christian world which was deeply rooted in their respective and, in important points, identical religious attitudes. The idea of God as the Creator, the Law-giver and Redeemer of the universe and mankind was common ground, and so was an *a priori* acceptance of theonomy-heteronomy as the mainstay of religion. For Jewish philosophy this meant the absolute validity of the received talmudic tradition and the unquestionable legitimacy of the claim of Torah and *Mitzvot* to obedience.

The philosopher-sages of Judaism over a period of more than 600 years had to deal to a much greater extent than it ever was incumbent upon the sages of Talmud and Midrash, with the confrontation of tradition with the philosophy and science of the various schools—Kalam, Neo-Platonic, Aristotelian—which dominated the thinking of the Middle Ages. The legitimacy and indeed religious importance of this confrontation were recognized by the great majority of writers. Even the minority, which denied this legitimacy, freely used both the method and terminology of philosophical inquiry. In the name of autonomous human reason, which was the progenitor of all philosophy and science, one studied not only the basic theological and metaphysical questions such as God and His attributes, the meaning of existence, body and soul, immortality, and, in particular, the place of revelation in the order of things, but also, and as a logical consequence, the reasons of individual or groups of *Mitzvot*. Reason is not, here as elsewhere, limited to intellectual processes, but includes and occasionally is conceived as the moral sense of man, as in Kant's Practical Reason. It is evident that the problem of autonomy as opposed to the heteronomy of revealed religion is implicit, if rarely explicit, in the philosophical labors of the Middle Ages. An occasional voice can even be heard as early as the 11th century, if not from rabbinic at least from Karaite Judaism, which makes use of "the whole arsenal of arguments which at [the] beginning of modern times have been advanced on behalf of the idea of an autonomous morality."[18] Reason, on the other hand, has to justify itself, its rights and functions, alongside revelation as its competitor as a source of knowledge and a guide in human conduct; and perhaps its greatest justification from the point of view of Torah lies in its being the chief instrument of investigation and interpretation of the meaning of Torah. But it is reason, too, that has to justify the need for revelation alongside or over and above what reason knows unaided. There could, of course, be no guarantee that reason would confine itself to exposition and justification. What if, like another "Sorcerer's Apprentice," the human mind would strike out on its own, as it were, and become the critic and rival of revelation instead of its faithful supporter and companion. Saadia, in fact, confines reason to this latter role and he was followed in this in modern times by S. R. Hirsch.

In this process of examination the medieval philosophers naturally arrived at a division of *Mitzvot* which we mentioned previously as having occurred already to the sages of the Talmud. This twofold division into those of Reason and those of Revelation (Tradition and Obedience), which from Saadia onwards we find in varying forms and contents with most of the philosophers, may not be identical in strictly philosophical terms with that of the Talmud and Midrash, but the connection cannot be denied. But to distinguish these two categories at once raises the question of their relative roles and importance. While the more rationalist were inclined to put the value of rational commandments above that of traditional ones, Judah Halevi, for instance, reverses this order. Both sides realize the danger which such a differentiation means to observance, and they try to counter this by laying great stress on observance of *Mitzvot*, whether their reasons are known or acceptable to reason, or not. On the other hand, when early teachers of Mussar such as Bachyah ibn Pakudah emphasized the duties of the heart as truly important in contradistinction to mere legalism and formal religiosity, then this was only another variant of the division and the dialectic of which we have spoken. Inquiring into the meaning and purpose of individual *Mitzvot* or Torah institutions sometimes involved advancing historical reasons (e.g., Maimonides' explanation of the sacrifices) which seemed to run counter to their eternal validity. Here, too, philosophers tried to guard against danger by stressing the unchangeable authority of Torah. But here again such differentiations among *Mitzvot* as to their relative importance and even their continued or time-bound validity had already been made by our sages in the Talmud and Midrash; and they, too, had thought it wise to warn the religious Jew not to allow such distinctions to influence his conduct.

Once more we have seen how in a vital period of Jewish continuity *and* creativity, a fine but essential balance was kept between Reason and Revelation, between the voice from on high and that from inside. Sure enough, in every generation there existed alongside the spokesmen of a philosophical and a scientifically based Judaism those rabbinic leaders who saw no need for philosophy to underpin a self-evident, self-supporting faith and way of life; who were content to look inward and let the great world go by, seeing only the dangers of heresy and religious estrangement lurking in the domain of rational inquiry. It would be facile to divide the medieval world into philosophers and halakhists. Most of the former were great expounders of Halakhah as well, and many purely rabbinical luminaries in those centuries had a good general education and were not hostile to philosophy and science. The frontiers often ran right through one personality as in Rambam-Maimonides. These men were perhaps less monolithic than we imagine, being only too well aware of the challenges and the dangers in them. They were above all deeply religious men, attached with every fibre of their being to the God and Torah of Israel. They could afford the courage and intellectual honesty required to walk the tightrope that swung between their intuitive, inborn, and often mystical union with Torah and *Mitzvot* and the inescapable demands of their intellect.

One cannot be sure to what extent the philosophical discussion of the Middle Ages—say from Saadia to Maimonides—affected Jewish communities beyond the intellectual elite. The explosion and controversies of the post-Maimonidean age show, in any event, that philosophical ideas had—in one shape or another—percolated to broader strata of the population with often undesirable effects on belief and practice. The opposition, whether violent or moderate, to philosophical inquiry now began to dominate Jewish life in

Europe, with the almost exclusive emphasis on Halakhah being reinforced by a growing interest in Kabbalah. But even to the end of the 13th century and the Expulsion, philosophical studies continued in Spain and southern France. The many important works written in this period—Levi ben Gershon, Crescas, Duran, Albo, Abravanel—presuppose a public interested in theological problems. Philosophy and science were blamed for the weakness and lack of *mesirat nefesh* (readiness to face martyrdom) shown by large sections of Spanish Jewry during the persecutions of 1391-1492. However that may be, it is equally true that some of the finest spirits and men of high education preferred exile to apostasy. The late flowering of Jewish thought in Italy after the Expulsion was largely due to Spanish emigrants. Little new, however, was added to the discussion of the problem of theonomy by the thinkers coming after Maimonides. And in the communities of northern Europe the problem did not exist. Jews were content and happy to perform the will of their Creator—with no questions asked.

Mendelssohn

The Renaissance, the age of humanism and Reformation which had conquered Europe and was followed in the 17th and 18th centuries by a revolutionary upsurge of the human mind and scientific discovery, made hardly any impression on the introverted life of the Jewish communities. Only as the 18th century advanced did intellectual and social cracks begin to appear in the armor, and "modern times" began to catch up with Jewry. The outstanding symbol of this development is Moses Mendelssohn, the man who unlocked the gates of European culture for himself and his people. It is, therefore, not without irony that it should be he, the Socrates of his time, who has been so much maligned by those in the Orthodox camp (who probably never read a line of his), who most strongly asserts the heteronomous character of Judaism by defining it as revealed *legislation* and *not* as a system of ideas and beliefs. In this distinction he was no doubt influenced by Spinoza who, in his *Tractatus,* had described the laws of the Torah as the state law of a no longer existing Jewish state and therefore no longer in force. Mendelssohn maintains the exclusive legal and practical character of Torah but insists on its timeless validity. The Torah, which merely tells us what to do or what not to do and not what to think or to believe, gives the philosopher absolute freedom in the realm of thought and inquiry. The eternal verities need no revelation except that which has its source in the human mind.

This was a doubtful gain for the principle of theonomy without any guarantee that the human mind will not use its freedom to question the assumptions and legitimacy of the divinely revealed legislation. Mendelssohn, in all his sincere loyalty to Torah and *Mitzvot*, is the model not of the Orthodox but of the "orthoprax" Jew who tries to keep his intellect and his religious observance in two watertight, non-intercommunicating departments. It is, of course, not true that the Torah does not require beliefs from us, that it has no dogmas. Mendelssohn himself has not been absolutely consistent in his assertion. But his ideology, which embodied much of the teachings of the medieval philosophers, suited his particular position, straddling European philosophy and Halakhah-controlled Jewish life. His was indeed a philosophy of transition leading to, but stopping at, the threshold of a new age.

Kant

The man whose philosophy heralded a true revolution in modern thought in general and in views on religion and revelation in particular was Immanuel Kant. After him, things would never be the same. His teachings, for better or worse, dominated Jewish thinking throughout the 19th century and beyond. Never before had the autonomy of ethics and anything that deserved the name of religion been asserted with such vigor and clarity. Not only were they autonomous, exclusive of external revelation, which was denied both as a fact and as a possibility, but religion was limited to and identified with ethical conduct as dictated by human conscience alone, thus depriving the greater part of *Mitzvot*, all that dealt with man's relations to God, of any meaning and value. The one-sided, over-rationalistic nature of Kant's Practical Reason and morality as a substitute for living religion was soon enough recognized, particularly by the Schleiermacher school and the romantic movement which sought to re-instate religious feeling as the sole basis of religion. But this was of small value to the believers in historical revelations and religious systems based on them. This is not the place to describe the deep religious inspiration that is one of the mainsprings of the Kantian system of religion and ethics and its undiminished religious value and potency for those who cannot conceive religion without a full commitment of man's rational faculties and his inborn conscience and sense of duty. All the more blatant is Kant's failure to give due recognition not only to the intuitive, affective and imaginative areas of the human psyche but to the role played by the historical religions and—by implication—by the acts of revelation and processes of tradition on which they are founded.

Quite apart from the overriding importance of Kant for the history of philosophy and for the philosophy of religion and our problem of autonomy versus heteronomy in particular, his influence on Jewish thinkers during the last century and a half has been decisive even where these went critically beyond their master's teachings. Essentially, the ideology of the Reform movement, with its rejection of ceremonial in favor of ethical religion, is based on Kant. The leaders of Reform, Geiger in particular, realized that this new conception of religion was diametrically opposed to what Judaism had meant in the past. They only lacked the philosophical consistency and clarity, and perhaps the courage (something which should not be held against them), to do away entirely, as a matter of principle and not of expediency, with Torah and *Mitzvot*. There were others, however, who presented a Judaism in which Kant was forcibly joined with the traditional concept of Jewish religion and ethics. Such was the achievement of Moritz Lazarus, and, above all, of Hermann Cohen. While the latter, in his published writings, would not go beyond the essentially Kantian concept of the Religion of Reason identified by him with Judaism, in his old age and in his lectures to students of the *Berlin Hochschule für die Wissenschaft des Judentums,* he felt constrained to admit that certain basic concepts of the Torah could not be explained and rationalized and were "wonders and miracles." Shades of Nachmanides!

S. R. Hirsch

Even S. R. Hirsch and S. D. Luzatto, who in the 19th century were the champions of heteronomy against the Kantian maelstrom of autonomy, would not go so far as to deny the existence of an inner autonomous revelation which was complementary to the theonomous one. Hirsch saw no need to differentiate between moral and purely religious duties. The philosophical fusion of all *Mitzvot,* of the entire Torah, into a harmonious ethico-religious system is his great achievement. That some essential ingredients of Jewish reality escaped him and found no place in his monumental structure need not concern us here. His overemphasis on heteronomy, his constant appeal to the obedience of the *homo Judaeus* to the will of God, is more apparent than real, more declamatory than systematically dominant. He often enough gave due weight to the voice of God that speaks *out of* man even if in general he stresses that voice that speaks *to* him. We have already pointed out, in our discussion of Saadia, whom Hirsch follows in this respect, how precarious the somewhat artificial restrictions are which they impose on the human mind in its relation to revelation and tradition. But one must pay tribute to the courage of Hirsch for proclaiming a new religious humanism, the human element in the Jew and his Torah, as well as the universalist concern and validity of our Torah. Hirsch, not unlike Mendelssohn before him, had to fight a battle on two fronts: against the radicalism of Reform and assimilation and the obscurantism and ossification of the surviving past. He was no less a son of the 19th century, the ideals of which he shared, than a sincere and enthusiastic exponent of an integral traditional Judaism. He was much more successful than Mendelssohn in harmonizing these two tendencies, whatever limitations his historical position inevitably imposed on his system and ideology.

The weak spot in that system is its lack of historical thinking. The facts of revelation are strictly confined in time and place, and three and a half thousand years of Jewish history have no part to play in that revelation. Here lies the cause of the violent controversy between Hirsch on the one hand and

Zechariah Frankel and the school of Positive-Historical Judaism on the other.[19] For the latter, history mattered. In those millenia Sinaitic Revelation had its chance fully to deploy and develop, particularly in the Oral Law and Tradition contained in rabbinic literature. For Frankel and his school this process of evolution continues and cannot be limited artificially. Hirsch, in his staunch belief in a once-and-for-all revelation, and in spite of what is called his "humanism," could only suspect heresy in the historical approach, an encroachment of the human element on what must be conceived as exclusively divine. But history should not be denied its meaning and value for the unfolding of truth and Torah, as a school in which the Jewish people—and humanity—learn to bring the potentialities of Sinai into more and more actuality. The yoke of the Kingdom of Heaven and that of *Mitzvot*, and this is what theonomy-heteronomy means, is so much easier to accept and so much lighter to bear as the partnership of man with the Giver of Torah becomes evident.[20] This dynamic view of Torah, though it has been adumbrated in the Aggadah, is no doubt the most fruitful contribution which the 19th century has made to the solution of the problem of religious heteronomy, breaking to a large extent the vicious circle of the either-or which had made the issue so intractable. It shall not be denied that the historical evolutionary approach has its dogmatic difficulties and indeed dangers. But so had earlier attempts to find a compromise between autonomy and heteronomy.

Franz Rosenzweig

Before we sum up, a few sentences ought to be devoted to that great Jewish thinker and *Baal Teshuvah*, Franz Rosenzweig. This mind and soul of a giant was not only heir to the fullness of philosophical tradition, both Jewish and general, but also an outstanding example of the perplexities which beset the Jew in the 20th century. This pupil of Hermann Cohen and the neo-Kantian school had undergone that great transformation which set him on the road of return to the God of Abraham, Isaac and Jacob and away from the

God of philosophers. Jewishness was for him not ideology and thought processes but experience, renewed and growing experiences. The European, the philosopher, and the poet in him demanded freedom of thought and action; the enthusiastic Jew, submission to God's Torah and his all-embracing, ubiquitous *Mitzvot*. For him, the acceptance of the yoke of *Mitzvot* was a deadly serious matter, confronting him ever afresh with the need for a decision whether to keep this or that *Mitzvah* or not. In the freedom of this decision, which was not always positive, he preserved his autonomy. Asked whether he was observing a certain *Mitzvah* his answer might be: no, not yet. He had not only to be willing, but also to be able, morally and intellectually, to accept the *Mitzvot* or any of them. He rejected the description of them as laws. Law demands unquestioning compliance. *Mitzvah,* for Rosenzweig, was a request, a demand, a direct personal approach. But man could do no more than was "humanly possible." Accepting the historical view of revelation, he believed that his own generation, as well that which went before, had a share in the God of Israel—according to its ability, conditioned by its particular historical circumstances and setting. As a Jew he felt himself a member of the Jewish community as well as a link in the chain of a tradition borne and passed on by preceding generations. While recognizing the compulsive element which lies in this double involvement, he nevertheless postulated for the individual a certain elbow room of autonomous freedom of decision. This intensely individualistic approach is open to many obvious objections. But it may still be a modus vivendi of sorts vis-à-vis a religious problem which confronts a certain type of modern Jew, a way which has the merit of keeping the doors open for many who wish to return and keep some attachment to Torah and *Mitzvot* without having to accept the all or nothing alternatives which systems such as Hirsch's place before the perplexed but searching Jew of our time.

The foregoing survey—in many ways sketchy and inadequate—of one of the most pressing problems of religious man, of the Jew who loves and believes with all his heart and soul in the Torah, has led us through the four principal periods of our spiritual history: the biblical, the talmudical, the medieval-philosophical—all abutting on this modern age. In all of these we found the problem of theonomy either adumbrated or discussed with various solutions or accommodations proffered or implied. Much of this was ephemeral, conditioned by transient circumstances, but below the surface there flowed a strong current of a conflict that is perennial. Modern Jew, no less than his predecessors, must return to the Bible and Talmud as the reservoir of living waters from which to draw the elements of both question and answer. The masters of the Middle Ages and their pupils not only brought the clarity and articulation of philosophy to an age-old problem, but it was their merit to have assured, once and for all, the legitimacy of the inquiring human mind facing what is superhuman and supernatural. The age which we call modern has broadened this intellectual freedom into the moral and social freedom of man who is called to master and mold not only himself but also his environment. We moderns have learned, as the logical result of that new freedom, to see in history humanity's striving towards its God-given goals, and the dynamism of the human spirit to which God has entrusted the unfolding and consummation of his Revelation.

Modern times, more than any other age have made man conscious of his hard-won inner freedom. But how is he to use it? Some of us are only too eager to surrender it forthwith and to accept freely and eagerly the shackles of theonomy, of the heteronomous way of thought and life as it is found in the selfcontained and timeless teachings of our masters, past or present. Others, the great majority, have cast off the yoke and arbitrarily break or fulfill God's law according to their hearts' desire. And there are those who strive to find the inner balance and harmony of the religious, God-serving man without having to jettison the freedom that they feel is theirs, the judgment of the heart and of the mind that makes them accept "every day anew" what was commanded of old. They feel that they live in today's world, not yesterday's or that of the day before, and as such have to shoulder the Jewish man's burden. Theirs is the harder road but, in this writer's opinion at least, the only one that is neither a cul-de-sac nor one that leads into outer darkness but to the broad uplands of a great future.

BIBLIOGRAPHY

JULIUS GUTTMAN—*Die Philosophie des Judentums*, Munich, 1933, (Hebrew edition, Jerusalem, 5711; English edition, Jewish Publication Society, Philadelphia, 1963).

ISAAC HEINEMANN—*Ta'amey Hamitzvot be-Sifrut Yisrael*, 1st vol., 3rd revised edition, Jerusalem, 5714, II, Jerusalem, 5715.

I. GRUNFELD—*Introduction to the English translation of S. R. Hirsch, Horeb*, I, London, 1962.

MAX WIENER—*Jüdische Religion im Zeitalter der Emanzipation*, Berlin, 1933.

JOSEPH WOHLGEMUTH—*Das jüdische Religionsgesetz in jüdischer Beleuchtung*, II, Berlin, 1912 & 1919.

NOTES

1. I made this criticism in a recent article in the *Jewish Review* of London, Vol. XIV, no. 412, pp. 6–7, in which I evaluated Dr. I. Grunfeld's English translation of Samson Raphael Hirsch's *Horeb*, the nineteenth century work by the father of modern Orthodoxy.

2. See Dr. Grunfeld's Introduction to *Horeb*, p. LXXVII.

3. Samuel I, 15:22.

4. Ex. 24:7.

5. *Shabbat* 88a.

6. *Sifra*, Lev. 20:22.

7. See also Malbim to *Sifra*, I, c. and II; 44, 45.

8. Or, of "revelation" (Klatzkin, Thesaurus IV, p. 133; so also Rosenblatt in his translation of Saadia, p. 145); or, of "obedience" (Guttmann, *Philosophie des Judentums*, p. 80).

9. *Yoma* 67b and *Sifra*, Lev. 18:2; *Pesikta de R. Kahana* (Buber, p. 40b) and parallels.

10. S. R. Hirsch, *Horeb*, 396–479, ed., Grunfeld, II, p. 279 ff.

11. *Kiddushin* 31a.

12. *Bava Kamma* 38a.

13. Nor does Rabbi Chanina deny his due reward to the latter, a side of the medal which has often been stressed, by, among others, Maimonides (*Guide to the Perplexed*, III, 17).

14. *Lifnim mishurat hadin* or *me'kadesh et atzmo be'mutar lo.*

15. Moritz Lazarus, *Ethik des Judentums*, I, p. 225 ff. and additional note no. 32.

16. In *Berakhot* 33b (cf. Yerushalmi, *ad loc.*) the Mishnah says, "If one says, 'May Thy mercies extend to a bird's nest,' we silence him." The Gemara explains this reproof of an apparently innocent expression with the criticism, "He presents the decrees of God as deriving from mercy whereas they are but decrees"—

certainly a heteronomous attitude. It should be noted, however, that this is only one of several explanations given in the Babylonian and Palestinian Talmud. The reason of mercy, rejected in the Gemara quoted, is in fact adopted by the Midrash (*Vayikra Rabba* XXVII), by one of the *Targumim*, and also by Rashbam. I refer the reader to the excellent discussion of this passage by Joseph Wohlgemuth in *Das jüdische Religiongesetz in jüd. Beleuchtung*, II, p. 31–32 and his suggestion that instead of decree one should read *din* (law), thus giving the statement a very different and more plausible meaning. On the basis of the present reading, however, the law regarding the sending away of the mother bird would have to be ranged with the group of statutes mentioned before (cf. Rashi, *ad. loc.*) and the idea expressed in the Gemara would lose its general character.

17. The distinction between man-made state laws and a natural, universal one is already made by Aristotle and by others before him.

18. J. Guttmann, *op. cit.*, p. 91.

19. For a critique of the underlying assumptions of the positive-historical position, see Walter S. Wurzburger's "The Oral Law and the Conservative Dilemma" in the Fall 1960 issue of TRADITION, pp. 82–88. The same article also shows how the Orthodox position can incorporate an awareness of historic processes.—*Ed.*

20. Man's creative role in the halakhic process is described in "Ish ha-Halakhah," the classic study by Rabbi Joseph B. Soloveitchik, *Talpioth*, 1944, pp. 651–735. Cf. also Rabbi Emanuel Rackman's "Israel and God, Reflections on their Encounter," *Judaism*, 1962, pp. 233–241 and "Truth and Wisdom: An Orthodox Approach," *Judaism*, 1961, pp. 148–50.—*Ed.*

The Natural Law Teaching of the Eastern Orthodox Church

Stanley S. Harakas

Noting that the Eastern Orthodox Church has never in its long history developed a systematic approach to the question of natural law, Stanley S. Harakas cites various church fathers to show that the church nonetheless has had a continuing concern with the question. Following his historical exposition, Father Harakas presents a discussion of the Orthodox Church's position regarding the source, content, and legal force of the natural law. Father Harakas' article, reprinted from the Winter 1963–1964 issue of *The Greek Orthodox Theological Review,** was first presented as a paper at "An Interreligious Clergy Dialogue on the Natural Law," sponsored by the Northeastern Region of the National Conference of Christians and Jews, May 21 and 22, 1962, at the Harvard Club in Boston. The church Father Harakas serves is St. Basil's Greek Orthodox Church in Peabody, Massachusetts.

IT IS a fact which cannot be denied that the Eastern Orthodox Christian Church, in its history of almost two thousand years, has failed to develop a comprehensive and thoroughly systematic approach to the question of natural law. Most writers refer to the teaching of natural law only in passing and, until recently, one could find on this topic only very little discussion and this usually limited to the prolegomena of the ethics handbooks and the studies in Canon Law. However, as of late, a more serious approach to the problems and exposition of natural law teachings has been noted in the Eastern Orthodox Church, in conjunction with a new return to the Fathers of the Early Church.

* 50 Goddard Avenue, Brookline 46, Massachusetts.

Men such as Kyriazis, Ioannides, Romanides, Lossky and Bulgakov have made substantial contributions in natural law studies, but as yet a full and complete and authoritative study of a definitive character has failed to appear. In spite of this, however, it is possible to present a paper such as this today, in exposition of the natural law teachings of the Eastern Orthodox Christian Church as sketchy as this may be. We will approach our topic in two sections. In the first we will give a brief definition of the natural law teaching of the Eastern Orthodox Church and examine the sources for this teaching. In the second we will examine somewhat more in detail the questions of the source of the natural law itself, the problems of diagnosis and content and the legal and judicial character of natural law. The paper will close with an attempt to relate the Eastern Orthodox position to that of other groups and positions.

I

The Eastern Orthodox Church accepts and teaches the reality of natural law found in the rational nature of man through which man may know the fundamental laws and rules of human moral and social life. This law has its source in the will of God, who created man in His own image and after His own likeness and may be discerned through experience and reason, and its content, as generally known and accepted, corresponds roughly with the Mosaic Decalogue. It has a binding and legal character to which all positive laws, secular and ecclesiastical, are subject and from which they obtain their authority.

The source of this teaching on natural law is the same as that for Eastern Orthodox teachings in all areas of its concern, that is, Divine Revelation as found in Holy Scripture and Holy Tradition; Holy Tradition being understood as the unwritten teaching of the Lord and Apostles as understood, lived and recorded by the early undivided Church. In actual practice, the sources for the Eastern Orthodox teaching on natural law are found primarily in the writings of Saint Paul and in the writings of the Fathers of the Church of the first five centuries of the Christian era.

The main New Testament source of natural law teaching is the passage in the Epistle to the Romans in which Saint Paul says: "All who have sinned without the law will also perish without the law, and all who have sinned under the law will be judged by the law. . . . When the Gentiles who have not the law, do by nature what the law requires, they are a law to themselves, even though they do not have the law. They show that what the law requires is written on their hearts, while their conscience also bears witness. . . ."[1] The understanding of this passage in the early Church was not subject to great differences in exegesis. The general patristic interpretation is, in the words of Kyriazis, "that the place which the Mosaic Law has for the Jews, that is the knowledge of the law and therefore of good and of evil, is the very same taken amongst the gentiles by their naturally given capacity for the knowledge of God and the knowledge of the main requirements of ethics which they are able to find in the law written in their hearts."[2] Thus, the core of the Mosaic Law, the Decalogue, and the core of the natural law written in the hearts of all men coincide, the contents being essentially the same. The difference is found in the fact that the written Mosaic Law was a step in the preparation of mankind for the acceptance of the future acts of salvation. There is a distinction, however, to be made between the natural ethical endowment, and the understanding of this ethical endowment as a law, binding upon human social behavior. The fact that the recipient of this ethical endowment is subject to judgment and condemnation on the same level as the recipient of the Mosaic Law, is reason enough to identify the ethical endowment as a legally binding requirement of life for those who are without the written law. There are other biblical sources of the natural law teaching of the Church. The teaching in Romans (13:1) and Peter (2:13) that the civil ruler is a servant of God for the Good, that the authority of the civil ruler is God-given (John 19:11), that "it is better to obey God than to obey man" (Acts 5:20) and Jesus' teaching in the form of the negative question, "And why do you not judge for yourselves what is right?" (Luke 12:57) have all indicated to patristic writers the existence of natural law precepts.

Which comment leads directly to the second source of natural law teachings, Holy Tradition, or more specifically, the writings of the Fathers of the Church of the first five centuries. Very briefly, I should like to survey the natural law teachings of the most important of these writers.[3] Perhaps the father of natural law patristic thought, Justin, may be understood best and most quickly by noting the main themes which he first used in approaching the subject at hand. Natural law exists and is identified in content with the ten commandments, though there is a differentiation made between religious and legal commands. This natural law is in effect everywhere and at all times. Justin introduces the concept of the logos into the concept in that the *"spermatikos logos"* or "spermatic word" is seen as the manner in which mankind is made aware of the content of natural law and natural theology. On the one hand, the concept of the spermatic word or logos leads to the source of natural law in the "Logos" of God and on the other, to the use of reason as the means by which man diagnoses the content of natural law. Thus, in Justin's presentation, "Christ is found, in seed (spermatically) in man, that is, in his logical and ethical nature. Therefore, that which is logical is at the same time morally good, and oppositely, that which contradicts ethics is at the same time against reason,"[4] in the words of Kyriazis. Thus the requirement to obey the dictates of reason becomes a requirement to obey and be subject to the moral endowment of man.

Irenaeus made further contributions in this field by distinguishing the natural moral law as natural commands and noting that Christ did not destroy these but rather expanded and completed them. Of importance is the comment that we do not find here a sharp division between "natural" and "super-natural" but rather a continuum. Clement carries this concept further by use of the concept of the logos. Since all persons share in the logos, all have some knowledge of the moral law. The difference between the Christian and the Gentile is one of degree. Because of his lack of saving divine grace the Gentile only knows part of the full moral law of God. Yet each individual is created in the image of God, in the image of the Logos, and because of this knows in greater or lesser degree the content of the moral law. The Christian, unified with the "Logos of God," the Son, is in a better position to recognize and implement the moral law. What is objectively the Logos, the Son, and second person of the Holy Trinity, is subjectively in each human being that which is called the human logos or reason or natural law in the heart of man. Origen also gives much attention to the question of natural law and sees it as the law of God, which however is subject to development in the individual human being. Origen contributes by differentiating the natural law from conscience by noting that the first is a rational power of the soul for discovery of the content of the law while the second is a spiritual power which serves as a guide to the moral life, praising the good and condemning the evil. Thus Origen is the first to seek to analyze the processes and functions of natural law.

Tertullian makes a special effort at diagnosing the content of natural law, and without ignoring the older tradition of the rational nature of natural moral law, he does add the observation that *all* of nature is included within the structure of natural law and that nature itself is law and requires obedience. Athanasius emphasized the natural law idea in connection with the creation of man in the image and after the likeness of God. Saint Basil, following Tertullian and expanding on the *Lex naturalis–natura legalis* concept, finds the law of nature in the order of nature which is at the same time an order of ethical values. It was Basil who first amongst the Fathers noted that the function of a judge was not only to make judgments subject to human positive law but also to obey the requirements of natural justice within his own heart. Gregory of Nazianzus and Gregory of Nyssa both touch upon but do not elaborate in detail natural law concepts. St. John Chrysostom, however, gave great attention and concern to natural law teaching. Though he did not contribute new understandings, he did express more clearly than anyone else the formal teaching of the Church on the question of natural law, or *nomos physeos* or law of nature as he preferred to call it. The law of nature for Chrysostom is a true law and any positive law opposed to it is not worthy of obedience as false. The law of nature is general, eternal and immortal. Special revelation is not needed to understand its precepts; it is known naturally. The freedom of man's will is understood as self-evident and the law of nature is identified with the natural logos or reason. The core of the content of natural law is identified with the last six commandments of the Decalogue. The natural law is a fundamental necessity for human life.

Cyril of Alexandria follows the teachings of Chrysostom generally but he also makes mention of the eternal law in God which will play an important role in later thought, especially in Augustine. Though it is not true that Augustine was the first to employ the concept of the eternal law in God (Justin, Origen, Lactantius and Cyril preceded him in this), it is true that in Augustine this concept was developed and crystallized. God, as creator and as provident, acts in accordance with His pre-existent plan and idea of creation and providence. This plan of creation is the *lex æterna* or *ainios nomos* which is implemented by the will of God. Through His will in the eternal law God created in all things the laws and principles according to which they function, or the laws of cause and effect. Logical beings, however, can and do discern the natural moral law within themselves. Though we are not able to know the full range of the eternal law we are able to know a part of it. This Augustine calls the natural law, of which he says, "The natural law is written in the logical soul of man." It is at this point, as we shall see shortly, that western and eastern positions divide. The point at question will be the place or nature of the eternal ideas or plan of the eternal law. Is this an objective body outside the will of God, or a part of His Essence, to which He necessarily conforms His will or which is to be found in God's stable will and activity, i.e. His "Energy"? The first was the answer of the West. The second, the answer of the East.

The purpose of this review of the positions of some of the major Fathers and Ecclesiastical Writers is two-fold. First, to show that the natural law teaching has been a continuous theme in the teaching of the Church from the beginning and, secondly, to indicate some of the basic elements which go into the make-up of the present day teaching of the Eastern Orthodox Church on the natural law.

II

We now come to an attempt in a more detailed and systematic manner to sketch the position of the Eastern Orthodox Church regarding (1) the source of the natural law; (2) the means of its diagnosis; (3) its content; and (4) its legal force and character.

1. The Source of Natural Law. The source of natural law is God and more specifically, the will and intelligence of God. Rejecting completely Platonic and Aristotelian concepts of an ideal, self-sufficient world of ideal, self-sufficient eternal ideas as perfect types according to which all things exist and have been created, the Orthodox Church teaches that all of creation is an act of the intelligence and will of God alone. This refers to all of creation and not alone to the natural and moral law. God is not bound by a plan outside of Himself. To quote Father Romanides, "From the dogma of the creation of the world from nothing by the will and energy of God, it follows that the world, visible and invisible, was created in a completely positive manner. This very existing world, and no other, was created by the will of God. It is not, therefore, a naturally imperfect copy of another, supposedly real world, nor is it the result of some form of fall or alienation from reality or a kind of emanation of ideas from the divine essence and their contact with matter. Biblical tradition is ignorant of the customary philosophical distinction between matter and form or between matter and reality."[5] Thus, all of creation is seen as an act of the will of God. But not as capricious will. "If," says the same author, "in nature there is noted a stability in natural phenomena, this is not attributable to some law of nature understood as a kind of blind fate, but just the opposite, it is attributable to the stable will and faithful energy (activity) of God. Thus, God acts not according to necessity and essentially (*kat' ousian*) but according to free will."[6] God creating according to His own plan and intelligence through a free creating and provident will is what is understood as the eternal law of God. "The *Lex Æterna* includes the order of the world and of things."[7] Man as part of the order of the world shares in the *Lex Æterna.* We discover the order peculiar to the rational and moral nature of man in the fact that God freely and as an act of His will "created man in His own image and after His own likeness." In Eastern Orthodox Theology this indicates not only the spiritual, moral and rational aspect of human personality, but also the possibility of its perfection and complete participation in the divine, or deification.

We would go too far afield at this point if we included in our discussion the Eastern Orthodox distinction between essence and energy in God and the concept of the idea of the individual within the Logos as the second person of the Holy Trinity. It suffices to note that since man is created in the image of God, he is characterized by a moral and rational nature. Professor Karmiris, commenting on St. John of Damascus' statement that the " 'according to the image' expresses rationality and free will and the 'after the likeness' indicates the potential to virtue," writes to the effect that "the above mentioned and other, especially ethical characteristics and abilities of man come from the spiritual and ethical nature and the whole personality of man to which the 'image' primarily refers, being an expression and a result of his reason and free will in his tendencies and efforts toward God and in his conformity to divine law."[8] Even after the Fall the ability and characteristic of man to live according to the moral law written on his heart was not completely destroyed, in the sense that, though darkened and weakened, man alone, without revelation, was able to do good and cultivate the ethical life. However, man can never regain the full potential of his moral and spiritual life, that is, union with God and deification, without the saving and sanctifying power of the Grace of God. In other words, it is only with the Grace of God that he can truly fulfill his nature.

Thus, natural law as a species of the eternal law preceded in time the Mosaic Law and governed the activities and thoughts of men long before the promulgation of the Decalogue which, in the present context, is referred to by some Eastern Orthodox writers as a portion of the "Divine Positive Law." There remains, finally, as a guide and light to the natural law in man, the voice of conscience which dictates to man the requirement to choose the good and avoid the evil.

2. The Diagnosis of the Content of Natural Law. We now ask to find the means by which the content of natural law may be known. The effort of unaided reason is seen by the Fathers of the first five centuries as the main and central means by which man discerns the content of natural law. Man's rational nature is effective for this purpose because he shares in the rational nature or Logos of God. Since God is rational, and wills what His intelligence decides, man who is also rational shares in the divine wisdom and divine law. Thus, the basic elements of natural law ought to be clear and evident to all men, though such understanding is subject to development. Another means, parallel to the above, is the order existing in creation which man is bound to view as good and which claims obedience of him. A third source may be recognized in the fundamental expressions of the Mosaic Law which, according to the Fathers, does not add anything new to natural law, but rather clarifies it and makes it specific as a preparation for the work of salvation. The fact, however, does exist that many individuals and even large groups of people have failed to recognize one or more of the elements of natural law. This is seen in some quarters as a serious objection to the whole thesis of the natural law teaching. Here, the Fathers simply see the effects of sin and the failure of men to use and cultivate their rational powers. Generally speaking, however, it is felt that all peoples and nations in practice recognize the precepts of natural law, and, as we shall note later, apply its principles to their peculiar situations in varying ways.

3. The Content of Natural Law. The Golden Rule, in its many forms implying a certain rule of equity, seems to summarize in the minds of the Fathers the essence of the content of the natural law. However, as we have seen, the natural law is seen to be the same as the Decalogue in a slightly broader perspective. Both are characterized eternally valid, and both require for their fulfillment attitudes of justice and piety. Thus, the natural law refers to man's relationship with God, with the need for truthfulness and trust in his relationship with his fellow-man, with the relationships between husband and wife, parents and children, employer and employee, the citizen and the political and social entity of which he is part. Thus, life, property, honor, the family and the social and political order are protected from disintegration and destruction. However, as we begin to discuss these social relationships a new perspective demands attention. For most of these areas are not only subject to natural law, but also to positive laws, whether they be understood as enactments of legally constituted authority, or of custom, the *ius gentium*. Our emphasis now shifts from natural law to justice.

4. *The Legal Character of Natural Law*. Though it is a question of debate in the Orthodox Church, it may be safely said that generally speaking Natural Justice is also an accepted teaching. By Natural Justice, *Ius Naturale* or *Physikon Dikaion*, is meant the teachings of the natural moral law which apply directly to the social life. Kyriazis writes, "Justice is a part of morality, which portion refers to the elementary acts of men, which assure the regularity and prosperity of social life. Therefore, insofar as the rules of natural law refer to the social sphere, to justice in the relations amongst men and more generally to the organized forms of human society, they are characterized as the rules of natural justice."[9] The contents of natural justice, therefore, are arrived at in the same manner as those of natural moral law. But further, under the pressure of ever-changing practical situations, man's rational-ethical nature cultivates the ability to apply the general principles of natural justice to special cases. The results of this effort become general operative principles sharing in the full character of natural justice. What relationship does this concept have to positive law? Since all authority is divine in origin,[10] the authority of the law-giver and law-maker in the sphere of positive law is subject to that of God. Thus, natural justice is not simply an advisory ideal for the law-giver, but one that demands implementation in the rules of positive law. Thus, a positive law, which is not in harmony with the spirit and rules of natural justice, is no law at all and is not worthy of obedience. Thus, to repeat MacIver's term used in his book *The Web of Government*, natural

justice is the "firmament of [positive] law." The judge must judge not only on the basis of the positive law, but must also speak and judge in terms of the dictates of natural justice.

III

There remains one final area of concern before this paper is brought to its end. It would be appropriate to deal with questions which arise from this teaching on natural law with special reference to the reading material and the general background of contemporary natural law discussions. The approach of the Eastern Orthodox Church is an almost purely theological approach. Does this preclude a philosophical approach to natural law? I would say that it does not, since the teaching itself sets at its foundation the rational nature of the phenomenon of natural law. I would venture to say, however, that it cannot be understood in its largest perspective if it is not approached theologically.

The strongest objection which can be raised against this approach is that it is not scientifically defensible. In fact, the rejection of any absolute referent outside the will of God seems at first glance to ignore the modern scientific achievement of a stable body of knowledge regarding the physical world. This, however, is not the case. The doctrine of natural law as outlined here, Eastern Orthodox theologians feel is independent of any particular scientific world view and can be expressed along with any position which does not outreach the necessarily limited bounds of scientific method.

We can also raise the question of how this position bears on the question of the bifurcation of the "is" and the "ought" since the time of Hume. We, of course, cannot go to the extremes of the Cambridge Platonists whose efforts failed in part because they sought to imbed their philosophy of the moral life in an order outside the will of God. Is and Ought are intertwined because of the rational imperative in both the nature of God and man seen in a theological perspective.

These last comments are simply a few areas which might be touched upon in the ensuing discussion and may be considered as starting points for any comments, criticisms and clarification to be made in the subsequent conversation.

NOTES

1. Romans 2:12, 14–15.

2. K. V. Kyriazis, *To Physikon hai Kanonikon Dikaion ex Epopseos Orthodoxou*, Part I, Volume I (Athens, 1957), pp. 6, 49. See also pp. 55 and 103.

3. Based primarily on Kyriazis, *op. cit.*, pp. 57–109.

4. *Ibid.*, p. 65.

5. John S. Romanides, *To Propatorikon Hamartema* (Athens, 1957), p. 51.

6. *Ibid.*, p. 56.

7. Kyriazis, *op. cit.*, p. 105.

8. Ioannes Karmiris, *He Dogmatike Didaskalia tou Ioannou Damaskenou* (Athens, 1940), pp. 36–37 and elsewhere.

9. *Ibid.*, Part II, Volume II, p. 10.

10. Romans 13:1.

Teilhard De Chardin:
A Philosophy of Procession

E. R. Baltazar

One of the most remarkable trends in recent Roman Catholic theology—a trend exemplified most notably in the work of the late Pierre Teilhard de Chardin, S.J.—is the effort to move away from the static categories of classic Aristotelo-Thomism and to consider man in terms not of "essence" and "nature" but of uniqueness and subjectivity, time in terms not of substance but of process. Such an approach does not issue in subjectivism, declares E. R. Baltazar, because process is the basic and objective structure of being. "Personality is not for the sake of nature, but nature for personality. . . . The basic flaw in the scholastic solution to the problem of nature and supernature was to relate grace to nature instead of to personality." Dr. Baltazar is Assistant Professor of Philosophy at the University of Dayton. His article is from the Spring 1964 issue of *Continuum*.*

THE VALIDITY and worth of the philosophy of procession[1] can be demonstrated by its ability to solve what may be considered as the central problem of human thought— the relation between reason and faith, nature and supernature, finite and infinite, immanent and transcendent, and now, in a new form, evolution and Incarnation. What is necessary, first, is a conversion from the Aristotelian to the Teilhardian or biblical philosophic pattern of thought. This attempt is not novel or original, since it is but an attempt to express modern man's new way of looking at reality on all the levels of his constructions and systematizations.

Aristotelian philosophy, as we know, was not a creation

* Saint Xavier College, Chicago 55, Illinois.

that was independent of its milieu. It was in fact a philosophic expression of the science of the day which aptly illustrates the maxim: as the physics so the ontology. The ancient view of the universe was Ptolemaic: the earth was the center and the sun and other heavenly bodies revolved around the earth. This geocentric pattern was reproduced in the classic view of man as the center of the world, with the lower forms of life about him. He was a microcosm, i.e., a universe on a small scale. Aristotle's genius was to integrate these views and give philosophic expression to them in a philosophy whose basic category is that of substance and whose dynamism, act and potency, is egocentric. Substance is the ultimate substratum which is no longer predicated of anything else;[2] it is a dynamic principle of identity, activity and organization;[3] it exists of itself and not in another and is the substratum of accidents.[4] We thus have a Ptolemaic view in which substance is the center and the accidents are the satellites. It was in this context that the medieval theologians integrated theology. As F. Crowe, S.J., notes: ". . . medieval theologians took over Aristotelian philosophy, which had already integrated the mathematical and physical sciences, and added theology to obtain a coherent and closely-knit view of the universe."[5] Again we have a Ptolemaic view of truth where the truths of faith (*substantia fidei*) were located at the center together with philosophic metaphysical truths, and outside were the contingent and particular truths of science, related to the universal truth as *instances*. The emphasis in theology became from henceforth the timeless and unchanging nature of Revelation, and the self-assigned task of theologians was to be champions and defenders of the timelessness and immutability of dogma. In line with this view, too, the theologians assumed the right to say what philosophy and science can or cannot do since they possessed the universal truths of reality.

Today we have moved far from this classic and medieval world-view. There has been a *conversion* in outlook. First on the geophysical level the conversion has been from the Ptolemaic to the Copernican; on the biological, from the Aristotelian eternal species to the Darwinian; on the physical from the Newtonian and Euclidean fixed and mechanical explanation of matter to the Einsteinian view of relativity and the conversion of matter to energy; and on the philosophical and theological levels there has also been a conversion but not as definitive as those in science. Thus there has been a shift in our view of man from the static, objective approach in terms of his nature to the dynamic, subjective approach in terms of his personality; in philosophy in general, there has been a movement from the idealistic and metaphysical to the empirical, phenomenal and existential. In theology there is a movement back to the Bible, a movement from treating theology as timeless truths to considering the mysteries as a history of salvation, as particular and contingent events, or even developing processes.

If we single out the main characteristic of modern thought it is its historical rather than timeless view of reality. This has been achieved progressively and is true on all levels. The conversion on the scientific level has already been accomplished: the Copernican, Darwinian, Einsteinian outlooks give us an integrated view of the physical world. There has been a shift from egocentricism to a centering in the opposite: from the earth to the sun, from the past to the future, from matter to energy. There has been a shift from the static and timeless to the dynamic: the earth in orbit, matter as energy, fixed species as evolving. However, on the philosophic level no comparable conversion has yet been made. The works of the empiricists, phenomenologists and existentialists are admirable but partial, and the only attempt that can be called a philosophy in the sense of being a synthesis is that of Teilhard's *The Phenomenon of Man*. The philosophy implied in this work has not been formalized, however; and before theology can attempt a conversion from the timeless to the historical, philosophy must furnish a framework.

The process of conversion is not going to be easy, due to the conditioning of centuries. Aristotelian philosophy is a philosophy based on common sense observation just as the Ptolemaic and Euclidean views of physical reality are based on common sense; and this explains their persistence and appeal, as is evident from the Galileo case. Those who opposed Galileo took the frame of reference of common sense observation as an absolute frame of reference, and within this context

Galileo was truly wrong. But his opponents were also wrong in considering this context as some kind of an absolute. Indeed, from common sense observation, the mountains and valleys are models of changelessness; the species of plants and animals are eternal and immutable. But the reason for this is that the time scale of our frame of reference is so small that within that scale no changes are perceived. But if we take a very long and wide time scale, and thus change our contextual situation, then we are able to see that everything is process. What we called permanent in what may be termed the two-dimensional setting (2-D) of common sense observation, is really process in a three-dimensional (3-D) frame of reference.

One may conclude then that substance is process. There is no contradiction here unless one takes the statement out of the context of 3-D. But even with this 3-D distinction, it is apparent that the notion of process is not correctly understood. Thus a distinguished Thomist has written:[6]

> I do not question that St. Thomas made no systematic use of the idea of development or evolution in the modern sense of these words. But for one thing, that idea itself is neither enlightening nor fertile except in the context of an ontological analysis, of reality. . . . to enclose a metaphysic in a compartment of history is not a way to give evidence of a sense of history; and it is no more proof of philosophic sense to think that there is nothing more in a metaphysic than the scientific imagery which in a given era permitted it to exemplify itself in the plane of phenomena, which plane never confined it.

It is clear from the above passage that evolution or process is relegated to the category of the phenomenal or accidental as opposed to the metaphysical or substantial. And having made this identification, what applies to phenomena, namely, that they cannot enclose a metaphysic, is also applied to evolution. Again we find the identification of evolution with activity in the following observation:[7]

> The subject is the reality which is principal . . . the power of operation is a complementary reality, secondary, subordinated, the principle of evolution of the individual, the

principle of the "accidental" order, or the order of "secondary" perfection. It exists by the subject, in the subject and for the subject.

The same view is held by Louis de Raeymaeker who asserts that evolution is an activity of the universe.[8]

What these statements represent is an attempt to hold on to the 2-D frame of reference and then try to assimilate process or evolution in it. The 3-D statement that reality is evolving, or that substance is process is made to mean that first we have substance or a subject and from it proceeds process as an activity. The reason for this is that in 2-D, substance and accident are comprehensive categories, so that any being within that context is either substance or accident. Accidents inhere in or proceed from substance; and process is placed in the category of accident. A conclusion which seems well supported by observation: eating, talking, typing, etc., are actions and they proceed from the subject or substance and are contained in it as the effect in the cause. Process is movement, hence logically it is seen as an activity of substance, and consequently, evolution or process is seen as proceeding from substance. The fallacy however is in identifying process with activity, relative to the 2-D context.

With regard to any given concrete being, one can look at it from a 2-D or 3-D frame of reference. Thus one can look at a being here and now, abstracting from his birth and death, and this would be a 2-D frame of reference. But one can look at it from a greater time scale which includes birth and death, and this would be in 3-D. Now in 2-D one can observe activities like talking, singing, typing, etc., and they do indeed proceed from substance; but can one say that birth proceeds from substance? To say so would be tantamount to saying that this substance gives birth to itself which is a contradiction. One is driven to conclude that birth cannot be assimilated within the 2-D context, for birth is not an accident that inheres or proceeds from substance, because the substance in question does not yet exist. It does not stand out from that which precedes birth; to say otherwise would be like saying that the chicken laid the egg from which it would develop.

Substance proceeds from birth and is therefore contained in birth. Now birth is not just a first event: substance is continually born to the next moment, and hence substance is always in the context of process. Similarly with death. Death is a complete cessation or it is a rebirth. If it is a rebirth, then substance is contained in it. If it is a cessation, then in like manner, death contains substance, and not the other way around. Substance does not perdure in such a way that death inheres in it as an accident, for death means and presupposes the nonexistence of substance. It is death that contains substance as the subject contains the predicate. As long as we abstract from birth and death, the 2-D category of substance-accident is all-comprehensive. But when it takes birth and death, which are the alpha and omega of process, into consideration, then it is unable to assimilate them and attempts to do so only at the cost of distorting the facts. It is more nearly true to relate substance to birth than birth to substance. What is true of our analysis is true for all beings, because all beings come to be by birth. Nothing comes to be simply an adult.

Let us consider another concrete example to illustrate how process does not proceed from substance. A seed corresponds perfectly to the Aristotelo-Thomistic notion of substance: self-enclosed, well-defined, able to exist of itself. Now, if one literally translates the substance-accident category with respect to the seed, so that process is an activity of the seed, then this would have to mean that the seed left alone is able to germinate itself, grow itself, flower and bear fruit, all by itself, i.e., without help from the "ground" (soil, moisture, heat, etc.). Given this example, one can see that the process of the seed does not proceed from the seed. What causes germination is the *union* of the seed with its "ground." It is the ground that germinates the seed, that makes it grow, matures it and lets it flower and bear fruit. Process is this continuous vital union of seed and "ground." That this *union* cannot be within the seed is obvious for it is the seed that is within the process and *is* the process, since this union is successively the seedling, the plant, the fruit. We have reached here the first stage in our conversion of the notion of substance. Thus the center of substance is process. In the example of the seed, it is not the seed that stays put, and the ground comes toward it; it is the seed that tends toward the ground. The ground is the center and the seed roots itself in it.

The second stage in this conversion is the destruction of the notion of substance as having its own act of "to be." Again, let us consider an example from the world of nature. If we look at a plant, abstracting from its rootedness in the ground, the plant seems to have its own act of "to be." But a little consideration is sufficient to show that it is the union of the plant with the ground which is the very existence of the plant. Uproot the plant and it is dead. Clearly there is no proper act of "to be" separate from the ground. All the things that we see and call substance, i.e., as having autonomous existence are really the result of *union*. Existence is not something locked up within a being or substance; this is merely the impression we get in 2-D. We see a dog move around and we say it has its own act of "to be," for it has a different existence from that of another. That observation is true in 2-D, but in 3-D, no object or substance in this universe can be understood apart from the evolutionary unity of the universe in which it is situated and from which it takes its meaning and existence. Outside of this context, it has no meaning. God is not an Aristotelian God that thinks of essences, dog, cat, man, etc., and who then puts them together to form a world. Although common speech and our common way of thinking abstract from the evolutionary context, we cannot argue from our common way of thinking to the way reality is. It is ideal to think of a single object as having an existence apart from the world; but existence is sharedness. All things are born into a world. They are not simply born, for without a "world" there is no existence. The foetus in the womb is born to the womb; its existence is continued union with the womb. When it is born, it is born into another world, and its existence is precisely this union; death being a separation from its world. The existence of what we call substance is always existence-with. *To be* is always to-be-with. Being is always being-with-another. Thus the very notion of substance as self-enclosed, as self-subsistent, as the principle of its own activities is simply a construct. We cannot define substance apart from its essential relatedness to a world.

What is true of the analysis of individual beings is true of the universe as a single evolutionary unity. The universe is a process: it is born. Yet we impose upon it the category of substance. The naturalistic evolutionists, unconscious of the philosophic pattern of their thoughts, think it to be scientific to consider the universe as self-sufficient, as able to evolve itself. But this is comparable to saying that the seed left alone can germinate itself, grow itself, and bear fruit; and in effect it is to say that the seed is its own ground, the foetus its own womb, the egg its own hen. And yet this absurdity is preferred to admitting that the universe needs a "Ground," and this "Ground" directs it, brings out its potentialities and leads it to fulness. The universe does not contain its process like some monad or self-enclosed seed, for such a view would be a metaphysical contradiction. As Corte notes of Teilhard: "to him and men of his way of thinking, evolution demands the continuous action of creative wisdom more imperiously than does fixity (of species), for we are clearly concerned with an evolution which has a purpose, a *directed* evolution, an evolution which itself suggests that once it has reached its summit, which is man, it has nothing more to do but to stop and leave man himself the task of following it through in the order of reflective consciousness."[9] Divine creativity, therefore, is not finished; the universe through man, participates and cooperates in its own creation. It in fact is a grander and more nearly true view of God's omnipotence that he can make a creature to create himself. In what sense after all is man an image of God if he is not able to create like God?

The final result of the preceding kind of analysis would be a new ontology. The notion of being would be converted from being as substance to being as process; from being as an island, to being-with-another; for existence is a sharing, is a union. The shift in perspective may be illustrated by the example of the seed alone by itself and the seed in union with the soil, for being is not the being of the seed alone, but being-with-the-ground. Since the being of the seed is not true being, when left alone the seed dies. Hence its being is a being-towards-death. We cannot build ontology on being-towards-death. The being-towards-the-"ground" is being-towards-life: and on this alone is true being founded. Thus the paradox which Aristotelo-Thomism with its philosophy of common sense cannot see is that not everything which exists is being. Being is being only when it is *born* to *its* world; and outside it, there is no being, only death. This truth is the primitive datum of ontology. Being is union-with-a-world, not substance. The biblical view of reality is founded on this view of being: being is covenanted; creation is covenanted; man is covenanted. As regards man, he is ordained towards God as his "Thou," or "Ground," and outside of this union he is nothing. This covenant, which is a bond of union, is the basic and central category of the Bible. As Johannes Pedersen notes:[10]

> For the Israelites, one is born of a covenant and into a covenant, and wherever one moves in life, one makes a covenant. . . . if the covenant were dissolved existence would fall to pieces, because no soul can live an isolated life. It not only means that it cannot get along without the assistance of others; it is in direct conflict with its essence to be something apart. It can only exist as a link of a whole, and it cannot work and act without working in connection with other souls and through them.

Through the preceding analysis we had come to this same conclusion. There is therefore need of conversion from the category of substance to the category of relation or process. But anyone cognizant of Aristotelian categories will know that *relation* is the most ignored and most maligned of all. It is labelled as a "debellissimum ens," i.e., as the weakest of beings, and the borderline between being and non-being. It is *substance* which has claimed principal recognition as the basic category; and so the goal of a new ontology is to restore to *relation* its birthright.[11]

Process or relation is not a passing thing, it is not accidental. Destroy process, and separation or death results. It is coterminus or coextensive with existence. "Rootedness" or "union" is existence itself. Again the Israelites have the same view: ". . . annihilation of the covenant would not only be the ruin of society, but the dissolution of each individual soul."[12] Process is also necessarily the basis of epistemology, of truth. It is only in process that being unfolds, reveals itself to itself and to others. To say that the essence of the seed is seedness is pure tautology. There is no revelation of being here, but concealedness. Substance then has no meaning in itself apart from its ground or world, for meaning is based on true existence and this is attained only in the union of substance with its world. To define is to relate, not to cut off and isolate. In 2-D individualization is freedom from essential dependency, so that to be united essentially is to lose one's individuality. This view is the basic philosophy of individualism. But deeper reflection will show that union differentiates; and this is the lesson of evolution. As Teilhard notes:[13]

> In any domain—whether it be the cells of a body, the members of a society or the elements of a spiritual synthesis—*union differentiates*. In every organized whole, the parts perfect themselves and fulfill themselves. Through neglect of this universal rule many a system of pantheism has led us astray to the cult of a great All in which individuals were supposed to be merged like a drop in the ocean or like a dissolving grain of salt. Applied to the case of the summation of consciousnesses, the law of union rids us of this perilous and recurrent illusion. No, following the confluent orbits of their centres, the grains of consciousness do not tend to lose their outlines and blend, but, on the contrary, to accentuate the depth and incommunicability of their *egos*. The more "other" they become in conjunction, the more they find themselves as "self."

The law that individualization is to be in union may be again illustrated by the example of a plant. The more it is rooted in the ground, the greater its growth, its differentiation, its fulness; and if we move to a higher level, we observe that the "I" becomes truly a personality when it is united with its "Thou," and the greater that union, the greater the personalization.[14] Outside the inter-personal union, we have an individual but not a person.

Existence, selfhood or individuality, and meaning are all therefore to be found in the context of union or process. The

Aristotelian notion of substance as autonomous, existing in and for itself, having an essence or meaning apart from any relation to the whole (evolutionary whole) is as philosophical as the observation that the sun sets and rises is scientific. The true philosophic view is that "all around us, as far as the eye can see, the universe holds together, and only one way of considering it is really possible, that is, to take it as a whole, in one piece."[15] "The distribution, succession and solidarity of objects are born from their concrescence in a common genesis."[16]

The third and last stage in the conversion of *substance* is the elimination of the view that substance (or nature) attains its end by its own powers alone. The end of being is *fulness* by a process of growth; but growth always presupposes a "ground," and hence it is through *union* that the end of being is attained. The plant attains its end not by its own powers alone but more fundamentally through rootedness in its ground; the foetus attains its birth through vital union with its womb; the feminine attains fulness through union with the masculine; and the "I" attains full personality through the powers of the "Thou" cooperating in fruition.[17] Being attains self-sufficiency only in union. Being, then, is not "proud"; the basic attitude of being is "gratitude." There is no being that can say: I stand alone.

Since *substance* tends to its "other" in order *to be* and be *true*, the dynamism of being is not a having but a giving. The conversion is from the dynamism of act and potency to the dynamism of love. "Love" in the popular conception is a sentiment or an emotion, but it is in its natural dynamism and evolutionary significance that it is considered here. In this sense, Teilhard observes:[18]

> Considered in its full biological reality, love—that is to say the affinity of being with being—is not peculiar to man. It is a general property of all life and as such it embraces, in its varieties and degrees, all the forms successively adopted by organized matter. In the mammals, so close to ourselves, it is easily recognized in its different modalities: sexual passion, parental instinct, social solidarity, etc. Farther off, that is to say lower down on the tree of life,

analogies are more obscure until they become so faint as to be imperceptible. . . . If there were no internal propensity to unite, even at a prodigiously rudimentary level—indeed in the molecule itself—it would be physically impossible for love to appear higher up, with us, in "hominised" form. By rights, to be certain of its presence in ourselves, we should assume its presence, at least in an inchoate form, in everything that is.

The universe then is in the framework of love rather than that of justice. The Aristotelian view of nature would put a claim, exigency, and title in nature for its natural end. This view is correct if nature attains to its end alone, for then it must have the necessary means to attain that end, and God cannot create a being in vain. Therefore, it is claimed, God owes it to Himself to give the means by which the creature attains its end. The relation is one of justice. In line with this view, nature is seen as an objective potency which fulfills itself by receiving acts or perfections which realize its potencies. But this dynamism is relative to, and for the sake of, the deeper dynamism of being which is in union. Being in its essence is a gift. Being must first be a *we* before it can become an *I*. The seed must die to itself and give itself to the ground before there is new life. This pattern and dynamism is repeated throughout the whole hierarchy of being up to the Infinite Being.[19] And thus the biblical view conforms to this analysis of the dynamism of being. The whole of reality from the lowest to the highest is *covenanted*. The universe is seen as feminine and its perfection is to be found in that covenant which is conceived as a marriage between Yaweh and all creatures. The whole of Christian spirituality conforms to this view that it is in giving that we receive.[20] The life of the plant exemplifies the pattern for being. It is in a state of constant rootedness which is a state of constant surrender, a constant giving of self; but it is only in this dynamism that it truly possesses itself.

Since being tends towards the other in order to be, being is not in itself but in the other. Its *presentness* is not being; its *future* is the place of being and truth. In the whole Greek tradition of philosophy, the present is the region of being; the future is non-being. This Greek view is, again, based on common sense observation. The present is the center of organization where we relate the past and the future to the present. We say, "my birth" or "my death," thus relating the past and future to the present. Again, ordinary speech refers to the future as coming: we speak of the "coming" week, month, year, etc.; we consider ourselves in the present as stationary. But the problem is whether the present is stationary or whether it is in orbit. For the Greeks, reality is seen as substantially finished. Thus present reality is being or substance and the future is purely accidental. It is this view that is integrated into the Ptolemaic and Aristotelian theories. But today, when reality is regarded as evolving and tending towards fulness and transformation in the future, then the weight of being is in the future. The Omega is the Future-Universal which is also Hyper-Personal,[21] the irreversible culmination of the movement of synthesis,[22] the Centre of centres where the universe fulfills itself.[23] The Bible expresses this philosophic view in its own language as the movement of creation, represented by man himself, towards the *Land*. The word "Land" has various levels of meaning: Jerusalem, the Holy Temple, Christ and the Church, Faith, Heaven. But on all these levels, there is a common symbolism, namely that *Land* is Truth (the land of truth), Being (the land of salvation flowing with milk and honey). Being is in a journey; man is a wayfarer; we are tent-dwellers.

For the Greek tradition, time is the place of opinion, of change, of non-being. Truth is in the unchanging and permanent. True knowledge is accordingly substantial or metaphysical knowledge because substance is the principle of permanence in being. The methodology for the attainment of truth and being is a flight from time by a metaphysical separation from temporality or by abstraction. All this is logical if we start with the presupposition that present reality is substantially finished. But in an evolving universe, to stay put is to die. Permanency is falsehood; process is truth. The reason is that the domain of being and truth is the future, and the only way to attain the future is to be in time. To be outside time, then, is untruth; while to be in time is truth. Instead of assimilating time into substance and so destroying its reality, we should bring substance into time, make it process, and thus restore to time its reality.

With this new view, there is now a metaphysical basis for involvement in time. In the past, the early Christians, in accordance with Hellenic philosophy, had no reason to involve themselves in time, since time was portrayed as the region of flux, error, change, non-being. There was, as a result, a physical retreat into the desert, into the monastery; a retreat into the region of the mind and the idea. Christians shunned public duties and civil affairs; and the ideal man was the thinking and contemplative man; thought was placed before action. Philosophy became a thinking philosophy and more and more withdrew from dealing with existential problems; theology likewise became a thinking theology, a textbook theology, instead of a history of salvation.[24] Our inheritance from the past resulted in a cleavage and a split in man: the duality of thought and action. Thought is substantial; action phenomenal. But in a non-Hellenic context, being as process is at once *existence and unfolding*; to act is to grow in being and be revealed to oneself.

For the Hebrew, time has always been the region of truth. Timelessness is likened to a barren woman and this state is untruth, death. To have time is to be true and it is likened to a woman with child.[25] Time was salvific for it is in time that God works his saving acts. Time matured and ripened Israel, the spouse of Yaweh, so that she gave birth to Christ, the Fulness of Time. (Gal. 4:4). In the Christian dispensation, it is through liturgical time with its seasons and cycles that the Mystical Body grows to the *Pleroma Christi*. It is in time that the truth longed for by all nations is revealed. Thus we see that biblical epistemology is the complete opposite of Greek epistemology, and this resulted ultimately in a cleavage between biblical thought and scholastic theology. It is in time that we see the universal who is Christ. To the Greeks this was a stumbling block: a universal could not appear in time, for time is the place of the contingent and particular. They therefore could not see Christ as God.[26]

Aristotelo-Thomism approached man wholly from the side of his nature.[27] Man was seen as an essence or being-as-object.

But such a notion does not reveal the deepest in man, his uniqueness and subjectivity; for to apprehend being-as-object is to apprehend it as a thing.

The major problem, however, is how to approach man as subject without being subjectivistic. It is the position here that subjectivity and uniqueness can be approached through the categories of process, namely of birth and death. Subjectivity is not attained through the dynamism of act and potency for then the person does not give itself. To know the subject one must catch it in the act of giving itself, and that act where the subject is given in its uniqueness is the act of love. The highest act of love is sacrifice or a form of "dying": that is, physical death or an act of faith where one dies to one's self-sufficiency and surrenders oneself totally to the "Other." It is in this act of immolation that the "I" is united with the "Thou" and through this union, the new "I" is born. And thus in the Bible, the categories of birth and death are the deepest of categories. On them are built the central mysteries of the Faith: the Incarnation and the Redemption. The categories of birth and death are eminently the categories that reveal being as subjective and personal.

There is no subjectivism here because *process* is the basic and objective structure of being. On the level of man, process takes on the categories of birth and death (commitment, immolation, sacrifice, suffering, love, hope, faith). The "I" is in process of birth; but to be born, there is the need of love, and love means a dying, a sacrifice. There are thus two levels in man: the level of the objective: nature; and the level of the subjective: personality. Personality is not for the sake of nature, but nature for personality. And the dynamism of nature which is that of receiving is for the sake of giving. Thus, man is not perfected by individualism but by love. The basic flaw in the scholastic solution to the problem of nature and supernature was to relate grace to nature instead of to personality.

NOTES

1. We prefer to call this philosophy that of *procession* rather than that of *process* in order to express the *verbal* rather than *substantival* character of reality. What is given here of the new philosophy is a sketch.

2. *Metaphysics*, V, 8.

3. *Sum. Theol.* Ia, Q. 4, art. 2 & 3; Ia. Q. 2, art. 3.

4. I *Sent.* d. xxiii, q. Ia. I; II *Sent.* d. xxxv, q. 2, a. 1 ad. 1.

5. Cf. "On the Method of Theology," *Theological Studies*, 23 (1962), p. 638.

6. Jacques Maritain, *Existence and the Existent* (New York: Pantheon 1948), pp. 45–46.

7. Fernand Van Steenberghen, *Ontology*, trans. Martin Flynn (New York: J. Wagner, Inc., 1952), p. 127.

8. Cf. his *Introduction to Philosophy*, trans. Harry McNeill (New York: J. Wagner, Inc., 1948), p. 49.

9. Nicolas Corte, *Pierre Teilhard de Chardin* (New York: Macmillan Co., 1960), p. 85.

10. Johannes Pedersen, *Israel, Its Life and Culture*: *I* (Copenhagen, 1926), p. 308.

11. There is an inherent contradiction in scholastic theology in that in its philosophy, relation is the weakest of categories and yet this weakest of categories is used to portray the highest of beings, namely the Divine Persons in the Trinity. It is true however that, scholasticism prefers to treat of the Godhead under the category of substance and its attributes under that of relation. And yet the central mystery of our Faith is the Mystery of the Holy Trinity. But the primordial mystery and the heart of the mystery is the *Eternal Procession*. This Being *is* an eternal procession. In the Godhead, process is the central category, not substance. The former category is revealed in Scripture, not the latter.

12. Pedersen, *op. cit.*, p. 308.

13. *The Phenomenon of Man* (Harper: New York, 1959), p. 262.

14. The greatest union possible according to Catholic theology is the eternal procession in the Godhead. So infinite is the union that the result is a differentiation into subsistent relations or personalities.

15. *Phenomenon*, p. 44.

16. *Ibid.*, p. 217.

17. The whole economy of faith and salvation is built on a metaphysics of process or interaction where finite reality is "I" in relation to God as "Thou." Opposed to this is the Aristotelo-Thomistic view where revelation is seen as an "It" which is accidentally related to man taken as "substance" or human nature.

18. *Phenomenon*, p. 264.

19. In the eternal procession in the Trinity, the dynamism is that of Love. As St. John says: God is Love. It is an eternal procession of love where one totally gives of Himself to the Others.

20. There is a cleavage, as many have observed, between theology where perfection is the *reception* of grace as perfective of nature and Christian spirituality where perfection is in union, in giving. The first is a dynamism of act and potency, the second, of

love. This cleavage can be healed with the view of being as including the dynamism of love.

21. *Phenomenon*, p. 260.

22. *Ibid.*, p. 270.

23. *Ibid.*, p. 294.

24. Crowe, *op. cit.*, p. 637.

25. Claude Tresmontant, *A Study of Hebrew Thought* (New York: Desclée Company, 1960), pp. 26–29.

26. *Ibid.*, p. 80.

27. Robert Johann, S.J., "Towards a Philosophy of Subjectivity," *Twentieth Annual Convention of the Jesuit Philosophical Association* (1958), p. 19.

III

The Churches
in Relation

Judaism and Christianity:
Then and Now

Krister Stendahl

Arguing that Judaism and Christianity are far more closely connected than we are apt to think when we speak about them as two distinct "religions," Krister Stendahl delineates an approach which would be conducive to renewed discussion between the two traditions yet would not sidestep the particularity of either. Such debate, he maintains, is both necessary and promising: "Not that we know where it will lead, but it should at least bring us to the point where we differ and disagree for the *right* reasons." Dr. Stendahl, Frothingham Professor of Biblical Studies at Harvard Divinity School, served as editor of the volume *The Scrolls and the New Testament*. His article, taken from the October 1963 *Harvard Divinity Bulletin*,* originally was a convocation address delivered on September 25, 1963, in Harvard's Memorial Church.

IN HIS recent book, *The Meaning and End of Religion*, Wilfred Cantwell Smith of McGill and, we may say, of Harvard, has drawn to a pointed conclusion the uneasiness which scholars have felt for some time when using the word "religion," not to say "religions." His warnings are much to the point when we try to speak about Judaism and Christianity.

"Christianity" and "Judaism" are abstractions. The given is not a religion but a people, a church, a community with its history, its traditions, its claims, its witness, its attempts to relate itself to an ever-changing world. If we were to use a not too attractive image we could say that the abstraction

---

* 45 Francis Avenue, Cambridge 38, Massachusetts.

"Christianity" is just the skin which the snake sheds every so often. It can be handled and studied in many ways. But the living reality is the church, the people with its organic continuity and the complexity through the ages. And the same applies of course to Judaism. To speak about Christianity and Judaism as two religions already forecloses many of the possibilities to understand what happened, happens, and might happen.

At the present time the popular image of the relationship between Judaism and Christianity is well expressed in two distinct habits of speech. On the one hand there is the reference to The Three Faiths of America: Catholicism, Protestantism, and Judaism. On the other hand there is the more academic construct "The Hebrew-Christian Tradition". Both of these "models" exert a powerful influence on our culture and our thinking. While theology is to many a highly technical and suspect term, it is evident that such expressions harbor whole theologies, partly conscious but mainly unconscious. It is reasonable to ask whether these theologies are well founded, sound and honest.

To speak about The Three Faiths is perhaps dubious already since it suggests that a Hindu, a Buddhist, a Muslim, an agnostic or an atheist could not be a true American. But it is not necessary to draw that arrogant conclusion. More serious is the implicit suggestion that the relation and the distance between these three faiths is somehow of the same order. This is further complicated by the fact that, due to the given majority/minority ratio in a community, we often get a constellation of Protestants and Jews versus Catholics. Yet, from many points of view, Catholics and Protestants would be expected to have a great deal more in common than such a pattern suggests. And also Judaism has *its* catholics and protestants. It becomes increasingly clear that the pattern of The Three Faiths is a construct in which the non-theological factors easily gain the upper hand. That does not diminish its significance. But it makes us anxious not to extend this significance beyond its own limitations.

The expression "The Hebrew-Christian Tradition" is more at home in colleges and universities, in the survey courses of the Humanities. It sees this tradition as having furnished the Western world with certain indispensable ideas and ideals, often epitomized as justice and compassion. It presupposes that the significant elements in Judaism and Christianity are those which they have in common, not those which divide them. If The Three Faiths are non-theological in the direction toward the sociological, The Hebrew-Christian Tradition is non-theological in the direction toward the philosophical and ethical. It should also be noted that the Christian imperialism exerts its pressure on how this tradition is usually handled in higher education. The component "Hebrew" often stands for what Christians call the Old Testament, and once Christianity is on the scene this "Hebrew" element is absorbed in the Christian tradition. Little or no attention is given to Jewish history and thought after 70 or 135 C.E. Maimonides may be a footnote to Thomas, the Jewishness a footnote to Spinoza, and Hasidism is not mentioned at all. Thereby the expression "The Hebrew-Christian Tradition" becomes more manageable, but the term pays little more than lip-service to the actual relationship between Judaism and Christianity. It does not need to be that way, of course, and it may well be that the formula "The Hebrew-Christian Tradition" could function more adequately in our search for a viable understanding of the relations between Judaism and Christianity. Even so, we should not forget that it of necessity puts a premium on similarities rather than differences, thereby prejudging the case before us.

Whatever the respective and relative assets and liabilities of these two models, habits of speech or even slogans, we cannot stress too emphatically that they are good and highly significant signs of a positive climate; a climate which the Western world has seldom known, and the Christian majority has seldom allowed; a climate in which we may be able to take a new look at the relationships. Without sounding more prophetic than we have the right to be, we could see the present situation in America as a unique and fresh challenge to our own generation of theological scholarship. The Jewish and the Christian communities find themselves side by side without many of the man-made walls which earlier separated them socially, culturally, intellectually. In both communities this proves to be a blessing, and it has driven us to a deeper grasp of our separate identities as believers. This is the time and the place and the climate in which we dare, and we must, question these models. We can and we must ask whether they are as well conceived as they were well-intentioned and have proven pragmatically beneficial.

It is my contention that, in the long run, a onesided stress on the common elements, or a non-theological acceptance of a sociological status quo with its mutual and, hopefully, increased respect for one another, cannot be the final chapter. That climate constitutes rather the first pages of a new volume in the history of the debate out of which the Christian Church was born. The time has come for resuming that debate which was cut off prematurely and transformed into an unusually grim history of everything ugly from name-calling to pogroms and holocaust.

I am not sure that the image is a happy one, but for whatever it is worth, we need a certain type of historical psychoanalysis, by which we are made aware of what happened in that most early infancy when the nascent church emerged out of its Jewish matrix and when the first steps were taken. Without serious attempts to recapture that most significant stage in the life of the Christian Church, new and free and fearless action may well be impossible.

We know a good deal more about those early years than we did a hundred years ago. But such knowledge is slow in affecting the sentiments and the systematic thinking of the present. Contemporary biblical and Jewish studies may have many weak points, but they have developed a very impressive ability to distinguish the actual issues of the past from the ways in which these issues appeared to later generations, our own included.

Let us then turn to a few areas where I think a changed picture of the past might affect the questions of the present and rectify the future debate between Judaism and Christianity.

1) The understanding of Jesus depends heavily on how one reads what we Christians call the Old Testament. In a

time when the red thread through that Old Testament was seen to be ethical monotheism and where the prophets were hailed and measured by that canon, Jesus became to the Christians the super-prophet. His greatness was asserted by demonstrating—often on shaky grounds—that his ethic was higher and his monotheism was purer and warmer than ever before in Israel or in the world at large.

We are now very much aware of how such a perspective on the Old Testament, while congenial to the 19th century in the West, is alien to the perspective of the Scriptures. We have learned to see the Old Testament centered in the people of the covenant, with its Torah, its cult, its psalms, its wisdom and proverbs, its prophets and their promises. We see an Old Testament which points toward an Age to Come, an Old Testament which leads to eschatology and messianism.

2) This new picture was mainly drawn on the basis of a better analysis of the Old Testament texts in their historical context, but it was highly confirmed and corroborated by the increased concern for, and knowledge about, the so-called Intertestamental Literature with its apocalyptic intensity and religious vitality. All this came to the attention of a wider public with the much celebrated find of the library of the Qumran community, the Dead Sea Scrolls. Here was a Jewish community in which the strict obedience to the Law was an integral part of its eschatology, even to the point of an anticipatory realization of the New Covenant. Their common meal was a foretaste of the messianic banquet.

3) Different in structure and yet not unrelated to the sentiments of the age, pharisaism can be understood in categories which had been utterly submerged in the anachronistic alternatives of legalism and grace. Pharisaism becomes a serious and honorable way of living in expectation and obedience, an obedience which is motivated and warmed by the expectation and an expectation which is made realistic and practical in concrete and flexible obedience.

4) In such a setting all that is said and came to be said of Jesus has its genetic center in the claim that he was the Messiah, that with him or through him the messianic age had drawn nigh. His teaching, his actions, his gracious and his

harsh words all relate to this one claim. It would be wrong to say that he came to teach a better concept of love, a deeper concept of repentance, a more spiritual concept of the kingdom. All these concepts were there, warm, deep and spiritual enough. But, to him, so close was the kingdom, so closely did he believe himself related to its coming, that he dared to apply its glorious gifts and standards here and now. And often—I think to his own surprise—the publicans and the sinners were more willing to listen and follow than were the professed religious. Thereby both the grace and the judgment were heightened immeasurably in the very structure of the gospel.

5) There is increasing evidence that the role of Pilate was considerably greater in the execution of Jesus than the tradition and even the gospels lead us to think. The precise role of the Jewish leaders we cannot assess. The nature of the sources makes it unlikely that we ever will. The crucifixion—a Roman execution—speaks its clear language, indicating that Jesus must have appeared sufficiently messianic, not only in a purely spiritual sense, to constitute a threat to political order according to Roman standards. At this very point we can discern one of the earliest signs of how tensions between Judaism and Christianity have affected the writing of history. Already in the gospels two tendencies are at work. The role of the Roman official, Pilate, is minimized—it was not easy in the Empire to have a founder who had been crucified by a Roman procurator; and the "no" of the Jews was the theological basis on which Paul and other missionaries claimed the right to bring the Gospel to the Gentiles. "He came to his own, but his own received him not . . ."—". . . and the vineyard will be given to other tenants who will deliver to him the produce when the time comes." Under the pressure of these two tendencies, one political and one theological, the exact events of history have been lost, as to the interplay between the members of the Sanhedrin and Pontius Pilate. But it is reasonable to see the latter as the key figure.

6) Thus the messianic issue in all its Jewishness stands in the center of Christian origins. What else could we expect when "Christian" actually is only the Greek for "Messianic."

I do not consider it an overstatement to say that the whole christological development of Christianity, even to that famous intensity of the 4th century, should be seen as a development from its original and Jewish nucleus: Jesus Christ. That is the creed: I believe that Jesus is the Messiah; and its chiastic correlate: the Messiah is Jesus.

There is one point in the early stages of this christological development which needs special attention. If we were to say, as we often do, that the Christian believes that the Messiah has come, while the Jew still lives in expectation, then we use at least highly unprecise language.

In one of the earliest christological expressions found in the New Testament we hear Peter say: Repent . . . that times of refreshment may come from the Lord and he may send the Messiah who was appointed for you, i.e. Jesus, whom heaven must keep until the time of consummation . . . (Acts 3:19–21). Here the coming of the Messiah Jesus is still future. Peter here shares with the Jewish community the faith in the Parousia, which is the consummation, the Age to Come. He announces that their Messiah will be this Jesus. While later Christians came to assert the "first coming" of Jesus in his earthly ministry but had highly divided opinion about the so called "second coming," the earliest Christians were clear about the Coming, the Parousia, which they looked forward to, together with their Jewish brethren. *Their* problem was to find the right answer to the question: In what sense and to what extent was the life and death of Jesus a coming of the Messiah? This is the problem to which the different gospels, and the traditions underlying them, give their answers, some tentative, some increasingly clear.

In the earliest stages of this development the claim that the messianic age had come and was truly inaugurated, that its powers were at work in the world through the church, centered around the resurrection and the spirit. These were the decisive signs that the new age was here. The general resurrection had begun, Jesus being "the first fruits from those who have fallen asleep," and the spirit was at work as the prophet Joel had promised, and the Messiah was now enthroned in heaven, and one prayed in the Lord's Prayer: let your will become

manifest on earth as it is now manifest in heaven.—Mara-
natha.

It may be suggested that this and similar layers of Christian thought, piety, and experience will prove significant to
keep in mind as we resume the debate between Judaism and
Christianity. No one could or should claim that such language
is an inadequate witness to Jesus as the Christ. Nor is it easier
to take than much of the later christological or trinitarian
development. But it is a language cut out of the same cloth
as that of Judaism. And Judaism, in turn, has had its own
developments. Yet one point at which to start is where the
communications broke off, perhaps for extraneous reasons.
This is not to turn the clock back; that neither should nor
could be done. But since the picture of that early history has
been one of the alienating and agonizing factors in the later
developments of our relations, let us at least get the record
straight. And let us compare similar things, i.e. first century
Judaism with first century Christianity. To compare Buber to
Paul, and Tillich to Akiba or Philo is nonsense from many
points of view. And so it is to compare Jesus to Maimonides,
and Hillel or Qumran to Origen or Chalcedon.

7) But what about Paul? In the more recent phases of
Jewish studies of Christian origins there has been a tendency
to recognize Jesus as somehow within the pale of Jewish
tradition: Jesus as one of the great teachers in the prophetic
tradition. Such an "Ehrenrettung" of Jesus has usually taken
place at the expense of Paul. Paul the Jewish renegade is
then blamed for having transformed and distorted the teachings of Jesus into a sacrilegious hellenistic mystery religion in
which the properly Jewish sentiment of monotheism yields to
claims of the divinity of Jesus. Or we hear about Paul's willful
or inadvertent misunderstanding of Judaism and its understanding of Law, Mercy, Repentance and Forgiveness.

It is striking that such assessments of Paul depend heavily
on an understanding of Paul which was set forth by apologetic
and tendential Christian interpreters. In such studies Paul's
words and attitudes have often lost their connections with the
specific issues which were Paul's primary concern. "Judaism"
and "Judaizers" became symbols of self-righteousness and

legalism as discussed in the controversies of the Western Church by Augustine, Luther, and Harnack. One could perhaps have expected Jewish scholars to be more sensitive to the primary setting of Paul's arguments than were their Christian contemporaries. Only recently, through the work of men like Johannes Munck, have we begun to see more clearly how Paul was positively related to Judaism even in his sharpest arguments in favor of the inclusion of the Gentiles into the People of God. And Paul's doctrine of a justification by faith without the works of the Law was primarily a scriptural argument, according to the exegetical principles of Judaism, in defense of his mission to the Gentiles. It was not a promulgation of a superior religion or of a deeper insight into the nature of grace, superior to that of "benighted pharisaic legalists."

Thus Paul's epistle to the Romans reaches its climax in chapters 9–11, where he gives his most explicit views on the relation between the Jews and the Gentile Christians. He, the apostle to the Gentiles, is not only full of what could have been a condescending concern for his "kinsmen according to the flesh"; as he looks toward the consummation of history, he cannot imagine that end without the final salvation of the Jews. He goes as far as to consider the mission to the Gentiles and the success of that mission in the name of the Messiah Jesus only as a detour which ultimately must lead to the point where the Jews accept this same Jesus as their Messiah. To him this is necessary; otherwise God would not be the God of Abraham, Isaac and Jacob. He reminds his Gentile Christians that they certainly have no reason to boast and to feel superior to the Jews. On the contrary, they should remember that they are wild branches, only engrafted on the true olive tree of Israel. "So do not become proud, but stand in awe."

It is of interest to note that Paul does not think about this final return of the Jews to their Messiah as the result of a mission from the Gentiles. At least he nowhere admonishes his congregations to such efforts. Nor does he intimate that it will come about by a spectacular display of virtue on the part of the Gentile Christians. In accordance with his good pharisaic training he looks toward this return as a mystery which lies in God's hands and which will happen in God's own time. But without such an end the Gospel could not be the Gospel and Jesus could not be the Messiah.

The Pauline panorama suggests to us and to our concern for the relations between Judaism and Christianity that these two are far more closely connected than we are apt to think when we speak about them as two religions. It suggests even that the Gentile Christian is what we might call "an honorary Jew." As Christians we speak to our Jewish friends and ask them to consider our claim to be fellow heirs to their promises. We claim that right by faith in Jesus the Messiah and for his sake. Such a claim appears to be well in accordance with the image which has emerged from our reconsideration of some of the earliest facets of our common and divided history.

Such a view has a strange effect on the present situation. First it reminds us that the New Testament has something to say about our relation to actual Jews. There are many good Christians who know their New Testament and the eleventh chapter of Romans quite well. But, to them, the "Jew" has ceased to be a real Jew; it has become that negative symbol for legalism and self-righteousness. The Church has so spiritualized its Scriptures that they have lost their original and concrete meaning. While this at points has a beneficial effect, it has also been impoverishing and misleading. The present discussion at the Vatican Council seems to follow a spiritualizing course when it expresses the conviction that all mankind shares in the guilt of Jesus' condemnation. The validity of such a *theological interpretation* of the gospels can hardly be denied by any Christian. It should become a corner stone in our catechisms and it will prove highly beneficial. But such an interpretation should not deprive Israel of its particular role in God's history, nor should it absolve the churches from listening obediently to Paul's warnings against Christian boasting and superiority feelings.

What is far more important is, however, the way in which Paul's vision somehow reverses the present sentiment of many Christians. The Gentile Christian now finds himself in need of defending his right and his claim to be one with his Jewish brother. With that attitude the debate which was drastically interrupted can be resumed. For the Christian there is an inner necessity to resume it. Not for the benefit of the Jews but for the sake of his own faith and identity. And that at the very center of the faith.

What good could come of such a resumed debate? The history of the debates between Judaism and Christianity has many chapters which make such encounters the last thing to be encouraged. *Vestigia terrent.* But if the general climate from which we took our point of departure is what I think it is, and if the attitude of which we have just spoken in the context of contemporary biblical studies is a valid one, then the debate is not only necessary for the reasons given but holds much promise. Not that we know where it will lead, but it should at least bring us to the point where we differ and disagree for the *right* reasons. In the atmosphere of the University such a result is a great and purifying achievement; in the hands of God it may prove fruitful and significant beyond our planning.

Our plea for such an approach should, however, never lead us to forget or belittle the unity of our common humanity. That unity is all the more significant for Jews and Christians since as human beings we have more things in common than many: the faith in God, a God who acts in history; the glorious and demanding values of what could be called the Hebrew-Christian tradition; with these we share in the common responsibility to our fellow men near and far. All these things bind us together in an all-embracing brotherhood with truly universal ties. And yet the future does not lie only in the attempts at letting all that is particular to each of us be swallowed up in an ever growing universality.

It seems that the power of religion in men's lives and in human culture lies in the specific, the particular, i.e. that which divides. Here philosophy and religion part ways and reach their intensity and identity in opposite directions. Worship and faith reach truth and creativity by intensifying the specific, the particular. I guess that is why we are apt to speak about a personal God, and that is why the language of worship must always be closer to myth and poetry than to philosophy.

Thus the particular—which is the divisive—is of the essence to our two traditions. We can only proceed by purifying our understanding and intensifying our grasp of the particular, even toward the point of transcending it; and yet we retain the specific, lest those who come after us be deprived of that transcendence.

RECENT LITERATURE

For the New Testament and the Early Church: Gregory Baum, O.S.A., The Jews and the Gospel, (1961).—Paul Winter, The Trial of Jesus, (1961).—Joseph Blinzler, The Trial of Jesus, (1959).—Johannes Munck, Paul and the Salvation of Mankind, (1959).—H. J. Schoeps, Paul, 1961.—I have given a fuller treatment of some of the New Testament problems relating to our topic in two recent articles in the Harvard Theological Review 55 (1962), 343–55, and 56 (1963), 199–215; and in the chapter on "Messianic License" in Paul Peachey (ed.), Biblical Realism Confronts the Nation (1964).

On the history and issues of Jewish-Christian relations: Jacob Katz, Exclusiveness and Tolerance: Studies in Jewish-Gentile Relations in Medieval and Modern Times, (1961); cf. idem, Tradition and Crisis, (1961).—H. J. Schoeps, The Jewish-Christian Argument, (1963).—Jakob Jocz, The Jewish People and Jesus Christ, (1949); cf. idem, The Spiritual History of Israel, (1961).—James Parkes, The Foundations of Judaism and Christianity, (1960).

Much of the recent development in the reconsideration of Jewish-Christian relations emanated from the programmatic study of Jules Isaac, Jésus et Israël (1948).—On the American scene Will Herberg's, Protestant, Catholic, Jew (1955) has been highly influential. See also the chapter "The Relations of the Christians and Jews in Western Civilization" in Reinhold Niebuhr, Pious and Secular America (1958).

The Significance of the Ecumenical Councils

William Nicholls

Anglican theologian William Nicholls discusses the ecumenical councils of the past, concluding that in recent times there has been a "general upgrading" of the status accorded them by Western non-Roman theologians and that the present-day ecumenical movement affords an insight "into the positive significance for theology of the method of solving problems by conciliar discussion." He then offers suggestions for future ecumenical councils that would include Roman Catholic, Orthodox, and Protestant churches. Dr. Nicholls' article, originally a paper given at the consultation between Orthodox and non-Orthodox theologians at Montreal in 1963, is reprinted from the April 1964 issue of the *Canadian Journal of Theology*.* The author of *Ecumenism and Catholicity*, Dr. Nicholls is Head of the Department of Religious Studies at the University of British Columbia.

THE SEVEN Ecumenical Councils have such importance for the Orthodox Church that it has been possible for some of her representatives to define her as "the Church of the Seven Councils."[1] No Western Church regards Ecumenical Councils with quite this degree of seriousness, nor does any single out these particular seven in the way that the Orthodox Church does. Councils have, of course, been retained in the Roman Catholic Communion, and a not inconsiderable number of them, including the Second Vatican Council, have been designated as "Ecumenical," both before and after they have taken place. Indeed, since the Middle Ages, any Council called by the Pope, and therefore representing the whole Roman Communion (i.e., in the eyes of its mem-

* University of Toronto Press, Toronto 5, Ontario, Canada.

bers, the whole of the Catholic Church), has been classed as ecumenical *per se*. But the surprise occasioned by the decision of Pope John XXIII to convoke the Second Vatican Council was a witness to the prevalence, within as well as outside the Roman Communion, of the opinion that the age of the Councils had been brought to an end by the new role assigned to the Pope himself by the developments of the nineteenth century. Even Vatican II was assigned no role of dogmatic definition, whereas when Pius XII considered that the time was ripe for a definition of the dogma of the Assumption of our Lady, he refrained from calling a Council, though it is understood that he consulted the Roman Catholic episcopate, without calling its members together. On the other hand, the willingness of the Roman Communion to continue the definition of dogma, with or without a Council, is an indication not merely of its confidence in its own full catholicity and ecumenicity, but of the failure of the Seven Councils to retain in the West that sacrosanctity they have assumed in Orthodox eyes.

Nevertheless, the Roman Catholic Church certainly accords to the Seven Councils of the undivided Church full dogmatic authority and indeed infallibility, even if she does not consider that they have said all that needs to be said about the content of revealed truth. The Anglican and Protestant traditions, with which the present paper is concerned, lack such a precise view of the authority of the Councils, nor are they altogether at one in the convictions they do hold. In view of the controversies of the time, most of the classical documents of the Reformation period say what little they have to say about the Councils in a somewhat negative form. They are concerned that the authority of the Councils shall not be set up against that of Scripture, and that they themselves should not be committed in advance to submission to the findings of a Council meeting under papal leadership or pressure, and without adequate representation from their own side. Fuller discussion of the ancient Councils is reserved for the literature of the second phase of the Reformation, when its doctrines have to be defended against the attacks of papalists and sectaries. At this stage a somewhat more positive tone is heard, and it emerges that four at least of the Seven are held in very high honour, and their pronouncements acknowledged to be in the fullest accord with Holy Scripture. But it does not appear to me that this more positive tone takes the theologians of the Reformation as far as an explicit definition of the authority of Councils, though at this point it may be said that certain Anglican writers, and certain Anglican official pronouncements, constitute something of an exception to this generalization. Here, however, we are confronted with a phenomenon that has marked Anglicanism right down to the curriculum of theological teaching, a reverence for the first *four* of the Seven Councils, coupled with virtual silence about the rest. This phenomenon, at first sight if hard to explain, at present seems to me to have quite deep roots in the Western attitude in general.

The Reformation view of authority, as we all know, lays very great stress upon Holy Scripture, as the supreme and in some sense sole authority in the Church. At the same time, nothing is more clear from the writings of the Reformers than the respect in which they hold the corporate mind of the Church, as expressed especially in the earlier periods of the Church, when the abuses of which they complain were less conspicuous, or non-existent. Whereas, however, in dealing with the authority of Scripture they are on their own ground, speaking positively about a crucial element in their own theology, in their references to Councils they are more guarded: *prima facie,* the Councils belong to the territory of their opponents, and they must show, first, that no such absolute authority attaches to the Councils as they have claimed for Scripture, and, second, that in any case the Councils speak for them rather than the papalists. But once these points have been made polemically, they are free to praise the doctrinal achievement of the Councils and make clear their own firm adherence to the doctrines and definitions there elaborated. Many of the references to Councils in the literature of the Reformation have in mind rather the possibility of a future Council than the authority of past ones. The Reformers inherited from the Conciliar Movement of the late Middle Ages the notion of a great council gathered together by the

Empire and committed to the reformation of the Church "in head and members."[2] In the previous century, the movement had had genuine success, limited and temporary though some of its victories were. The Church had not been turned into a constitutional monarchy, but some of the worst scandals of schism had been brought to an end. All the Reformers, Lutheran, Reformed, and Anglican, alike appealed to a free General Council to discuss and settle the issues raised by them and others. But in such an appeal lay the risk that the Council would be captured by the forces of conservatism, and that its decisions would be unilaterally arrived at under papal control. The Reformers had to guard themselves against being committed to signing a blank cheque for a Council in which their case might never be heard properly, as indeed it was not properly heard when Trent met. Undoubtedly some of the discussion of the Councils of the past is carried on with a glance over the shoulder at future possibilities. The authority of Councils is no academic question for the Reformers.

It follows that the most frequently urged position about Councils in the literature we are considering is the negative one: The Councils are not Scripture, and they can neither contradict it nor add to it; likewise, not being Scripture, they may err. In any case, so fresh and dynamic is the Reformation view of Scripture, at its most typical, that it must, for those who feel its excitement, inevitably thrust any other or relative authority into the background. The Reformers are innovators, in relation to the earlier advocates of reform whom they superficially resemble, in holding a dynamic view of Scripture as a living Word of God which speaks directly to faith, and indeed elicits faith, where it is rightly preached and expectantly read. Their predecessors, including such men as Wyclif and Hus, seem to have regarded Scripture rather as a legal document containing the constitution and ground-rules of the Church, and in this sense certainly an instrument for the reform of both doctrine and manners. If, however, Scripture is a legal document, it needs an interpreter, to decide doubtful questions, just as Parliamentary law needs courts and judges. To the extent that Reformation writers do regard Scripture as a legal document—and it must not be forgotten that they sometimes do speak in his way—they see a need for Councils as a court of final appeal.[3] More characteristically, however, they find in Scripture a living, self-authenticating Word of salvation, which needs no authority outside itself, either to support or to interpret it. It is this experienced capacity of Scripture to be God's saving Word which goes far to justify the extreme Reformation assertions of the sufficiency of Scripture, summed up in the phrases *sola Scriptura, Scriptura Scripturae interpres, perspicuitas Scripturae.* Extract these slogans from the experience of hearing and believing God's living Word of judgment and mercy, and you have no problem in refuting them. Within that experience, it makes perfect sense to say, with the Anglican Article VI, "Holy Scripture containeth all things necessary to salvation," and to refuse to admit any authority external to it. As the vehicle of the Gospel, Scripture needs no support. The doubts which may arise over the details of doctrinal interpretation, or through the findings of historical criticism today, need not obscure the Word in its essential content, the proclamation of Jesus Christ.

However, the Reformers recognize that the voice of Scripture is heard within the community of the Church, and that they are not the first to hear it. The Word has always created for itself a company of believers, and at no time in the history of the Church, even at its blackest, have true believers been lacking to the Church. Indeed, the Reformers accept from the traditional Western church the assumption that the Church has a teaching authority. What they are concerned to deny is that it extends to the creation of doctrines or moral precepts not contained in Scripture. Calvin grants that the Church cannot err "in so far as, having forsaken its own wisdom, it allows itself to be taught by the Holy Spirit through God's Word."[4] But Luther, Calvin and the rest are at one in asserting that a Council cannot invent any new doctrine whatever. This is the theme that runs, for example, through Luther's lengthy discussion in *On the Councils and the Churches.* When he finally comes to summarize his position in ten points, he begins by the general assertion that a Council has no power to establish new articles of faith, because the four chief Councils did not do so, and drives home the point, again by reference to the ancient Councils, in his first two: "A council has no power to establish new articles of faith, despite the fact that the Holy Ghost is with it," and "A council has the power, and is bound, to suppress and condemn new articles of faith, according to Holy Scripture and the ancient faith."[5]

Calvin denies the infallibility of Councils on the best of theological grounds, namely the eschatological one that the Church is not yet the perfect Church, without spot or wrinkle or any such thing.[6] And, of course, Councils may err by forsaking Scripture; the *latrocinium* of Ephesus II frequently recurs to the mind of the Reformers. But, this said, Calvin can be surprisingly positive:

> I venerate (the Councils) with all my heart, and desire that they be honoured by all.
>
> We willingly embrace and reverence as holy the early Councils, such as those of Nicaea, Constantinople, Ephesus I, Chalcedon, and the like, which were concerned with refuting errors—in so far as they relate to the teachings of faith. For they contain nothing but the pure and genuine exposition of Scripture, which the holy fathers applied with spiritual prudence to crush the enemies of religion who had then arisen. In some of the later councils also we see shining forth the true zeal for piety, and clear tokens of insight, doctrine and prudence. But as affairs usually get worse, it is to be seen from the more recent councils how much the church has degenerated from the purity of that golden age.[7]

But the test of a Council's work is Holy Scripture, and this test must, of course, be applied by others as well as by the fathers of the Councils themselves. A Council may not interpret Scripture without appeal.[8] Clearly Calvin would have welcomed the notion that a Council is not to be regarded as ecumenical in advance, but must obtain recognition from the corporate mind of the Church in the light of Scripture and the common tradition.

If we now turn to the Church of England, to seek its mind on the significance of the Councils, we are confronted, as I have suggested, with a special case in relation to the Reformation Churches as a whole. How special, and in what way, is notoriously a disputed question. Those who have been most concerned to claim a Catholic character for the Church of England have often sought to show that she does not in fact hold the distinctive Reformation positions, or that she took the first opportunity to get rid of them. To me, this is no more convincing than the position of those who deny that Anglicanism is a special case at all, and see it without qualification as one of the three main traditions emerging from the Reformation.[9] It seems to me neither possible nor desirable to deny that the Anglican Church is committed to such Reformation positions as the supreme authority of Holy Scripture, and justification by grace alone, through faith alone. The question that Anglicanism raises, both in relation to the continuing Catholic tradition in the West, and to the other churches which underwent the Reformation of the sixteenth century, is whether these doctrines are so incompatible with Catholic Christianity as both sides have been apt to suppose, and it is gratifying for an Anglican to note the way in which the same question is being adumbrated today by such Roman Catholic theologians as Hans Küng.

Anglicanism is at least special in this, that an explicit affirmation of the doctrinal authority of the four first General Councils is contained in an important document of the Elizabethan settlement, the Act of Supremacy of 1559. "Provided always . . . that such person or persons to whom your highness . . . shall . . . give authority to have or execute any jurisdiction, power or authority spiritual . . . shall not in any wise have authority or power to order, determine or adjudge any matter or cause to be heresy, but only such as heretofore have been determined, ordered or adjudged to be heresy, by the authority of the canonical Scriptures, or by the first four General Councils, or any of them, or by any other General Council wherein the same was declared heresy by the express and plain words of the said canonical Scriptures."[10] Likewise the canon which imposed subscription by the clergy to the XXXIX Articles also declares that they are "to be careful that they never teach ought in a sermon, to be religiously held and believed by the people, except what is agreeable to the doctrine of the Old and New Testaments, and what the Catholic fathers and ancient bishops have collected out of the same doctrine." The theologians of the time, Hooker, Jewel, and Field, echo in their several ways this respect for tradition and in particular for Councils.

The recognition of the first four General Councils seems somehow to have become a distinguishing mark of Anglicanism, and since as a theological decision it is not self-explanatory, it is interesting to enquire how it came about. The question appears to be a somewhat obscure one, and I can only tentatively suggest where an answer might be sought.[11] The origin of the position within Anglicanism may well lie in the Act of Parliament just quoted, as is implied by King James I in his *Premonition*.[12] J. T. McNeill, in a footnote in his edition of Calvin's *Institutes*, on IV, 9, 8, suggests that Calvin's own recognition of the authority of these four influenced Bullinger to set an account of these Councils at the head of his *Decades,* a work that is known to have had a great theological influence in England, and was indeed commended by Convocation in 1586 to the study of unlicensed preachers.[13] Certainly the standard theologians, with few exceptions, seem to concentrate their approval of the Councils in these four, and as recently as 1930 we find the bishops in conversation with the Old Catholics seeking and receiving from them an assurance that they regard the first four Councils as the most important.[14] Likewise, Anglican theological students tend to end their study of the doctrinal developments in the early Church with the Council of Chalcedon.

Luther, writing a few years earlier than the composition of the passage in Calvin just referred to, lays the same stress as Calvin on the first four: "To be sure, I have not read all the Councils, and shall not read them all and lose all that time and effort, since I have read the four chief councils thoroughly, better than any of them have done. Also I make bold to say that, after the four chief councils, I will hold all others of small value, even though I would hold some of them to be good." And again, "in all the books there are not more than four of these councils that are famous or well-known, and so the Roman bishops compare them to the four gospels, as they cry in their decretals."[15] According to the editor of the Philadelphia Edition of Luther's Works at this point, C. M. Jacobs, the reference is to *Decret. Grat.* dist. 15, c. 2, where Gregory the Great's celebrated allusion[16] is quoted. Here, conceivably, lies the clue to the nature of the tradition about the four chief Councils which so strongly influences Luther, Calvin, and through them the Anglican tradition. Once the West continued the series of Councils reckoned as ecumenical beyond the number of seven, the fifth, sixth, and seventh did not stand out so clearly from their successors as the first four may be admitted to do. And Gregory's remark about the four Gospels, made at a time when two of the other Councils had not taken place, and while the fifth remained in certain aspects highly controversial, seems to have greatly influenced the West. Nor, surely, are the Reformation writers wrong in seeing something altogether fundamental in the work of the first four Councils, as having basically refuted all the principal heresies that could logically arise in connection with Christology.[17] If these suggestions are well founded, it remains puzzling why the four Councils in question are regularly described as undisputed. Clearly someone has disputed every Council, if only those whose doctrines were anathematized. And granted the disputes which took place in connection with the Fifth and Seventh Councils, they hardly exceed those which arose over Ephesus and Chalcedon, as a result of which the Church was faced with schisms hardly less grievous than that between East and West, or those of the Reformation period. Perhaps "undisputed" should be taken to mean, "not disputed by Luther or Calvin and their followers!" This, if true, might be a somewhat embarrassing conclusion.

One of the writers I have mentioned, Richard Field, takes a more favourable view of the later Councils than his predecessors, and it is noteworthy that his opinion seems to be based on very thorough study. At any rate, his is the first well-known study of the authority of Councils within Anglicanism that goes into real detail; his essay, indeed, amounts to several thousand words; it appears in the fifth book, published in 1610, of his work on the Church.[18] Field, with characteristic commonsense, points out that Councils can scarcely be necessary to the Church, since she got on quite well without them to the time of Nicaea. "Notwithstanding," he goes on, "General Councils are the best means of preserving unity of doctrine, severity of discipline, and preventing of schisms, where they may be had . . .; and howsoever there may be a kind of exercise of the supreme jurisdiction that is in the Church by the concurrence of particular synods, and the correspondence of several pastors, . . . yet the highest and most excellent exercise of the supreme ecclesiastical jurisdiction is in General Councils."[19] Field shares the reluctance of the Reformers, and of the Anglican tradition generally, to admit infallibility anywhere outside Scripture. He will not grant to General Councils an authority equal to that of Scripture.

> Though the inspirations and resolutions of Bishops in General Councils proceed from the same Spirit from which the Scriptures were inspired, yet not in the same sort, nor with the like assurance of being free from mixture of error. For the Fathers assembled in General Councils do not rely upon immediate revelation in all their particular resolutions and determinations, as the writers of the books of Holy Scripture did, but on their own meditation, search and study, the general assistance of Divine grace concurring with them. . . .[20]

However, though Field thus attaches the authority of Councils to the general authority of the Bishops and other ministers taking part in them, and to the ordinary grace by which these are guided at all times, he is not reluctant to accord to Councils a very high degree of authority:

> Yet when there is a lawful General Council . . . we are so strongly to presume that it is true and right that with unanimous consent is agreed on in such a Council, that we must not so much as profess publicly that we think otherwise, unless we do most certainly know the contrary.
> Concerning the General Councils of this sort that hitherto have been holden, we confess that in respect of the matter about which they were called, so nearly and

essentially concerning the life and soul of the Christian faith, and in respect of the manner and form of their proceeding, and the evidence of proof brought in them, they are and ever were expressly to be believed by all such as perfectly understand the meaning of their determination.[21]

Field reckons six Councils[22] as being worthy of this sort of assent; the seventh he regards as dealing with manners, not faith, and as suspect through what he conceives to be its later consequences in the West. Field's study as a whole is especially impressive, and should be mastered by anyone attempting to reach a conclusion on the matters he deals with.

The great spokesmen of the Reformed tradition today, Barth and Brunner, have little expressly to say on the Ecumenical Councils, since the question is for them absorbed in the larger one of the authority of the confession of faith. Looking at the Scriptures today in the light of the ancient Councils and of the Reformation Confessions, which reiterate the authority of the creeds of the early Church, the Protestant theologian can acknowledge that the Word was rightly heard and borne witness to by the men of the past. The Councils are to be commended, precisely because of their fidelity to Scripture. Brunner argues that the Reformed Churches possess no dogma, in the sense of *credendum,* but only confessions of faith, in the sense of *creditum,* and argues that the form of the earliest Protestant Confessions bears him out.[23] However, it is not so clear that the Confessions differ in this respect from the Ecumenical Councils themselves. Barth, on the other hand, admits the term dogma, but rather characteristically grounds its authority on the commandment: "Honour thy Father and thy Mother."[24] His massive discussion of authority under the Word in *Church Dogmatics* 1/2, 20, 2, shows an awareness of the humble responsibility incurred by those who dare to recognize that they are in a *status confessionis,* that reminds us of his own experiences in Germany in the 1930's, and of his part in the Barmen Declaration. His insistence upon the necessity for seriousness of the *damnamus,* the *anathema,* may contain a valuable lesson for the Ecumenical Movement as it approaches the point of crystallizing the results of years of debate. For Barth, the authority of Confessions does not bind, as Scripture does, but none the less must be respected and taken seriously, and not lightly controverted. A biblicism which ignores the findings of the Church receives no respect from Barth. I have not been able to find in these writings any separate doctrine of the Councils; they fall into place in the general doctrine of the authority of church tradition, which is the authority, for them, of the past hearing of the Word.

In the final portion of the paper, I turn to the consideration of the influence of the Ecumenical Movement upon the Western non-Roman traditions in their view of the Councils, and to sketch out the kind of view which I think might now emerge. Those who have followed the proceedings of the Christ and the Church Commission of Faith and Order, which were recently reported to the Fourth World Conference, will note the way in which its discussions have implicitly accepted as authoritative not only Scripture but at least the four first Councils. In particular, there has been much play with a Christological analogy, which can be valid only if the Chalcedonian formula is certainly true. One of the most striking developments in the last period in ecumenical theology has been the growing appreciation of theologians for the work of the fathers and the Councils, and particularly for Chalcedon. A generation ago, so great a man as William Temple could say of Chalcedon that it "represents the bankruptcy of Greek patristic theology." Few would echo that sentiment today. Apart from a general renewal of scholarly interest in the patristic period, the major credit for this development is probably to be assigned to Karl Barth. Not only does Barth take Chalcedon as the basis for further reasoning, he is prepared to make use of post-Chalcedonian refinements such as those associated with the name of Leontius of Byzantium. In short, there has been a general upgrading, as it were, of the status accorded to the Councils by Western non-Roman theologians. As we leave the stage of biblical theology, which has held sway since the end of the war, and enter the realm of true dogmatics, we become more ready to appreciate not only the faith but the professionalism of the conciliar fathers.

Secondly, the ecumenical movement itself has given us an

insight not only into the procedures of Councils, but also into the positive significance for theology of the method of solving problems by conciliar discussion. Basic to the ecumenical movement is the practice of meeting in conference, face to face.[25] We have learned that we cannot expect to understand the point of view of a theologian of another tradition merely from reading his books. Only when we meet him, and engage in dialogue with him, so that our interpretations of his position are subject to his instant correction, can we seriously expect to know what he means, or correspondingly to be able to explain ourselves to him. Many of the disputes of the patristic period turned in part at least on differences in terminology; while some of the greatest men were able to see this, there were exceptions. It seems to be a step forward when the Fifth Ecumenical Council is able to incorporate such different emphases within its own thought, while warning against the onesided conclusions that might be involved in each way of speaking if it ignores the witness of the other.[26] More positively, many have toyed with the idea that the World Council of Churches may be the seed from which will grow a renewal of the practice of the authorized teachers in the churches conferring with each other right across Christendom, and coming to agreement about the faith which they teach. Some, like Professor T. F. Torrance of Edinburgh, look forward to a definition of the Church which might join the series of Christological definitions undertaken by the ancient Councils.[27] Similarly, the Second Vatican Council has brought the idea of a council, and particularly one with an ecumenical aim, vividly before the consciousness of Western Christendom.

Before turning in conclusion to the question of whether the West might come to a more positive appreciation of the Seven Councils venerated by the Orthodox, it might be helpful to consider some of the problems which would arise for the West if the suggestion of a future Ecumenical Council ever reached the stage of seriousness. Outside the Roman Communion, there could certainly be no question of a Council being regarded as ecumenical in advance. One could conceive of a highly representative body being gathered together in connection with the World Council of Churches, especially if it were to come about that the Roman Catholic Church joined in the Council, as so many of the Orthodox Churches have now done. Such a body might be called a Council, and it might be regarded as ecumenical in the modern acceptation of the term, as in the phrase, "ecumenical movement." But its authority, great as it would obviously be for us all, could hardly be accepted unconditionally in advance. It would be a very different Council, from the Anglican and Protestant viewpoint, from Trent, inasmuch as it would include the Orthodox and ourselves, on equal terms. Clearly we should look to it with very high hopes. But to enrol it in the select list, whether the list now be four or seven long, would be a matter for the subsequent judgment of Christendom. However, I take it that if we adopted this attitude we should only be returning to what has always been the Orthodox practice.

Secondly, even if the non-episcopal churches did not take part, and my assumption is that they would, we should not want the Council to be confined strictly to bishops, if the utterances of some of our most influential past theologians are to guide us today. Not all our bishops are very highly educated theologically, and, if they are not, they are not always willing to submit to the guidance of their theologians. While the bishops for us too retain the right of final decision as to what is of the essence of the Christian faith, they have no sort of infallibility, and their decisions can have no validity if they ignore Holy Scripture. Many theologians are in plain fact far more competent to read the mind of Scripture on the points now at issue than the vast majority of bishops. So priests and laymen should be present at such a council, and their voices clearly heard. By the same token, the representatives of the non-episcopal churches would have to take part if the Council were to have any usefulness in resolving the kind of problems that divide us in the West. But untraditional in certain ways as such a Council might be, I do not see what is to prevent the Church at large from subsequently recognizing that it had indeed succeeded, if such were the case, in determining and resolving the matters hitherto under dispute, and in bringing about a union between the separated churches. If so, I cannot see why it should not come to be regarded by all parties as an "Ecumenical Council" in the sense of those of the past. As we have seen, the West is not altogether at one in the significance which it attaches to these past Councils.

I have just implied, and I should want to stand by this implication, that the role of such a Council would for us be limited to declaring the mind of Scripture and the past witness of the Church, especially in its undivided state, upon the matters under dispute. Likewise, no infallibility could be claimed for it. Infallibility is even less acceptable to us now, since the rise of historical criticism, than it was at the time of the Reformation, and I am confident that the vast majority of the Western theologians associated with the Ecumenical Movement would echo Calvin's eschatological objection to the idea. Moreover, we hardly accord infallibility in all matters even to Holy Scripture. Whatever our formularies may say, it had better be faced that most of us feel not only free but obliged to read Scripture in the light of the most rigorous and scientific historical criticism that we can bring to bear upon it. All this raises large questions about the nature of revelation, which in my judgment are far from having been solved even by the rather extensive literature on the subject produced in the last thirty years. However, we should all agree in believing that the gates of Hell shall not prevail against the Church, and that divine Providence will always prevent the whole Church from falling into grievous error in a matter affecting our salvation. There may well be a kind of infallibility which is not the same as the verbal inerrancy of a theological formulation.

More positively, the authority of such a future Council would derive for us very largely from its representative character. One reason that we have for rejecting the ecumenicity of the Western councils which have taken place since the schism with the East is precisely that they are purely Western, and we do not reckon the West to be the whole Church. This does not exclude the possibility that the whole Church might later come to accept some of them as ecumenical, on the ground that they correctly declared the common faith. Similarly, Anglicans at least have not dared to claim for their own synods any such ecumenicity, and we have avoided the making of confessions of faith, since we do not regard ourselves as a body competent to make them. Perhaps we should listen more carefully to Karl Barth here, and admit that even quite a small group of Christians may find themselves forced into the *status confessionis*. Even so, and in spite of the loyalty which we ought to accord to such a confession if we found ourselves shut up by God in the necessity of making it, we should have to await the judgment of all the churches before we could ask them to regard it as binding also upon themselves. But with all these qualifications, I seriously believe that we should all regard a truly representative Council as competent to decide and pronounce upon the most important at least of the matters which divide Christendom today.

If this is our view of a possible future Council, what of the past? I have shown that the first four Councils are already held in very high honour, under Scripture and short of infallibility. I do not believe that we are likely at any time to accord them more authority than we now do. We may come to use their formulations much more frequently in our teaching than at present. What of the other three? This seems to be a question on which the West might well be invited to re-examine its mind. Here I should not be justified in speaking other than personally, beyond the reminder that there is, at least in Anglicanism, a minority tradition of regard for the authority of at least the Fifth and Sixth Councils. I believe that we shall in fact come to have an increasing regard for the theological work done at Constantinople in the sixth and seventh centuries, as we in general get more deeply once more into the problems of Christology than we have in recent years. I am bound to say, however, that the condemnation of the Three Chapters is likely to present in our time something of the problem it created in the West at the time of its enactment, if the matter is now pressed. As for the Seventh Council, it might be embarrassing if I were to quote some of the utterances of Protestant theologians and formularies in its regard. None the less, for myself I look forward to its increasing acceptance, for it seems to me that it was on sure ground when it invoked the Christological analogy in favour of the icons, and that the Eastern church, in its stricter interpretation of that Council, has gone along a surer way than the West. Had the Reformers known of the Eastern attitude to icons with the same intimacy which they had with the Western use of images, it is possible that they might all have followed Luther in his more tolerant attitude in these matters. But I doubt if such a development is to be looked for outside the Lutheran and Anglican traditions for a long time to come, and if it does come, I think it will be the fruit of a liturgical movement, rather than of dogmatic theology.

The question which the "other three" Councils pose for the non-Roman West is, I believe, this: Can we ignore the representative voice of the Church, speaking through Councils which have been accepted as ecumenical in both East and West? If we are *sure* that they are against Scripture, we ought to do it. But are we so sure?

NOTES

1. Cf. Timothy Ware, *The Orthodox Church* (Penguin Books, 1963), p. 43. But presumably a full definition of Orthodoxy would include the liturgical witness.

2. Decree, *Sacrosancta* of the Council of Constance, 1415.

3. E.g. Luther, *On the Councils and the Churches* (*Works of Martin Luther*, Vol. V, Philadelphia Edition, 1930–43), p. 253; Hooker, *Ecclesiastical Polity*, I, x, 14.

4. *Institutes*, IV, 8, 13.

5. *On the Councils and the Churches*, pp. 243f.

6. *Institutes*, IV, 8, 12.

7. *Ibid.*, IV, 9, 1, 8.

8. *Ibid.*, IV, 9, 14.

9. It is interesting to read Karl Barth to the contrary in *Church Dogmatics* (Edinburgh: T. & T. Clark, 1956), 1/2, p. 610.

10. Quoted, for example, by R. H. Bainton, *Age of the Reformation* (Princeton, N.J.: Van Nostrand, 1956), p. 147.

11. Since this article first went to press, my attention has been drawn to the explanation given by B. J. Kidd, *History of the Church to 461 A.D.*, Vol. III, p. 338–9. Interested readers are advised to consult Kidd's authoritative account.

12. P. E. More and F. L. Cross, *Anglicanism* (London: S.P.C.K., 1935), p. 3.

13. G. W. Bromiley, *Zwingli and Bullinger* (Philadelphia: Westminster Press, L.C.C. Vol. 24, 1953), p. 284.

14. Lambeth Conference, 1930, meeting with bishops of the Old Catholic Church: *Lambeth Occasional Papers*, 1931–38, p. 31.

15. *On the Councils and the Churches*, pp. 109, 145.

16. Ep. 25, to John of Constantinople and the other patriarchs.

17. Hooker, *Ecclesiastical Polity*, V, iv, 10.

18. Quoted at length in More and Cross, *Anglicanism*, pp. 142–155.

19. *Ibid.*, p. 144.

20. *Ibid.*, p. 151.

21. *Ibid.*, p. 152.

22. Cf. Cosin, More and Cross, *Anglicanism*, p. 55.

23. *Revelation and Reason* (Philadelphia: The Westminster Press, 1946), p. 156; but cf. *Dogmatics* (London: Lutterworth Press, 1949), Vol. I, pp. 52ff.

24. *Church Dogmatics*, 1/2, p. 585; *Dogmatics in Outline* (London: S.C.M. Press, 1949), p. 13.

25. Cf. the Constitution of the Faith and Order Commission.

26. Anathemas 7, 8, 9.

27. *Conflict and Agreement* (London: Lutterworth Press, 1959–60), Vol. I, p. 233.

Ecclesiology and Roman Catholic Renewal

George A. Lindbeck

What is the dynamic behind the *aggiornamento*—renewal—
currently at work within the Roman Catholic Church? In the
view of Lutheran scholar George A. Lindbeck, it is a new
understanding of the nature of the church—a vision which
sees the church not as "a state or army embarked upon the
conquest of the world," but as "the humble servant of all
mankind, Christian and non-Christian alike." This vision is
new also in its view of the church's internal life: "the bishops
are the servants of the people, and the pope is the servant of
the servants of God." Dr. Lindbeck, Associate Professor of
Historical Theology at Yale Divinity School, has served as
delegated observer from the Lutheran World Federation to
the Second Vatican Council. His article, reprinted by permission, first appeared in the Summer 1964 issue of *Religion
and Life.**

AN ECCLESIOLOGICAL revolution is now taking
place in the Roman Catholic Church. The revolutionaries, to
be sure, are transformists and gradualists, not despisers of
tradition nor rebels against authority. Nevertheless, their vision
of the church is profoundly different from the one that has
been dominant in the post-Tridentine period, and this leads
them to press for radical reforms. Further, their chances of
success are considerable. The present Vatican Council will
probably, at most, take only the first steps towards the reformers' goals, but they have the currents of history and the
younger generation on their side.

* 201 Eighth Avenue South, Nashville, Tennessee 37203. Copyright © 1964 by Abingdon Press.

In this article we shall deal with the role of theology in this upheaval. For Roman Catholics, as for Protestants, technical theology has often seemed irrelevant. The administrators who run the churches are not interested, the laity is uncomprehending and the secular world contemptuous. Then sometimes, as in the present Catholic situation, the work of the academicians becomes decisive. What had seemed of no importance to anyone but esoteric bands of specialists creates the possibility of transforming ecclesiastical power structures and altering almost beyond recognition the way Catholics and non-Catholics experience and understand the Roman Church. One is reminded of the relation between the years Karl Marx spent in the reading room of the British Museum and the Russian Revolution, or of the link between Einstein's abstruse mathematical computations and the atom bomb.

I

To be sure, ideas alone never transform a social or ecclesiastical system. Deeply rooted traditional patterns must be gravely threatened before they can be substantially changed. Yet the mere fact that they are under pressure does not guarantee change, and certainly not creative change. Many a church body, like other social groupings, has clung to the old in the face of the new to such an extent that it has become a reactionary, defensive ghetto, isolated from society as a whole, irrelevant to 90 per cent of the lives of its own members. This has happened to a considerable extent to Roman Catholicism and—at least as far as irrelevance is concerned—to Protestantism. A second type of inadequate response to challenge probably afflicts Protestantism more than Catholicism. A church may make pragmatic, undirected adjustments to modernity with the result that it loses the vision it had of itself without gaining a fresh one. New ideas are necessary if a community is to respond creatively to new situations. Great leaders like John XXIII are also needed, but in the present context it is the theological contribution to the new self-understanding of the Roman Church which concerns us.

It is always difficult to change one's self-image, even for individuals. In case of communities it is even harder. When the community is as large and ancient as the Roman Catholic Church, the task seems almost impossible. Its unity and continuity have become dependent on the unity and continuity of a highly intellectualized self-understanding, that is, on the traditional theological theory of the church. To question this doctrine has seemed equivalent to questioning the church. To change this doctrine is, for many Roman Catholics even to this day, equivalent to destroying the church.

It is because of this close connection between theory and the realities of the church that the contribution of seemingly ivory-tower theology has been decisive in the current Roman Catholic renewal. It has had to devise the new ecclesiological theories, the new conceptual frameworks, which have made change conceivable and given it guidance.

This task has required an immense expenditure of intellectual energy. The new ecclesiological developments have not been the product of one man, or even of a few men, but of large numbers of scholars writing specialized articles and books and criticizing one another's efforts. The most thorough survey of recent literature in this field has 210 pages of bibliography listing well over 6,000 titles, and this is relatively complete only for the German language and only for the period from 1920 to 1960.[1] Some major figures stand out, and a few names have become known outside of academic halls, but their work would have been impossible without the collaboration of multitudes of quite ordinary and, in many cases, "dry-as-dust" scholars.

Scholarship on this scale is possible only where there is a strong tradition of fostering intellectual work for its own sake quite apart from its immediate practical usefulness, and where there is also relative freedom for new ideas. Within Roman Catholicism, these conditions are best fulfilled in the French and Germanic cultural areas of Europe. It is in these lands that the theological renewal in general, and the ecclesiological renewal in particular, has proceeded farthest. However, its influence, especially since the last war, has spread throughout the world and is capturing the younger generation everywhere, even in Latin America, Spain, and, to a certain extent, Italy.

The success of the new theological movements depends on their ability to meet three highly demanding conditions. First, they must show that they are not in contradiction to the magisterium, i.e., the official ecclesiastical teaching authority. Second, they must show that revelation is on their side, i.e., that they are better based in Scripture and the total Christian tradition than is the inherited theology. Third, in order to win their way against carefully elaborated traditional ideas, they must be rationally persuasive.

The first condition is what makes a genuine change in Roman Catholic ecclesiology seem impossible, not only to Protestants but also to conservative Catholics. Parts of the traditional doctrinal theory have been dogmatized. No Catholic can question that the basic structures of the church are of divine institution, and therefore unchangeable. He cannot question, for instance, the decree of Vatican I (1870) that the pope is infallible and has universal and immediate jurisdiction over the church. This dogma was, in its origins, part and parcel of a monarchical-hierarchical view of the church according to which all power, initiative, and direction passes downward from the papal apex to the lower levels of the ecclesiastical pyramid. The new concept of the structure of the church is not monarchical but "collegial." The advocates of collegiality must try to show that the papal dogmas can be detached without logical self-contradiction from their original monarchical context and inserted into the new conceptual framework. In this process of reinterpretation the meaning of the papacy changes markedly. Its emotional connotations and practical implications are in some respects revolutionized. To cite examples which are familiar from press reports on the current council, collegiality suggests that the administration of the church should be decentralized and that a permanent "senate" of bishops be associated with the pope in the government of the church, so that the bishops rule the church together with the pope rather than simply in subordination to him.

This does not destroy, but it does transform, the operative

significance of papal supremacy and infallibility. In the new view the supreme doctrinal and jurisdictional authority would normally be exercised by the college of bishops (which, of course, includes the pope). Only when a dispute arises which cannot be handled by ordinary procedures, and which threatens the unity of the church, would the pope serve as the supreme judge. His decision would then be final. There is no higher authority to which one could appeal. But it would only be under these limited circumstances that he would define doctrine infallibility "from himself, and not from the consent of the church" (as Vatican I puts it) or, in the case of an administrative problem, actually exercise his universal and immediate jurisdiction.

Thus the new view does not deny papal supremacy but rather advocates a system in which that supremacy would be exercised far less frequently and far more cautiously than heretofore. The papacy's functions would resemble those of a combined Supreme Court judge and troubleshooter, rather than those of an absolute monarch.[2] The present council will not make these changes, but there are many bishops, not to mention others, who are in favor of them.

This illustrates the possibilities of incorporating old dogmas into new conceptual frameworks, but we should remember that even one change of this kind has repercussions throughout the theological system. For instance, how reconcile the new approach with the affirmation that the church never changes? It would seem that if its organization became explicitly monarchical in the course of centuries, this must be because it was from the beginning implicitly monarchical. According to this view, St. Peter's successors have always been supreme potentates by divine right even though it took a long time for the church to become fully conscious of this fact. Already in St. Thomas we find this kind of explanation of doctrinal development (though not applied to this particular case). Similar theories became unquestioned convictions in the nineteenth century, because the church was thought of as analogous to an organism whose structural changes represent irreversible progress, the exfoliation of the germinal. This would make it impossible to abandon monarchalism.

In order to handle this difficulty Roman Catholic theologians have had to learn a new way of thinking of changes in the church. Historical categories have replaced organismic ones. The church necessarily adjusts to the different periods in which it lives. It was inevitably influenced by the hierarchical and monarchical thought patterns and structures of the past. Centralizing and authoritarian tendencies were reinforced by the struggle to maintain institutional independence and unity against the efforts of secular powers to gain control of the church. However, so the argument goes, the Constantinian era has come to end.[3] Centralized authoritarianism is no longer necessary in democratic, pluralistic societies where there is freedom of religion and the state does not try to determine policy and the election of bishops and popes. Further, monarchical patterns are repugnant to the modern mind, and therefore not only unnecessary but positively harmful. Most serious of all, these patterns obscure the true nature of the church. Thus the organizational structures of the church, as well as its theology, must be thought of as much more relative to particular cultures than was previously supposed. They are not the products of a continuous and necessarily good development, but can be distorted and must be changed (within limits) as the times change. That which is unalterable in ecclesiastical structures lies at a deeper level than had previously been thought.

We have said enough to illustrate the kind of complexity of the difficulties which must be dealt with in order to adjust a new view of the church to the dogmas of the past. At the same time, we also have illustrated the way in which the newer ecclesiologists meet the third of the conditions for success which we mentioned. They are more "reasonable," more convincing, than the proponents of the older views because they take account of modern developments and use both the techniques and the insights of contemporary thought. In addition, they are intellectually rigorous, taking as much pains to be coherent and logically consistent as did their scholastic forebears. To be sure, they frequently lack scholastic clarity and neatness, but this is not usually a weakness. It is more often a strength resulting from the recognition that scholastic clarity was often a pseudo virtue which really consisted of mistaking abstractions for reality.

The second, and central, prerequisite for the success of a new ecclesiology must now be dealt with. The only way in which an ecclesiology can claim real authority is by showing that it is based on revelation. If it were simply an intellectual construct consonant with the modern mood and, by logical manipulation, reconcilable with dogma, it would be quite unpersuasive. For one thing, the modern mood changes too much from time to time and place to place. It was one thing in the 1920's, another in the 1960's, and varies greatly from country to country and from continent to continent. No, the strength of new ecclesiological developments is that they are based on the assiduous historical study of what the Roman Catholic considers the sources of knowledge of revelation: first of all, the Bible, and secondly, the total tradition of the church.

The theologians study history both to liberate themselves from a partial view of the past and to gain a new vision of the church. They have become aware that the "traditional" monarchical conception is really very recent, first becoming general, perhaps, only with Bellarmine in the seventeenth century and by no means undisputed even at Vatican I. With the help of modern historical scholarship (in large part, of course, Protestant) they have rediscovered the various biblical views. Their use of modern critical techniques, so different from the old proof-texting methods, has opened up new vistas on the early fathers and even on the medieval scholastics. The ecclesiology implicit in St. Thomas, for instance, appears to be radically different from what the so-called Thomists have often taught.

Drawing on this historical work, the systematic theologians have elaborated, often in highly abstract form, new theories of the church. They try to develop conceptual frameworks which make it possible to give due weight not only to dogma and the past and present situation of the church, but also to biblical and patristic evidence. These frameworks differ, but instead of being antagonistic they are complementary. They in some ways resemble scientific hypotheses each of which tries to give the most adequate account of much the same set of facts.

For this reason each of the recent ecclesiologies has contributed to one and the same new vision of the church, although none can be equated with it. This vision is much more pictorial and imagistic than the academic work from which it is largely derived. It is charged with emotion and inspires action even for those who do not know or understand the scholarship which lies behind it. In what follows I shall briefly describe the theological developments which have helped produce the vision and then sketch the vision itself.

II

We have spoken of the traditional Counter Reformation theory of the church as monarchical, but this is only part of the story. It is also static, juridical, and externalistic. These are the terms in which society in general was viewed at the time this theory was developed, and consequently it is not surprising that the church was thought of as basically analogous to a legally constituted state. In Bellarmine's well-known phrase, the church is a society "as visible as the Commune of Rome, or the Kingdom of France, or the Republic of Venice." Reinforcement for this approach came from the fact that Roman Catholic theology was at that time overwhelmingly defensive and apologetic, absorbed in the struggle to defend the juridical structures of the Roman Church against Protestant attacks.

In the nineteenth century new views of society developed. Through the growth of historical awareness and, especially in Germany, of romanticism and idealism, society came to be understood as comparable to a developing organism in which the inner life, the "spirit" (of a nation, for example), is of decisive importance. Institutional structures and changes were conceived as the self-expressions of the evolving *Geist*. Newman and Möhler, as well as Protestants such as Schleiermacher, applied analogous ideas to the church. Their stress on inwardness and growth was encouraged by their patristic studies, while the use of organic analogies received biblical support from the Pauline image of the church as the body of Christ. Scheeben especially made this notion central to his ecclesiology. He was the one who launched the famous characterization of the church as the continuation of the Incarnation.

However, Roman Catholicism as a whole was not yet ready for these novelties. A proposal at the First Vatican Council to define the church as "the Mystical Body of Christ" was mercilessly attacked by large numbers of bishops as obscure, mystical, and dangerous. After all, it was a favorite image of such heretics as the Jansenists! It will be recalled that Vatican I was prematurely interrupted by the outbreak of the Franco-Prussian War. This was fortunate because it left room for later developments; but the immediate effects of what the council did do, namely, dogmatize papal infallibility, was to strengthen the Bellarminian view of the church and reinforce its monarchical features.

It was not until after the First World War that newer ideas once more became common. The theme of the Mystical Body was taken up again with increased energy and enthusiasm. Scholastic-juridical concepts of the church were contrasted unfavorably with the vital-pictorial categories of Scripture and the fathers. The church as mystery was set over against the church as institution, the church of love against the church of law, and a spirit-filled community against a legally consti-tuted society. Sometimes these emphases were presented in a clearly orthodox Roman Catholic way, as, for instance, by the greatest theologian of the Mystical Body, Emile Mersch. This was not always true, however, and in Germany controversy became so acute that Archbishop Gröber of Freiburg appealed to Rome in 1943 to settle the disputes. The response came the same year in the encyclical *Mystici corporis*, which attempted to neutralize the new concepts by saying, in effect, that these simply refer to the inner reality of the Roman Catholic Church. The Roman Church is still to be understood in its outer aspects as essentially the kind of fundamentally juridical society which Bellarmine thought it to be. This, at least, is the interpretation of the intention of this encyclical which is suggested by the works of its original drafter, Sebastian Tromp,

who to this day remains one of the right-hand men of
Cardinal Ottaviani in the Holy Office.

In part because of *Mystici corporis,* in part because of
the war, there was a pause in the ecclesiological discussion
during most of the 1940's, but it has since been pursued with
ever greater vigor. Previously neglected themes have moved
to the center of attention. Of these, we shall deal briefly with
the "people of God" and with two attempts to define the
church, in one case as "communion" and in the other as
"sacrament."

First, however, we should note the decline in the theology
of the Mystical Body during the postwar period. This happened, in part, because further historical study has made it
clear that even though "body of Christ" is important for St.
Paul and the early fathers, still it does not represent their
fundamental conception of the church. Further, the dangers of
this metaphor have been recognized, not only by Protestants
but by some Roman Catholics who have pointed out that its
incautious use can lead to the "obliteration of all distance, . . .
the effacement of all difference" between Christ and the
Church.[4]

Perhaps the decisive difficulty, however, is that this image
is too ambiguous to serve as the basis for a definition of the
church. If one centers attention on the highly organized, unified, and centralized character of an organism, then the closest
social analogue would be a disciplined army in which each
member unquestioningly carries out the commands of the
head. This is the way in which conservative theologians tend
to think of the "body of Christ," thus interpreting it in a way
directly opposed to the intentions of the original Mystical Body
theology.

Some of those who have abandoned the attempt to define
the church as the body of Christ now use "people of God" on
the grounds that this notion is ecclesiologically fundamental
for the Bible and the early fathers. However, "people" does
not really serve as a definition. It also can be understood in
different ways, depending on the conceptual framework into
which it is inserted. For example, Michael Schmaus, author
of the biggest current Roman Catholic dogmatics, shifted from

"body" to "people" in successive editions without really changing his basic doctrine of the church.[5]

Yet this growing emphasis on the church as the people of God is important. It stresses the historical-eschatological aspect of the church in contrast to the ontological aspect which is underlined by the "body of Christ" image. In the latter, it is Christ's continued presence in and through the church which is thrown into relief, while "people of God" reminds us that the church, like Israel, is a wanderer through time, moving toward the eschatological kingdom, subject to historical vicissitudes and sometimes unfaithful to its Lord. It is hard to think of the body of Christ as needing reform, whereas the pilgrim people of God is obviously the *ecclesia semper reformanda*. This last phrase is not only being used more frequently by Roman Catholic theologians but was recently employed by one of the Roman Church's leading cardinals, Doepfner of Munich.

There are other themes which are now under active discussion: for example, the church as "mystery," or the relation of the church to the kingdom of God. Important though these are, we shall now turn to attempts to develop genuine theories, genuine definitions, of the church.

The first which we shall mention claims the authority of St. Thomas and has been developed especially by the French Dominicans Congar, Le Guillou, and Hamer.[6] According to it, the primary or direct referent of the word "church" is the interior community of saints in faith and love. This interior communion, to be sure, cannot be separated from the exterior elements which are its generative causes; but these elements themselves are fundamentally communal, i.e., structures of a fellowship of persons, not of an impersonal society. The visible church, in other words, is most vividly present, most fully actualized, in the worshiping community, especially in the celebration of the Eucharist. Juridical and magisterial institutions are secondary and instrumental rather than fundamental. Of course, the Roman Catholic proponents of this view insist that the true church is that ecclesiastical community which is subject to the successors of Peter, but this is not its essence. Indeed, even in reference to the papacy, it is more accurate to speak of "communion" with the pope than of "subjection." In brief, according to this view, the one-sidedly monarchical organizational developments of the last centuries have not altered the essential constitution of the church. This remains, and will always remain, communal or collegial.

The other major theory now under discussion is, at first glance, less congenial to Protestants. It is chiefly associated with the names of two German Jesuits, Semmelroth and Rahner.[7] Their ecclesiology is sacramental, which means that for purpose of definition they emphasize the exterior aspects of the church, not the interior community. Like the individual sacraments, the church is described as the visible and efficacious sign of invisible grace. It is not itself primarily that invisible grace, i.e., the communion of saints in faith and love. On the basis of these premises, Rahner has produced a definition of church membership which is strikingly like Bellarmine's. Even those who without living faith participate in ecclesiastical rites and submit to discipline are to be considered authentic members of the church.

While this sounds shocking to Protestants, it can be made to stress that the church is the people of God in the same thoroughly concrete way that Israel is.[8] Just as Jews remain in a real sense part of the chosen people even when they are inwardly unfaithful, so also in the case of Christians. The basic tenor of this ecclesiology is utterly different from Bellarmine's view of the church as a perfect (i.e., complete) society comparable to a state. To be sure, a sacramental people is, in a sense, just as visible as a state, but it is not self-contained, and it cannot be thought of as existing for its own sake as so often happens in the case of a state. Understood sacramentally, the whole being of the church is unmistakably directed toward something beyond itself. The purpose of its existence as a visible people is to serve as a comprehensive and efficacious sign of God's grace in Jesus Christ, and God continues to rule and overrule in using it for this purpose even when many of its members are tragically unfaithful.

Because this grace must be understood as the reconciliation and union of man with God and man with man, the sacramental theory can equal the *communio* ecclesiology in the emphasis it places on the interior communion of the saints. In another respect it is superior. The exterior elements of the church are not only said to cause the interior grace, as the *communio* theory asserts, but the nature of this causation is specified as sacramental symbolization. This means that the central question in ecclesiology is that of effective symbolization. The church should manifest, express, and witness to God's grace in Christ in every aspect of its visible structures and life. Just as major liturgical reforms are necessary in order for the sacraments effectively to symbolize, and therefore communicate, grace, so also in the case of the church. Further, from this perspective, the missionary task of the church becomes part of its very definition. It is in its essence "a sign lifted up among the nations."

We have given a most inadequate account of these two ecclesiologies, but this is perhaps excusable in view of the fact that our intention is simply to suggest how they have contributed to a new Roman Catholic vision of the church. It is this vision, as we said earlier, which is the dynamic force in the current renewal. It is by creating the possibility of this vision that the theological work which we have outlined is exerting a decisive role in present developments. We must therefore, in conclusion, pass from the world of technical ecclesiology to an attempt to sketch an image which lives more in imagination and feeling than in abstract reason.

The new vision of the church is not that of a state or army embarked upon the conquest of the world, but rather that of the humble servant of all mankind, Christian and non-Christian alike. The church's role is that of symbolizing, imitating, witnessing in all aspects of its life to a Lord who conquers through suffering, who gave his life that the world might live, who was more concerned with the poor and the oppressed than with the rich and the mighty. No phrase arouses more emotion in the hearts of vast numbers of contemporary Catholics (including the bishops in the council) than "Church of the Poor." No proposals are greeted with greater enthusiasm than the suggestion that the baroque, baronial splendors and ceremonials of the church should be abolished. There is an increasing passion for social reforms, an identification with the oppressed rather than the oppressors, with the poor, under-developed nations rather than the rich, so-called Christian ones. Those who feel this way are, of course, also convinced of the rightness of religious liberty and the disastrous results for the basic health of the church of such situations as exist in Spain and Colombia. Lastly, there is an astonishing openness developing in many Roman Catholic circles to so-called secular ideas and values, as well as to the contributions of non-Roman Catholic Christians. Those who wish to serve cannot be arrogant or defensive. They must be willing to learn from those with whom they want to join in the search for human brotherhood in obedience to God.

This vision is new, not only in the way it looks at the relation between the church and world but also in its view of the internal life of the church.

Bishop Edleby, a uniate participant in the council, effec-tively summarized the difference between the old and the new (even though he spoke of "western" and "eastern"). "The Western Church has supposed that Christ established Peter as supreme head—a kind of Roman emperor in cassock —and then gave him apostles as colleagues, and, finally, the clergy and laity as subjects. We in the East reverse the order: first Christ calls believers to whom the preaching of the gospel rightfully belongs, then he gives them apostles, and finally chooses a head of the apostolic college so that this will remain united."[9] In short, the bishops are the servants of the people, and the pope is the servant of the servants of God. These are traditional phrases, but now there is a great desire that they be made organizationally effective. We have already described how this might be done by establishing a collegial relation between bishops and pope, but this is only the beginning. The cry is arising to make the relation of bishops, clergy, and people collegial also; and above all, to give the laity real responsibility and initiative, not only in the practical domain but also in theological and spiritual matters.

There is no knowing what changes may eventually result from this new vision. Many hope for a transformation as complete as that which occurred after the church emerged from the catacombs. Perhaps this will happen in the next generations. The vision, aided by theology and abetted by the pressures of history, is pushing in that direction.

Protestants, of course, can only rejoice at these developments and hope for their fulfillment. The reforms which we have mentioned are still insufficient from our point of view, but if put into effect, they would represent immense progress. Further, there is obviously much that we can learn from the new Roman Catholic vision and theology of the church.

NOTES

1. Ulrich Valeske, *Votum Ecclesiae* (Munich: Claudius, 1962).
2. This is an approximate statement of the view of the papal office developed by Hans Küng, *Strukturen der Kirche* (Freiburg: Herder, 1962).
3. This has become a favorite slogan in Roman Catholic circles. See, e.g., M. D. Chenu, "La fin de l'ére constantinienne," *Un Concile pour notre Temps* (Paris: Cerf, 1961), pp. 59–87.
4. E. Przywara, "Corpus Christi mysticum—Eine Bilanz," *Zeitschrift für Aszese und Mystik*, XV (1940), 209.
5. Cf. the 1940 and 1958 editions of Schmaus's *Katholische Dogmatik*, III/1.
6. For this approach, see especially Jérome Hamer, *L'Eglise est une Communion* (Paris: Cerf, 1962).
7. In English, only the following is available: Karl Rahner, *The Church and the Sacraments* (New York: Herder, 1963).
8. See my forthcoming article "A Protestant View of the Ecclesiological Status of the Roman Catholic Church," in the recently established *Journal of Ecumenical Studies* (Duquesne University Press).
9. *Informations catholiques internationales*, November 15, 1963, p. 14.

IV

Biblical Trends

A Survey of Recent Gospel Research

Harvey K. Mc Arthur

"What may be said with confidence about the historical Jesus?" This question continues to concern New Testament scholars. It is Harvey K. Mc Arthur's contention, however, that before this question can be answered some basic issues must be isolated, clarified, resolved. Though in his essay dealing with these issues he does not attempt to move beyond clarification to resolution, he makes no secret of his own somewhat skeptical stance. Dr. Mc Arthur, whose essay first appeared in the January 1964 issue of *Interpretation: A Journal of Bible and Theology,** is Hosmer Professor of New Testament at the Hartford Seminary Foundation, Hartford, Connecticut. Among his other published writings is *Understanding the Sermon on the Mount.*

THREE RELATED but distinguishable questions are at the heart of contemporary discussion concerning Jesus of Nazareth, the One who stands at the center of the Christian faith. *Question one:* What may be said with confidence about the historical Jesus? *Question two:* How are the biblical affirmations about Jesus to be translated into categories of the contemporary world? *Question three:* How are the certainties of faith, or the kerygma, to be related to the uncertainties of our historical knowledge of Jesus?

It is a sign of the peculiar greatness of Rudolf Bultmann that he has answered each of these questions in so radical and distinctive a fashion that subsequent discussion can proceed only after coming to terms with his answers. His answer

* Published by Union Theological Seminary in Virginia, 3401 Brook Road, Richmond, Virginia 23227.

to the first question is in terms of radical form criticism; radical demythologizing is his reply to the second. His response to the third question cannot be summarized so simply; but apparently Bultmann is saying that while the kerygma emerged as a response to that which God did through the career of the historical Jesus, it is not *theologically* necessary for us to know the specifics of that career. While stressing the role of history in the emergence of the kerygma, he is concerned to insist that the recapture of that history can neither establish nor destroy the validity of the kerygma. The Word became flesh before it became kerygma, but for us of the subsequent generations the essential encounter is through the kerygma and not through the "flesh," which may be variously resurrected by various historians.

Current New Testament discussions might be clearer had it been possible to reach an agreement on the answer to the first of these three questions before being compelled to proceed to the second and the third. But the three are closely related, and Bultmann's provocative answers have brought them all into the debate at the same time. This study deals solely with the first question, that is, with the strictly historical question. More precisely, it deals with the issues which are prior to the answering of the first question. Since the solution of problems depends on the isolation and clarification of the separate issues, this study seeks to define and to arrange in sequence the basic issues which must be resolved in order to answer the first question: What may be said with confidence about the historical Jesus?

Five issues basic to this problem are presented in the following pages. In each case the issue is stated, its significance is indicated, and a brief comment is made concerning the relevant arguments. Where names are mentioned they are mentioned as representative figures. Generally I have allowed my own views to be obvious. This was not done to persuade the reader but rather to warn him of my conclusions and my bias; the purpose of the study is to clarify the issues rather than to resolve them. For convenience the five issues are listed here:

1) Are the Gospels primarily community tradition (the Bult-

mann circle), or do they contain substantial eyewitness tradition (T. W. Manson)?

2) Was the community tradition transmitted by anonymous and miscellaneous individuals (the Bultmann circle), or was it handed down by professional or semiprofessional persons (Riesenfeld, Gerhardsson)?

3) To what extent does the evidence of contemporary materials serve to corroborate items in the Gospel tradition (Jeremias versus Stauffer)?

4) Are there criteria by which authentic material may be distinguished from inauthentic in the Synoptic Gospels?

5) Do the sources permit the historian to reconstruct the development of the career of Jesus, or is only an impressionistic portrait possible?

The First Issue

Are the Gospels primarily community tradition (the Bultmann circle), or do they contain substantial eyewitness tradition (T. W. Manson)?

Methodologically, this is the first issue which must be resolved if we are to know how to use the Gospels as sources. Tradition has assigned the names of authors to the Gospels and has identified the sources through which they obtained their information. Thus Matthew and John were identified as eyewitnesses who recorded their own memories and those of their immediate associates; Mark and Luke were not eyewitnesses, but Mark reproduced the preaching of Peter, while Luke was an associate of Paul. As Tertullian said, ". . . our faith is based on John and Matthew, it is built up on Luke and Mark, followers of the apostles."[1] Nineteenth-century "Introductions" to the Gospels discussed at length the merit of these identifications, but it is a characteristic of some recent Gospel studies that they display a magnificent disinterest in such matters. This is partly because it is assumed that the contents of the Gospels prove them to be collections of community traditions, and consequently the identity of the final collectors is of subordinate importance.

The significance of this shift cannot be overestimated. If

the Gospels were written by eyewitnesses, or were based on sources derived from such, then the problem of the historian is quite different from the problem of dealing with Gospels collected by community tradition. Eyewitnesses are not always accurate, but, if their general integrity and intelligence may be taken for granted, their testimony may be assumed to be grounded in historical fact. Community tradition is notoriously unreliable in matters of fact, although it may reflect the significance which a person or event had for the community repeating the tradition.

Both within and without the Bultmann circle there has been a widespread abandonment of belief in any substantial eyewitness element in the Gospel tradition. Nevertheless, there is still a wing of thoroughly respectable New Testament scholarship which refuses to take this step. An excellent statement of this continuing belief in eyewitness sources for the Gospels appears in Manson's posthumous volume, *Studies in the Gospels and Epistles*.[2] With respect to Mark, Manson takes the position (a) that it was written by the John Mark known to us elsewhere in the New Testament, (b) that he incorporated the discourses of Peter, and (c) that it is possible to identify this Petrine material within the body of the Gospel. Manson labels some three hundred verses, or nearly fifty per cent of the entire Gospel, as Petrine. He begins his study of Matthew's Gospel with a detailed investigation of the well-known statement by Papias: "So, then, Matthew compiled the oracles in the Hebrew language; but everyone interpreted them as he was able." This statement is wholly inappropriate, Manson concludes, if applied to Matthew's Gospel but wholly appropriate if applied to an Aramaic Q document which underwent various translations into Greek. He therefore argues that the Q document was probably written by Matthew the Apostle, and that the Apostle's name was subsequently transferred to the Gospel which we know under his name.

If Manson is right, then Q, plus a substantial portion of Mark, represents eyewitness material. In this case the difficulties associated with community tradition are eliminated, or at least greatly reduced. Certainly five hundred verses of eyewitness material would provide a relatively stable foundation for research into the career of the historical Jesus. Thus a decision between Manson and the Bultmann circle is a necessary preliminary to any further consideration of the use of the Gospels as documents for the reconstruction of the career of Jesus.

While Manson's arguments are developed with his usual acumen and lucidity, I find them basically unacceptable. Undoubtedly this is in part a reflection of individual understanding of what an eyewitness might be expected to have said about the historical Jesus. In the sections which Manson had labelled "Petrine," the content and phraseology seem to refute his conclusion. In this category could be included the Feeding of the Five Thousand (Mark 6:30-44), the Walking on the Water (6:45-52), the Passion predictions (8:31; 9:30-32; 10:32-34), the Taking-Up-the-Cross saying (8:34), the Strange Exorcist (9:38-41), and the Withered Fig Tree (11:12-14, 20-25).

The internal evidence against the Matthean authorship of Q is much less clear-cut since, as is generally conceded, the Q material reflects an early strand of the tradition. Exceptions to this may be the Temptation narrative (Luke 4:1-13), the Great Thanksgiving (10:21-24), and the Cross-Bearing saying (14:27). But the basic weakness in Manson's argument for the Matthean authorship of Q is its highly speculative character. The hinge of Manson's argument is his contention that the expression "the oracles" (*ta logia*) cannot refer to a gospel containing a mixture of narrative and sayings. But if neither Papias nor Eusebius recognized this inappropriateness, may it not be a little presumptuous for us to insist that it could not originally have been intended as a reference to Matthew's Gospel? It may be that the comment of Papias does not correctly describe the First Gospel, but it is two long jumps from there to the conclusion that the comment was originally intended to describe a quite different document, and that we can identify that quite different document with Q.

However this question is resolved, the crucial character of the issue is clear. If the Gospels contain primarily community tradition, then the historian must handle them in one way; but if they contain a substantial and identifiable amount

of eyewitness material, then they may be utilized in a more
simple and direct fashion. If a decision is made in favor of
Manson's view, or some similar view, then some of the
following issues will become irrelevant. But those who reject
the eyewitness assumption must move on to consider other
issues.

The Second Issue

Was the community tradition transmitted by anonymous
and miscellaneous individuals (the Bultmann circle), or was
it handed down by professional or semiprofessional persons?

If the Gospels contain community rather than eyewitness
tradition, it is essential to determine, insofar as possible, what
the process was by which this tradition was repeated. For the
present purpose the answers to this question may be classified
in two groups. On the one hand, there are those who contend
that the transmission was carried out in an essentially un-
controlled form as the stories were repeated by various individuals in response to the numerous situations arising in the
life of the community. On the other hand, there are others
who affirm that the transmission was controlled by individuals
with a conscious technique for preserving the integrity of the
tradition. The former alternative has been tacitly accepted
by those following Bultmann's general approach. However,
in recent years a strong protest has been raised against this
assumption, particularly by Scandinavian scholars.

The clearest brief statement of this protest may be found
in a lecture by Harald Riesenfeld published in 1957 under
the title *The Gospel Tradition and Its Beginnings*.[3] The essence
of Riesenfeld's position is as follows: (a) The Jewish community handed on its own oral tradition by a rigidly controlled
process from teacher to pupil; (b) References in the New
Testament indicate that a similar process operated in the
young Christian community; (c) This process of formal
transmission began with Jesus, who was himself a teacher and
who undoubtedly initiated the process of repetition and
memorization among his immediate disciples. The implications
of this reconstruction of the transmission of the Christian

tradition should be obvious. While it is conceded that the Gospel materials are community tradition, the usual problems associated with that view are avoided by affirming that the tradition was transmitted in a controlled manner by professional techniques. Riesenfeld goes so far as to suggest that when Paul made his brief postconversion visit to Jerusalem, his chief concern was to be examined and approved by Peter for his mastery of the oral tradition concerning the things said and done by Jesus! The Riesenfeld lecture has now been supplemented by a full-scale study, *Memory and Manuscript*,[4] by B. Gerhardsson. Here the evidence from Jewish literature and the New Testament has been assembled and analyzed in detailed fashion. There is, however, some question as to whether the evidence is adequate to support the thesis.[5]

It is generally conceded that within rabbinic circles there was a relatively careful process by which a teacher handed on to his pupils the tradition in which he had been trained and which he himself had developed. But it is not clear that this procedure was as highly developed in the first century as it was in the second or third centuries and later. When one turns to the New Testament it is not at all certain that anything like such a rigid transmission pattern is apparent, despite the occasional occurrence of the technical terminology used in connection with the formal transmission of a fixed tradition. Jesus was unquestionably a teacher, but the Gospels suggest that he was quite different from the professional teachers of his day, and it cannot be assumed that he used their techniques unless this can be specifically demonstrated. To put it differently: a distinguishing mark of his ministry seems to have been that his method was informal rather than formal. It may still have included the formal technique of memorization, but this must be proved and not assumed.

There are other difficulties with this theory of a professionally controlled oral tradition. If such control occurred, how is it possible to explain the enormous differences between the Synoptic and the Johannine versions of that tradition? If Paul had mastered this technique, it is curious that there is no reference to this fact when he defends his authority. If Paul transmitted such a fixed oral tradition to his churches, why do his letters so seldom reflect the use of this tradition? (Surely it is inadequate to reply that Paul is silent because he had already given the oral tradition to the churches, or because the tradition had a sanctity which prevented its being quoted in informal letters.)

However the arguments are evaluated, the choice between the theory of a professionally transmitted tradition and that of a tradition transmitted by the general community is one of great importance. The Riesenfeld-Gerhardsson thesis is entirely different from that of Manson, but it would result in approximately the same confidence in the historical reliability of the Gospel materials. Such confidence cannot exist where the conclusions of radical form criticism are accepted. Instead, other devices must be found to distinguish authentic from inauthentic strands in the tradition.

The Third Issue

To what extent does the evidence of contemporary materials serve to corroborate items in the Gospel tradition (Jeremias versus Stauffer)?

All scholars agree that contemporary documents might provide evidence to corroborate items in the Gospel story. However, since Jesus played no major public role except perhaps at the time of his crucifixion, it is not surprising that contemporary documents fail to make direct references to incidents in his career. The comments in Josephus, Tacitus, and possibly Suetonius are too cursory to be of value here. Those in Jewish literature are rare in the early period, and even in these few cases it is not easy to determine whether they reflect independent, historical memory of Jesus, or whether they were polemic replies to the Gospels or to Christian propaganda. Nevertheless, it is possible that contemporary evidence may indirectly refute or confirm the historicity of elements in the Gospel tradition. At the very least, a knowledge of contemporary Jewish life and thought will enable the historian to identify anachronisms which may have been introduced into the tradition as it was shaped or revised by the primitive Christian community.

While most would agree on these general observations, there is marked difference in the way various scholars utilize the evidence from contemporary sources. By way of illustration I have named two scholars who agree on the value of the contemporary evidence but who differ dramatically in their specific utilization of that evidence. Both J. Jeremias of Goettingen and E. Stauffer of Erlangen use contemporary Jewish materials in their reconstructions of the life and teaching of Jesus; but the former uses these materials with cautious reserve while the latter, in the judgment of his critics, uses them with reckless abandon.

Jeremias is best known for his theories concerning the Aramaic *abba* and the Hebrew *amen*, both of which terms have been retained in the Greek New Testament and may go back to Jesus himself. In each case the usage attributed to Jesus is related to standard Jewish usage, but a significant change has occurred suggesting the creative action of some outstanding individual. Jeremias, along with others, argues that these terms must have been used by Jesus in the distinctive fashion reflected in the New Testament, and he goes further to argue that the new usages reflect significant aspects of his character and self-consciousness. Thus, according to Jeremias, the use of *amen* in the phrase "Truly, I say unto you" reflects Jesus' sense of unique authority; while the new use of *abba* in prayer to God reflects his sense of unique intimacy with God. It may not be as clear to all as it is to Jeremias that these two terms provide a Christology "in a nutshell," but certainly his analysis of contemporary Jewish usage sheds significant light on the thought and claims of Jesus.[6]

In principle, Stauffer simply carries further the methodology which Jeremias had employed so successfully. But those who have read his *Jesus and His Story* will have noted from the opening pages that, for Stauffer, an astonishing number of items in the Gospel tradition are confirmed by a knowledge of contemporary culture. The difficulty is that when others recheck his references they do not seem as conclusive as one would assume from Stauffer's confident statements. Thus, Stauffer insists that the two phrases "glutton and drunkard" and "son of Mary" indicate that Jesus was being attacked as illegitimate.[7] While it is conceivable that the phrase "son of Mary" had some such connotation, the evidence which Stauffer cites is something less than conclusive. (He ignores entirely the textual question in Mark 6:3.) The evidence on "glutton and drunkard" is even more precarious. Stauffer states without qualification, "In a genealogical table dating from before A.D. 70, Jesus is listed as 'the bastard of a wedded wife.'"[8] But the reference which he gives from M. Yebamoth IV, 13 is: "R. Simeon b. Azzai said: I found a family register in Jerusalem and in it was written, 'Such-a-one is a bastard through [a transgression of the law of] thy neighbour's wife.'" It is *conceivable* that Rabbi Simeon had reference to Jesus, but the unwary reader would never suspect how large an element of speculation was involved in Stauffer's assertion. The difficulty is not with the evidence but with the type of logic Stauffer applies to it. This may be illustrated by the use Stauffer makes of a New Testament passage. He cites the comment of Mary to the servants at the Wedding in Cana ("Do whatever he tells you") as evidence that the Fourth Evangelist and Mary were familiar with the story of the miraculous birth![9] Much of the material collected in Stauffer's book is of value, but it is difficult to believe that it can all be used to corroborate the Gospel tradition except by flagrant, special pleading. Some will disagree with this conclusion since, presumably, Stauffer does not walk alone.

The student of the Gospels must decide between the methodology of Jeremias and that of Stauffer, although there are obviously compromises between these two positions. If the more cautious approach of Jeremias is followed, it will be only occasionally that outside materials provide significant corroboration. Usually these materials indicate whether the Evangelist's narrative conforms with the general situation existing in Palestine about A.D. 30. If it does not conform, then the historicity of the narrative is suspect—but the reverse is not necessarily true. A narrative is not proved authentic because it conforms with the general situation existing at the time of the event. Not every later creation of the community was guilty of observable anachronisms.

The Fourth Issue

Are there criteria by which authentic material may be distinguished from inauthentic in the Synoptic Gospels?[10]

Since historical research is an art and not a mathematical science, the criteria suggested here cannot be applied in mechanical fashion. They serve as general guides. When they are used in combination by experienced individuals, the results suggest that they provide a significant degree of objectivity. But these results are far from infallible: scholars of equal competence may disagree with one another in their application of the principles; and the work of one generation must be tested by that of another. There is some consensus, nevertheless, concerning the four criteria which are outlined below.

First, there is the criterion of *multiple attestation*. For centuries the church assumed that the four Gospels were independent witnesses to the ministry of Jesus and that multiple attestation occurred when two or more of these Gospels reported the same incident or motif. But the argument from this simple form of multiple attestation disappeared when the interrelatedness of the Synoptic Gospels was recognized. If Matthew and Luke used Mark as a source, then their accounts of events in Mark are clearly not independent witnesses to those events. However, the sources which stand behind Synoptics may be regarded as having a relative independence. (For the present purpose the Fourth Gospel is ignored.) Thus Mark, Q, M (special Matthean material), and L (special Lucan material) may be examined to determine which motifs in the ministry of Jesus have multiple attestation. Generally, the identical incident or saying was not repeated in more than one source, so this methodology is more useful for determining the historicity of particular motifs than for determining the authenticity of specific incidents or sayings. For example, the incident of Jesus' eating with tax collectors and sinners as reported in Mark 2:15-17 is not repeated, so far as we can determine, in Q, L, or M. But the general motif of his concern for the tax collectors and sinners is solidly documented in all strands of the tradition. On the other hand, the Passion predictions, while reappearing in Matthew and Luke, are generally borrowed from Mark. Luke may have had one or two traces of this motif from L, but even these sound like echoes of Mark. Consequently the historicity of the Passion predictions is far less certain than Jesus' concern for tax collectors and sinners.

Admittedly a motif might occur in all four strands of the Synoptic tradition without being authentic; that is, it might have emerged in the earliest Palestinian-Christian community and so have influenced all strands of the tradition, even though unhistorical. Some scholars would place certain types of "Son of Man" sayings in this category. On the other hand, it is conceivable that a completely authentic motif might happen to be documented by only one strand of the tradition. But this is merely a way of saying that some material may be authentic even though, from a methodological standpoint, the extant evidence is inconclusive. This is a situation which continually confronts the historian.

It is worthy of note that the Bultmannians do not display any great interest in this multiple-attestation criterion, apparently preferring more esoteric guides. Having indicated some scepticism of British tendencies in Gospel research I should comment that, in my judgment, their regular and faithful use of this criterion is to be commended. While not infallible, it is the most objective of the proposed criteria and one which will undoubtedly have a permanent place in the task of Gospel research.

Second, there is the criterion, or principle, that *the tendencies of the developing tradition should be discounted.* A study of the Gospel tradition from Mark and Q through Matthew and Luke and on to John or the Apocryphal Gospels reveals certain "tendencies" which operate with a fair degree of consistency. Since one may assume that these same tendencies were operative during the earlier, hidden stages of the tradition, the researcher must make allowances for these tendencies when evaluating the earliest available form of the tradition. The tendencies identified here must be stated in highly oversimplified form. Only extended work with the details of the canonical *and* apocryphal Gospels can give any real awareness of the varying degrees to which the following statements are true.

1) Changes in place, time, and sequence of incidents were made without serious historical concern.
2) The beginnings and endings of narratives were subjected to the greatest change; or, conversely, the central section of an incident remained the most stable.
3) Sayings of Jesus changed less than narrative material.
4) Names tended to be added to narratives.
5) Aramaisms tended to disappear.

Perhaps it is necessary to warn the unwary that these tendencies are like actuarial statistics. They indicate what happens on the average; they cannot state categorically what must happen in a specific instance. For example, names may tend to become more numerous as the tradition develops; but this does not mean that every name in the tradition is secondary, or that there may not have been instances in which names were dropped from the tradition. Another necessary caveat is that the tendencies listed here have been identified from a study of the *written* tradition and its development. They may not have been applicable in precisely the same manner during the development of the oral tradition. Nevertheless, they were probably operative in a broad sense during the "tunnel period" of the tradition, and the historian who attempts to recover the earliest version of an incident will need to bear them in mind.

Third, there is the criterion of *attestation by multiple forms*. This criterion was utilized extensively by C. H. Dodd in his book *History and the Gospel*,[11] but it does not appear to have received extended subsequent discussion. Using the insight of form criticism that the Gospel materials fall into a number of literary forms, Dodd argues that if a motif is present in several different literary forms it is more apt to be authentic than if it appears in only one such form. Actually, this criterion points toward a special type of multiple attestation, that is, an attestation not of multiple sources behind our Gospels but of multiple forms within those sources. By way of illustration, Dodd cites six motifs and lists a variety of passages to demonstrate that each of these motifs is attested by its appearance in multiple literary forms.

Many scholars would agree that the motifs he cites are authentic, but that this does not of itself validate his criterion since there is an ambiguity in his evidence. The ambiguity arises from the fact that motifs which he has identified appear not only in a variety of literary forms, but also in a variety of sources. Would it be methodologically sound to argue that a motif is authentic if it appears in a variety of literary forms even though all appearances of this motif were confined to a single source? Is the motif of the Passion prediction, which (as has already been said) derives primarily from Mark, made appreciably more secure historically by the fact that it appears in a variety of literary forms in that Gospel? Perhaps a fair answer would be that while the variety of literary forms does not prove that the Passion predictions are authentic, it does prove that they were deeply embedded in the Markan tradition and not simply editorial additions of the final author or editor. Thus the criterion has some value in distinguishing comparatively early from comparatively late traditions, but it is not as decisive as that of multiple attestation by a number of sources.

Fourth, there is the criterion which suggests *the elimination of all material which may be derived either from Judaism or from primitive Christianity*.[12]

This is the most difficult of all the criteria to apply since it may easily be construed so as to leave no space between the Scylla of Judaism and the Charybdis of primitive Christianity. It is a radical criterion since much of the teaching of Jesus must have been more or less standard Judaism, and the elimination of this from the portrait leaves only a fraction of his original teaching—though perhaps the most distinctive fraction. Finally, it is an ambiguous criterion since scholars differ as to whether a particular item is more "natural" against the background of primitive Christianity or against the background of the ministry of Jesus. Nevertheless, this criterion has received widespread support, and some of its applications are relatively clear-cut.

It is easy to see that the question of the payment of the Temple tax (Matthew 17:24-27) is more natural against the background of primitive Christianity than as an authentic incident during the ministry of Jesus. Of course Jesus and his disciples paid the Temple tax! But as the early Christians steadily differentiated themselves from the main Jewish community, the question may well have become critical. Similarly the saying about cross-bearing is difficult to understand before Good Friday and Easter, but its symbolism is entirely intelligible in the life of the developing church. Again, Mark 9:41 reports that Jesus referred to those who "bear the name of Christ." Even if Jesus was regarded as the Christ by some during his earthly ministry, this particular phraseology seems to suggest a later period when this terminology was in general use. To many scholars these illustrations will seem entirely clear, but there are innumerable passages where a decision would be more difficult to reach.

On the other hand, the idea of eliminating from the words attributed to Jesus those sayings which reflect regular Judaism poses problems of principle as well as of application. Is it too drastic a rule? Should the Markan saying "The sabbath was made for man, not man for the sabbath" (Mark 2:27) be denied to Jesus because similar sayings can be found in Jewish literature? Even if the principle is accepted, the problem of application remains. Is Jesus' reply to the question about the Great Commandment (Mark 12:28-34) an expression of Judaism, or is it something distinctive?

Those who accept both halves of this criterion are aware that it is radical, particularly in its elimination of "Judaism" from the materials to be regarded as authentic. They concede that its application eliminates all except a minimal amount of material. However, they accept this limitation for methodological reasons; that is, they are anxious to establish as firm a base of certainty as is possible, even if only for a small amount of material. Some believe that once this minimum has been established with a high degree of probability, it may be possible that materials previously rejected can be reclaimed because of their congruity with elements in the established base.

The Fifth Issue

Do the sources permit the historian to reconstruct the development of the career of Jesus, or is only an impressionistic portrait possible?

In 1600 a German Protestant mathematician published a Harmony of the Gospels in which many of the events were dated not only by year but also by month and day. Thus, Bartholomaeus Scultetus dated the incident recorded in Luke 5:1-11 as having taken place on June 18, A.D. 30. Such confidence in the ability of the scholar to establish an absolute chronology for the ministry of Jesus was rare even in the sixteenth and seventeenth centuries. Most scholars, however, despite the insights of Bucer and Calvin, assumed that a relative chronology could be established by the proper arrangement of the material in the four Gospels. The nineteenth-century discovery of the priority of Mark encouraged the assumption that the Markan chronology should be followed as authoritative, but this assumption has been challenged by developments in twentieth-century Gospel research. There has been a wide response to the contention of the form critics that, outside the Passion narrative, the individual pericopes circulated without chronological links and were subsequently arranged in an artificial, or at least non-chronological, order. Others have contended that the interests of the Evangelists themselves in their sequence arrangements were topical or liturgical or theological—but certainly not chronological.

Today no competent scholar would attempt a detailed chronology of the ministry of Jesus. But there continues to be a decisive difference between those who feel that a broad chronology is possible and those who are sceptical about even such a limited possibility. Stauffer defends the view that chronology is both possible and essential for a history of Jesus.[13] In general, British scholars such as Dodd, Manson, and Vincent Taylor[14] share his view though they are considerably more cautious in their development of that chronology. On the other hand, the members of the Bultmann group are sceptical about chronology and development, although this scepticism is not as extreme in some as it is in

Bultmann himself. There is more chronology in G. Born-kamm's *Jesus of Nazareth*[15] than Bultmann would have in-cluded, but both scholars are in broad agreement on this problem. It is striking that M. S. Enslin, who is notoriously disinterested in the theological concerns of the Bultmann group, parallels at many points their attitude toward the possibility of determining the chronology of the career of Jesus. This is evident in his book *The Prophet from Nazareth*.[16]

Presumably, the differences over this issue reflect differ-ences in connection with some of the issues discussed earlier. Those who resolve the first two issues listed at the opening of this study by asserting that the Gospels contain anonymous community tradition will inevitably be sceptical about the chronological framework. But those who hold there is sub-stantial eyewitness material in the Gospels, or that the com-munity tradition was transmitted by professional techniques, are able to defend the *possibility* of authentic chronology in the tradition. These prior decisions affect *only* the possibility of an authentic chronology, and other considerations are necessary to demonstrate its actuality. For example, the presence of extensive eyewitness material in Mark does not establish the accuracy of Mark's outline unless one knows that the crucial eyewitness was interested in the question of chronology.

The trend of current scholarship is away from confidence in the Gospel chronology. However, this trend will need to be tested by the challenges of a new generation before it can be recognized as permanently valid. The question of chronology remains one of the basic issues in Gospel research.

Conclusion

Three topics have not been discussed which might have been expected in this context.

First, the generally accepted results of source criticism (Mark, Q, L, and M) have been taken for granted. There has been a vigorous attempt to reopen the discussion with challenges to the existence of Q and even to the priority of

Mark. But these challenges, while interesting, have not yet resulted in any substantial dislocation of the traditional critical position. Unless there are new and striking developments, source criticism should not be regarded as a basic issue in Gospel research.

Second, form criticism has not been considered as a separate issue. This does not indicate any lack of respect for the contributions of this methodology, which is undoubtedly here to stay. The controversy concerns the implications which may be drawn from form criticism, and these have been taken into consideration in nearly all of the issues discussed above.

Third, there has been no discussion of the "new historiography." The writer assumes that some of the emphases of Dilthey and Collingwood will be taken into consideration by any who are concerned with the "quest of the historical Jesus." However, it is not clear that the contrast between the "old historiography" and the "new historiography" is as sharp as one might imagine from the comments in J. M. Robinson's *A New Quest of the Historical Jesus*.[17] The leaders of the old quest were interested in the intention of Jesus as well as in the sequence and development of his career; the leaders of the new quest will, if they are wise, be happy to use any available information concerning even the externals of Jesus' career, since "intention" is visible only as it is embodied in concrete acts or sayings.

The quest of the historical Jesus raises theological as well as historical questions for the Christian community. In the normal life of the community these levels cannot, and should not, be kept isolated from each other; but for methodological purposes it is necessary to deal with questions on one level at a time. The present study has been concerned exclusively with the historical level.

BIBLIOGRAPHY

BORNKAMM, G., *Jesus of Nazareth* (New York: Harper & Brothers, 1960).

BOWMAN, J. W., "The Life and Teaching of Jesus," *Peake's Commentary on the Bible* (London: Thomas Nelson & Sons, 1962), pp. 733–747.

BULTMANN, R., *Jesus and the Word* (New York: Charles Scribner's Sons, 1934).

——, *History of the Synoptic Tradition* (New York: Harper & Row, Publishers, 1963).

BULTMANN, R., and KUNDSIN, K., *Form Criticism* (New York: Harper & Brothers, 1962).

COLWELL, E. C., *Jesus and the Gospel* (New York: Oxford University Press, 1963).

CONZELMANN, H. "Jesus Christus," *Die Religion in Geschichte und Gegenwart*, 3rd edition (Tübingen: J. C. B. Mohr [Paul Siebeck], 1957—).

DAHL, N. A., "Der historische Jesus als geschichtswissenschaftliches und theologisches Problem," *Kerygma und Dogma*, Vol. I (April 1955).

DAVIES, W. D., "A Quest to be Resumed in New Testament Studies," *Christian Origins and Judaism* (Philadelphia: The Westminster Press, 1962).

DIBELIUS, M., *Gospel Criticism and Form Criticism* (Edinburgh: T. & T. Clark, 1936).

——, *Jesus* (Philadelphia: The Westminster Press, 1949).

DODD, C. H., *History and the Gospel* (New York: Charles Scribner's Sons, 1938).

——, "The Framework of the Gospel Narrative," *Expository Times*, Vol. 43 (June 1932).

ENSLIN, M. S., *The Prophet from Nazareth* (New York: McGraw-Hill, 1961).

FULLER, R. H., *The New Testament in Current Study* (New York: Charles Scribner's Sons, 1962).

GERHARDSSON, B., *Memory and Manuscript* (Lund: C. W. K. Gleerup, 1961).

GRANT, F. C., "Jesus Christ," *Interpreter's Dictionary of the Bible*, George A. Buttrick, editor (New York: Abingdon Press, 1962). Vol. E-J, pp. 869 ff.

JEREMIAS, J., "The Present Position in the Controversy Concerning the Problem of the Historical Jesus," *Expository Times*, Vol. 69 (August 1958).

——, "Kennzeichen der ipsissima vox Jesu," *Synoptische Studien*, in honor of A. Wikenhauser (München: Karl Zink Verlag, 1953).

MANSON, T. W., *The Teaching of Jesus*, 2nd edition (Cambridge: Cambridge University Press, 1945).

——, *Studies in the Gospels and Epistles* (Philadelphia: The Westminster Press, 1962).

——, "The Life of Jesus: Some Tendencies of Present Day Research," *Background of the New Testament and Its Eschatology*, W. D. Davies and D. Daube, editors (Cambridge: Cambridge University Press, 1956).

RIESENFELD, H., *The Gospel Tradition and Its Beginnings* (London: A. R. Mowbray, 1957).

STAUFFER, E., *Jesus and His Story* (New York: Alfred A. Knopf, 1960).

TAYLOR, V., *The Life and Ministry of Jesus* (New York: Abingdon Press, 1955).

——, *The Gospel According to St. Mark* (London: Macmillan & Co., Ltd., 1952).

ZAHRNT, H., *The Historical Jesus* (New York: Harper & Row, Publishers, 1963).

NOTES

1. *Against Marcion* IV, 2.
2. Manson (Philadelphia: The Westminster Press, 1962).
3. Riesenfeld (London: A. R. Mowbray).
4. Gerhardsson (Lund: C. W. K. Gleerup, 1961).
5. See the critique by Morton Smith, "A Comparison of Early Christian and Early Rabbinic Tradition," *Journal of Biblical Literature*, Vol. 82 (June 1963).
6. See the brief reference in Jeremias' article, "The Present Position in the Controversy Concerning the Problem of the Historical Jesus," *The Expository Times*, Vol. 69 (August 1958), pp. 333–339. A more detailed statement is found in the German article, "Kennzeichen der ipsissima vox Jesu," *Synoptische Studien*, in honor of A. Wikenhauser, 1953 (München: Karl Zink Verlag, 1953), pp. 86–93. A similar view on *amen* has been presented by H. Schlier in the appropriate article of *Theologisches Wörterbuch zum Neuen Testament*, G. Kittel, editor (Stuttgart: W. Kohlhammer, 1933), Vol. I, pp. 339–342.
7. Stauffer (New York: Alfred A. Knopf, 1960), p. 16.
8. *Ibid.*, p. 17.
9. *Ibid.*
10. See the article by N. A. Dahl, "Der historische Jesus als geschichtswissenschaftliches und theologisches Problem," *Kerygma und Dogma*, Vol. I (April 1955).
11. Dodd (New York: Charles Scribner's Sons, 1938), pp. 91 ff.
12. See H. Conzelmann, "Jesus Christus," *Die Religion in Geschichte und Gegenwart*, 3rd edition (Tübingen: J. C. B. Mohr [Paul Siebeck], 1959), Vol. III, col. 623; also R. H. Fuller, *The New Testament in Current Study* (New York: Charles Scribner's Sons, 1962), p. 33; also H. Zahrnt, *The Historical Jesus* (New York: Harper & Row, Publishers, 1963), p. 107.
13. Stauffer, *op. cit.*

14. See Dodd, "The Framework of the Gospel Narrative," *The Expository Times*, Vol. 43 (June 1932); Also Manson, *The Teaching of Jesus*, 2nd edition (Cambridge: Cambridge University Press, 1935), pp. 12 f., 320–323; also Taylor, *The Gospel According to St. Mark* (London: Macmillan & Company, Ltd., 1952), pp. 145–148.

15. Bornkamm (New York: Harper & Brothers, 1960).

16. Enslin (New York: McGraw-Hill, 1961).

17. Robinson (London: Student Christian Movement Press, 1959).

Rudolf Bultmann and Post-Bultmann Tendencies

P. Joseph Cahill, S.J.

In this survey of recent developments in New Testament studies, P. Joseph Cahill, S. J., focuses on the "New Quest for the Historical Jesus" as it finds expression in the thought of students of the biblical theologian Rudolf Bultmann. Father Cahill also discusses Bultmann's reactions to these new developments, as well as making some observations and criticisms of his own in regard to both Bultmann and the post-Bultmannians. One of the happy aspects of the post-Bultmann movement, says Father Cahill, is a tendency to return to a type of theological understanding "that could be called more scientific and objective than the subjectivism of existentialism." Father Cahill, whose essay first appeared in the April 1964 *Catholic Biblical Quarterly*,* is a Lecturer in Religion at Loyola Academy, Wilmette, Illinois.

INTRODUCTION

At an age when other men might be satisfied to vacation at the German spas or to gather notes for their memoirs, Professor Emeritus Bultmann continues to exercise an unprecedented influence on German theology. Three years ago Bultmann wrote that the relationship of the primitive Christian kerygma to the Jesus of history has currently and in quite a new sense turned out to be a vital issue.[1] With this beginning Bultmann enters the theological arena where the battle centers on "The New Quest for the Historical Jesus." The renewed critical study of the life of Jesus has gained countenance as a

* Catholic Biblical Association of America, Washington 17, Cardinal Station, D. C.

"New Quest" and survives Albert Schweitzer's seemingly pessimistic assertion of fifty-eight years ago that, "There is nothing more negative than the result of the critical study of the Life of Jesus."[2]

Rudolf Bultmann has spanned the period of the old quest for the historical Jesus. He has contributed to diverting the mainstream of Gospel study from the purely historical to the kerygmatic approach. But now many of Bultmann's former students feel that the new quest for the historical Jesus goes beyond strictly Bultmannian principles and his resultant theological synthesis. Bultmann's former students, the Marburgers, have therefore called the period from 1953 to 1964 the post-Bultmann era.[3] Although Bultmann shows no interest in attaching his name to movements or periods, his own answers to his students make it clear that Bultmann is somewhat less than enthusiastic about the goal and procedures involved in the so-called new quest of the so-called post-Bultmann era.

This paper is an examination of the post-Bultmann evolution, an effort to analyze the new quest.[4] Four major points guide this attempt: first, a schematic history of the problematic of the Jesus of history; secondly, a brief presentation of the thought of Bultmann's former students; thirdly, Bultmann's reaction to the recent developments; fourthly, observations on two aspects of the new quest.

Part I: The Jesus of History

FORMATION OF THE PROBLEM

Until approximately the eighteenth century one does not encounter a technical problem with the historical Jesus or the relation of the Jesus of history to the kerygma. Paraphrases, harmonies of the Gospels, as well as lives of Jesus were produced from the time of Tatian. Elements obviously puzzling to a later day, for example, the cleansing of the temple, rejection at Nazareth, three paschs in the fourth Gospel, and the relatively late dates of the written Gospels, were not formulated as problems,[5] but, if acknowledged in any way as difficulties, they were viewed as parts of a mosaic that could ultimately be harmonized. So too the influence of the Easter perspective did not raise any distinction between the historical Jesus and the Christ of faith. And what might now seem an excess of optimism assumed that one could easily write the life of Jesus.[6]

When Lessing in 1778 published the last of seven fragments of Hermann Samuel Reimarus (1694–1768) entitled *The Aims of Jesus and His Disciples,* critics stood face to face with an emerging problem of the Jesus of history.[7] Rationalistic and imaginative lives rushed to defend the historical Jesus. But in 1835 David Friedrich Strauss (1808–1874) published a life of Jesus in which he claimed that the Gospels were a texture of myth and therefore largely unhistorical. Strauss, anticipating a later development, felt that the New Testament was not an archive document as was evident from the lack of historicity in the miracle accounts where it seemed that laws of causality, succession, and psychology were either violated or ignored. Strauss becomes the definitive line of cleavage between the nineteenth century and all preceding generations. Fifteen years after Strauss' work, Ernst Renan could say, " 'If we try to put down all that the Gospels contain of actual fact, we could scarcely obtain one page of history about Jesus.' "[8] Though Strauss surveyed the wreckage and salvaged "the idea of Christ," that is, man's oneness with God, critical research stood in doubt and hesitation before the apparent impossibility of reaching the historical Jesus described in the Gospels.

LITERARY SOURCE CRITICISM

In exactly the same atmosphere as the clouds of doubt rising from the work of Reimarus and Strauss, literary source criticism opened a patch of blue sky. Strauss had attributed the mythological and unhistorical character of the Gospels to the inconstant oral tradition which generated the Gospels. If the critic could recover or reconstruct original written documents at the source of the Gospels, then he could well hope to dissipate the darkness surrounding the historical Jesus. We need only mention the work of Karl Lachmann (1793–1851) who in 1835 inferred that Mark was the source of Matthew and Luke, a malleable theory to be further shaped by Gottlieb Wilke (1786–1854) and Christian Hermann Weisse (1801–1866) in 1838 and moulded into the classical two-source theory.

The notion of Mark and possibly a reconstructed Q as ultimate, underived, uninterpreted sorts of archive documents suited the historicist temper of the nineteenth century. At this moment the "Nestor of Historians,"[9] Leopold von Ranke (1795–1886), was teaching a seminar in the critical study of the sources. "History, he taught, should be written only from the 'purest, most immediate documents.' "[10] In the nineteenth century there was hope that the classical two-source theory could provide the purest and most immediate documents and thus reveal the Jesus of history.

MARTIN KÄEHLER

If the two-source theory seemed to put the historical Jesus within reach of critical research, Martin Kähler (1835–1912) was to erect the architecture of the Jesus of history problem in a form that has endured up to the present moment. Kähler's book, *Der sogenannte historische Jesus und der geschichtliche, biblische Christus*,[11] first published in 1892, did not exercise its full influence until very modern times. There is, for example, not one reference to this significant book in Schweitzer's *The Quest of the Historical Jesus*. According to Kähler, the standards and requirements of biography make it impossible to write a scientific life of Jesus. The Gospels and their sources are confessional and kerygmatic.[12] Precisely because the Gospels are documents proceeding from faith, documents of a believing Church preaching her belief, "Kähler thought it nothing less than naïve or preposterous for the historian to establish the ground and content of faith."[13] The foundation and basis of faith does not emerge from scientific or critical-historical reconstruction but rather "must be a Jesus Christ as proclaimed by the apostles in the preaching which established the Church."[14] To clarify the difference between history and kerygma, Kähler distinguished between *Jesus* and *Christus*, between what is *historisch* and *geschichtlich*. Only the biblical, preached, *geschichtlich Christus* of the kerygma is permanently significant for belief. In fact, as experience should have taught, man can encounter only the kerygmatic Christ. Bultmann would assume Kähler's perspective and add the existentialist modifications.

SUMMARY

Before turning to the Marburgers and to Bultmann's response, we may summarize the nineteenth century quest of the historical Jesus, apart from Kähler, as a search based on the feasibility of a history and life of Jesus or a psychological reconstruction and interpretation of the character of Jesus from the Gospels or their literary sources. Wilhelm Wrede (1859–1906) in *Das Messiasgeheimnis in den Evangelien* (1901), Karl Ludwig Schmidt (1891–1956) in *Der Rahmen der Geschichte Jesu* (1919), and Bultmann in *Die Geschichte der synoptischen Tradition* (1921), effectively buried the original quest for the Jesus of history. Before Kähler and Bultmann, critics approached the Gospels as history; subsequently the Gospels are taken as kerygma.[15]

Part II: The Position of The Marburgers

INTRODUCTION

Before presenting the position of Bultmann's former students over the period extending from 1953 to 1964, we must note three points. First, apart from a general agreement on the possibility of establishing by historical method a continuity beween the earthly Jesus and the kerygma, there is no settled, constant, and fully developed Marburg position. What at times seems to be a moving viewpoint in the process of formulation appears to resist, if not totally elude, definitive explanation. Secondly, for those who have not worked or pursued their studies in the existentialist atmosphere, there is the haunting difficulty of Heideggerian categories, terms and concepts. If, however, we are to speak at all of Bultmann and the Marburgers some use of Heideggerian terminology is inevitable. Thirdly, and at the risk of seeming to recede from the irenic ecumenical atmosphere, one cannot fail to wonder if the thoughts expressed in the new quest could not be susceptible of clearer explanation. For example, I have in mind some interminably long sentences, with quotations within quotations, dashes, hyphens, semicolons—and the whole array ending with a question mark. Then there is the further question of terms, such as the *Christus-kerygma*, the *Christusverkündigung*, the *Christusbotschaft*, the *urchristliche kerygma*, and simply the *kerygma*. What some readers might regard as a conspiracy of fluid terminology is rather a perfect example of the Heideggerian emphasis of the element which is *mitgesagt*, *mitgeteilt*, that is, explictly unexpressed but still communicated, in the use of words. With this in mind, occasional and brief references will attempt to stabilize some of the more mercurial terms.

ERNST KÄESEMANN

At a meeting of the "old Marburgers," October 20, 1953, Ernst Käsemann delivered a paper[16] suggesting that despite the difficulties of historical study of the life of Jesus, one cannot admit that only resignation and scepticism should have the final word and be allowed to lead to a disinterest in the earthly Jesus.[17] Käsemann was not hinting at a desire to construct a life of Jesus; such a life, demanding an explanation of both outer and inner development, remains impossible.[18] But scepticism not only neglects the primitive Christian concern to identify the exalted Lord with the humble Lord—the evangelists believed the Christ they preached was the earthly Jesus—but also overlooks the ascertainable fact that in the synoptic tradition there are passages which any sincere historian must recognize as significantly authentic.[19] Though the description of the exalted Lord, in a movement not unlike osmosis, practically absorbs the features of the earthly Jesus, still the primitive community intended identification of the two.[20] To resolve the compound one must seek the differences and similarities between the preaching of Jesus himself and the kerygma. According to Käsemann the question therefore of the earthly Jesus is "the question about the continuity of the gospel . . . and the variation of the kerygma,"[21] that is, the noticeable change whereby the historical Jesus who preached now becomes the exalted Lord who is preached. For the moment we may assert that the term kerygma here may be understood as the theologically interpreted presentation of God's activity in Christ as found in the Gospels.

ERNST FUCHS

Ernst Fuchs agrees that the kerygmatic proclamation is in continuity with the preaching of Jesus. Fuchs seeks the basis of this correspondence in the conduct or behavior of Jesus.[22] Fuchs maintains that how a man behaves or conducts himself indicates what grasp the man has of who and what he is. This may broadly be compared to the traditional assertion *agere sequitur esse* and its implications. We come to the being or existence of the individual through and in his activity. Critical-historical research is capable of reaching and asserting what grasp Jesus had of his own being, his existence, by considering his conduct. Later Fuchs will point out that the kerygma offers man a particular understanding of any and all human existence. The point of continuity, therefore, seems to be in the analogous understanding of existence found first in the earthly Jesus and subsequently available to all believers through and in the kerygma. God offers a new possibility of existence to men. Jesus verifies in his own person the new possibility in a unique way. In the kerygma which preaches Christ, the new possibility of human existence is accessible to man. Part of the proof of continuity in the understanding of existence is found in the terminological resemblances between the Gospel tradition and the kerygma, and in the common structure of commonly agreed authentic material in the Gospel tradition.[23]

To take an example: Jesus' understanding of his existence appears in the parables. In the parable of the Prodigal Son, for instance, Jesus teaches that God is gracious and forgiving; thus the parable illuminates Jesus' behavior in receiving sinners by putting himself in God's place, identifying his behavior with the will of God. But primarily Jesus' behavior clarifies the will of God by a parable which becomes intelligible in and through Jesus' conduct.[24] Thus the behavior or conduct of Jesus is, strictly speaking, the real context or structure of his preaching,[25] the element which throws light on his message. "In the message and action of Jesus is implicit an eschatological understanding of his person, which becomes explicit in the kerygma of the primitive Church."[26] The eschatological understanding that is clearly present in the kerygma—that is, Christ is here acknowledged as God's definitive action, the ultimate salvific event—is also discernible in Jesus' message and in his actions. The continuity, therefore, is in the eschatological understanding manifest both in the earthly Jesus and in the preached Christ.

GÜNTHER BORNKAMM

In November, 1956, Günther Bornkamm published *Jesus von Nazareth*,[27] "the first book on the historical Jesus to issue from the Bultmannian school since Bultmann's own *Jesus and the Word* appeared thirty years earlier."[28] Bornkamm admits, "No one is any longer in the position to write a life of Jesus."[29] He concedes that the search for "what actually happened," rather than bringing man to a knowledge of the Jesus of history actually leads man astray.[30] Bornkamm in principle accepts Kähler's position that the Gospels are kerygma, and he adds that the kerygma describes Jesus as "the risen Lord, present with his will, his power, his words."[31] Thus the proclamation affirms who Jesus *is* rather than who he *was*. This evangelical emphasis on the presence and contemporaneity of Jesus, as well as the concern of the evangelists to avoid recounting a timeless myth, involves a deep solicitude to point out that the earthly Lord is now in the kerygma and is the "once and for all" action of God. "Because the earthly Jesus is for the Church at the same time the risen Lord, his word takes on, in the tradition, the features of the present."[32] Amid all the emphasis on the fact that the Gospels are post-Easter creations and that they recount everything in the light of

Easter, one must keep in mind that it is precisely the Jesus of history who lived and acted before Good Friday and Easter who is seen in the Easter light.

While using Fuchs' observation that Jesus' conduct is the framework of his preaching, Bornkamm attempts to show that both Jesus' message and his conduct are related to the kerygma. If Bornkamm agrees with Bultmann that Jesus made no claims at all to the messianic titles, he goes on to affirm "that the Messianic character of his being is contained *in* his words and deeds and *in* the unmediatedness of his historical appearance."[33] Bornkamm means that even though Jesus did not use messianic titles, his words and deeds awakened messianic hopes. By word and deed he generated a hope that he was the messiah. " 'But we hoped that he was the one to redeem Israel' (Lk. xxiv. 21) seems to express quite accurately the conviction of the followers of Jesus before his death."[34] But because nothing in the ordinary Jewish hopes and expectations was capable of leading the Jews to an understanding of the total messianic mystery of Jesus—for example, ordinary categories could not grasp ignominy and suffering as messianic—it is only through the resurrection that the full messianic mystery of Jesus could possibly be disclosed and understood. Messianic hopes that Jesus aroused by his words and deeds were now corrected, modified, and transformed to appear in their true light. Or, one might say, what Jesus said and did was messianic but so sublime and so totally unprecedented that the Easter light was necessary to grasp his messianic character. In this one point therefore there is continuity: messianic hopes aroused by the Jesus of history are fulfilled by the exalted Lord who is one and the same person.

CONZELMANN AND EBELING

Other students of Bultmann refine the thread of continuity between the kerygma and the earthly Jesus. For Hans Conzelmann Jesus linked the hope of salvation to his own person in as much as in his deeds he sees the kingdom of God present and in his preaching sees the ultimate and definitive word of God. Jesus, therefore, is man's confrontation with God. After Easter the Christian community transforms this indirect Christology into direct statements about Jesus' person and work: they make explicit what was implicit. Thus Conzelmann establishes continuity between the kerygma and the Jesus of history on the fact that Jesus associated salvation with his person, and the kerygma is the explicit formulation and preaching of this definitive salvation that took place in Jesus Christ.[35]

Gerhard Ebeling, in common with other Marburgers, confesses that the state of the New Testament sources and historical understanding itself urge a quest behind the New Testament witness.[36] Ebeling distinguishes "elements in the message of Jesus—the nearness of the rule of God, the clarity of his will, and the simplicity of discipleship with joy, freedom, and lack of anxiety. . . ."[37] The historical Jesus is a witness to these elements and hence a witness to faith; after the resurrection-ascension this witness becomes the basis of faith.

SUMMARY AND OBSERVATIONS

The non-Bultmannian, Joachim Jeremias, in summarizing the present state of the problem of the historical Jesus, observes that in the preaching of Jesus we meet exactly the same claim for faith made by the kerygma. Every line and verse of the sources hammers in the fact that something unique, individual and totally unprecedented has taken place. The message of Jesus, including God's intimate dealings with sinners and the authority that dares to address God as Father is without either parallel or analogy. Even the mere acknowledgment that the word of Jesus, *Abba*, is actually *ipsissima vox*, puts man before the transcendent claim of Jesus. Every critical effort to reach the historical Jesus puts the investigator before an ultimate: he stands before God himself. Belief is neither made easier nor taken away by exegesis which indicates precisely how Jesus' transcendent claim is the basis of all his deeds and words. But critical, historical and exegetical work does put man before the question of faith.[38] Moving beyond this there is a growing agreement on the general stream and direction of Jesus' message as well as a tendency to agreement on the genuinity of individual logia. "If the prevailing character of the parables can be related to the dominant consensus as to the basic direction of Jesus' message, and this convergence can be identified and traced as a structuring tendency through the individual logia sifted by form criticism, probably as high a degree of historical reliability will have been attained as can be expected at the beginning of a new period of research."[39]

Most of the Marburgers would agree with James M. Robinson who claims that the possibility of resuming the quest for the historical Jesus comes basically from a newer and more developed concept of history and selfhood,[40] or from what might better be called the existentialist approach to the human personality in the world. The more recent concept of history, in contradistinction to the simply objective and disinterested recovery of past historical facts—places, times, dates, external sequences, causes and effects—focuses on the distinctively human elements of purpose, intention, will, desire, choice, and commitment[41] which go into the making of history, both of the person and of the world. As there is an evolution in history itself, so too there is an evolution in the understanding of what history is. The evolving understanding leads to different definitions of history. We may note here that the static and the dynamic concepts of history are both of service; each may lead to understanding which is the goal of theology. Acceptance of a broader basis for history, something beyond a history which simply seeks to reproduce events as they were, tends to eliminate false dichotomies. But there should be no attempt to abandon absolutely the nineteenth century concept of history to which we owe so much, but rather the effort to remove its imperfections and to acknowledge its limitations by confrontation with the modern and more refined concept of history.

Beneficial too is the existentialist emphasis on man as a being in the world quite different from the objects around him, a being oriented towards death, a being who must, by willing and choosing, almost literally take hold of his existence to live an authentically human life. As we come to know that a man discloses himself perhaps more by his conduct, by his deliberate choices, by his habitual orientation, even by the effect he has on other people, than in his words considered purely in the objective sense of *la langue* as opposed to *la parole* which is part of his conduct and character—as the knowledge of subjectivity increases there opens up a genuinely new possibility of understanding the Jesus of history from the available sources. Thus the larger horizon in which the exegete questions the New Testament will frequently enough determine the answer to be given. A more developed concept of history and the emphasis on man as an historical being, as well as investigation of the interpreter and the perspective from which he puts the questions and interprets, may enlarge the horizon of possible questions and therefore broaden the possibility of new answers.

Implicit in the procedure of the Marburgers is an emphasis on theological theory, that is, something which is neither true nor false in itself, but must be judged on whether it is adequate or inadequate, suitable to explain the data or unsuitable. This healthy distinction, though largely implicit in the new quest, will stress understanding rather than certitude as the aim of scientific and biblical theology. Thus also theories can lead to a clearer distinction between faith and theology—points to be considered in our concluding postscript. Faith is religious, intersubjective, and saving; faith apprehends its object unhaltingly and directly in easy transcendence of the vicissitudes of scholarship. Specifically theological activity is notional, scientific, objective, abstract, imperfect, analogous, and must make large use of converging probabilities. Should these distinctions between faith and theology become explicit there is hope for more synthesis of the amazingly varied and rich but nonetheless analytic proliferation of scriptural investigations.

While this is not the place to detail the Heideggerian existentialism permeating the Marburgers' new quest,[42] it is significant to observe in passing that the new quest is now explicitly opening out onto broader horizons and larger dimensions. In October, 1959, at Höchst, Germany, at the annual meeting of Bultmann's former pupils, Dr. Heinrich Ott launched a new discussion—the potentialities of the later Heidegger for theology.[43] This discussion is largely concerned with biblical and theological methodology. There are very clear signs that the above methodological questions are leading to the use of systematic and objective modes of thought, as well as other modes of thought, which can restrain some excesses of the more intersubjective, existentialist categories.

Part III: Bultmann's Reaction: Two Questions

What has been Bultmann's reaction to the "new quest"? In 1960 Bultmann published *Das Verhältnis der urchristlichen Christusbotschaft zum historischen Jesus.*[44] This pamphlet is a clarification of his own position as well as a response to critics such as Althaus and to his former students.

TWO QUESTIONS

Bultmann begins with the observation that there are two closely allied but distinct questions operating in the current discussion (p. 6). The first is the issue of the historical continuity between the work of the historical Jesus, especially his preaching, and the primitive Christ-kerygma. The second question is that of the essential relation between Jesus and the kerygma. *Sachlich* is the word we translate by essential. But *sachlich*, adequately expressed by essential or objective or basic or more often by material, also connotes the German *inhaltlich*. Thus the second question would concern the basic, the fundamental relationship between Jesus and the kerygma. Phrased another way: what is the relationship between the contents of the works of Jesus to the content of the kerygma (p. 9)? Bultmann himself poses the second question in a still more congenial fashion: "Is the historical Jesus identical with the Christ of the kerygma (p. 9)?" The answer given to the first question, that of historical continuity, is not at all necessarily an answer to the second problem, that of essential continuity.

HISTORICAL CONTINUITY

Bultmann grants that there is an historical continuity between the historical Jesus and the primitive preaching. Each is a phenomenon within history. And the kerygma presumes the historical Jesus as should be evident from the fact that the kerygma substitutes mythical features of the God-Son for the Jesus of history. Were one to deny this historical continuity, he would make the Christ of the kerygma into a myth. This historical continuity consists in the fact that for the first disciples the resurrected one preached in the kerygma was identical with the earthly Jesus. For the disciples the Christ of the kerygma bore the characteristics and basic features of the earthly Jesus. Hence Bultmann reasserts a continuity between the historical Jesus and the primitive preaching. The kerygma assumes and presents one aspect of the historical Jesus— namely the *that,* the fact of Jesus' historical existence. There is no interest in anything beyond the historical event of Jesus who turns out to be God's decisive action.

ESSENTIAL CONTINUITY

But those who would assert that the historical Jesus is in essential continuity with the Christ of the kerygma, therefore identical with the Christ of the kerygma, neglect the basic fact that historical-critical method is simply incapable of showing that God has made Christ the Lord. The Christ of the kerygma simply cannot stand in continuity with the Jesus of history because the Christ of the kerygma is accepted by faith and not proven by critical-historical method. Thus Bultmann denies not the historical continuity between the Jesus of history and the kerygma but the essential continuity between the Jesus of history and the Christ of the kerygma. Here it is worthwhile to note that Bultmann again and again returns to a methodological principle that is less clearly emphasized by his students—namely the inability of establishing continuity between the Jesus of history and the Christ of the kerygma by *purely historical reconstruction.* For Bultmann holds that it is precisely the paradox of the kerygma to assert that an historical event—the historical Jesus and his history—is eschatological occurrence, God's decisive action, the change of eons and all that is thereby implied (p. 8). Further, both Paul and John simply preach the *dass* of Jesus, that is, the fact that

God has acted in this historical man, Jesus. They make no attempt at biographical illuminations of the Jesus of history. Paul preaches the cross as occurrence and saving event. There is no effort to make the cross, the central salvific event, illuminate the *Was* and *Wie*, that is, the details of Jesus' human nature in its concrete historical manifestation.

POSSIBILITIES OF INDICATING ESSENTIAL CONTINUITY

Those who seek to transcend the simple fact, the occurrence of the saving event, the *dass*, and to show that the Christ-kerygma, in addition to the *dass*, the simple fact, contains more—a plus requirement or value, we may say—have two possibilities open to them. The critic may first show that the kerygma not only contains plentiful biographical details (the *Was* and *Wie* of the Jesus of history) but proclaims biographical details as necessary for an understanding and acceptance of the kerygma. But this effort to reach the Jesus of history is destined to founder because the synoptic Gospels to which appeal must be made do not give the necessary portrait of Jesus; there is simply not enough of the *Was* and *Wie*, not enough accurate historical detail to reconstruct his human personality. And as a matter of fact, in the sources, the Christ who is preached is not the historical Christ but the Christ of worship and belief.[45]

And the greatest objection to this first method is that we do not know how Jesus understood the supreme and central salvific event, his death. This essential salvific event and fact is refracted through the prism of the Easter belief; and the prophecies of death are *ex eventu*. Bultmann singles out the difficulty about Jesus' death on the theory that either you thoroughly explain and understand this event, or you do not understand anything, except perhaps minor details. It is fruitless, for example, to talk of Jesus' relation to the Jewish world and to be able to say nothing definite about Jesus' own understanding of the supreme saving event. The critic does not know how Jesus understood his death; he does know how the primitive community understood it.

A MORE GENERAL OBJECTION

Here Bultmann, in what is almost an aside, goes on to say that even if the interpretation of Jesus' death as a willingly accepted expiatory sacrifice were correct, what is gained? Nothing at all, because this would be an attempt to legitimate the kerygma by historical-critical means, substituting research for faith. One must observe here a certain shifting of ground in which Bultmann's radical Lutheran orientation in his stark emphasis on justification by faith only comes to the fore. And it must likewise be recalled that Bultmann's concept of demythologizing theoretically does to objective knowledge about God what Luther's doctrine on justification did to works.[46] The attempt to legitimate the kerygma suits the modern mind but poses a question in which the kerygma is not interested, the kerygma shows no concern with objective historicity beyond the fact, the *dass*; nor should one force an alien interest on the kerygma. The interest to legitimate the kerygma is alien because the New Testament says that we accept God's action in Christ by faith and by faith alone, with no support from historical-critical work. This position, incidentally, is perfectly consistent with Bultmann's statement in 1929, in the essay, "The Concept of Revelation in the New Testament," that, "The revelation consists indeed in nothing else than in the fact of Jesus Christ."[47]

THE SECOND METHOD OF PROVING AN ESSENTIAL CONTINUITY

The second method of procedure in proving an essential continuity between the Jesus of history and the kerygma will strive to show that in the works of Jesus the kerygma is already contained *in nuce*, as, for example, Conzelmann seeks to do. The effort here will be to show that Jesus' deeds and his words had kerygmatic characteristics. Against this type of approach Bultmann shows a marked restraint since Bultmann feels that it is evident that Jesus appeared as a Prophet with an eschatological message (p. 15). Further, both Jesus' appearance and his preaching implicitly involve a Christology because he demands a decision about his person as the bearer of God's word. What Bultmann does specify, however, is that one should complement the traditional historical-critical approach by means of the existential encounter with history. If the critic uses only historical-critical method to show that Jesus' deeds and words contained the kerygma *in nuce,* how does this objective approach make the kerygmatic Christ relevant for later generations? Further, the historical-critical approach must remain on the level of historical phenomena. But the kerygma proposes an eschatological occurrence that transcends the realm of the purely historical. Therefore the historical-critical method can never prove the essential unity of the works and words of Jesus with the kerygma.

BULTMANN'S CONCLUSION

Bultmann concludes that an answer to this vexing problem is provided only when the critic perfects historical-critical consideration of the work of Jesus through an interpretation of history (*Geschichte*) based on the truly historical (*geschichtlich*), that is, the existential encounter with history (*Geschichte*) in which man accepts or rejects the kerygma. Salvific history is direct address (*Anrede*) and understanding this salvific history consists in response (*Hören*), not in attempting to see it or to look at it after the fashion of empirical science or disinterested, objective history.[48]

Moreover, if the preaching and works of the Jesus of history placed the hearer before a decision and offered man the possibility of a new existence, why did not the apostolic preaching simply repeat Jesus' preaching? Why did the Jesus who preached become the preached one? What was grasped in the kerygma and what transcends historical-critical method was that the "once" (*einmal*) of the Jesus of history must be rendered into the "once and for all" (*ein-für-allemal*); that is to say, because the primitive community saw with increasing clarity that Jesus was the decisive eschatological event and therefore could never be reduced to a simple past action but must always be present occurrence, event taking place here and now, the primitive community preached Christ, not the message of Jesus. He became present and definitive and ultimate in their preaching. The kerygma presents Jesus as the Christ, the Lord, the decisive action of God, as eschatological occurrence. The kerygma claims that Christ is present in Jesus, and thus the kerygma takes the place of the historical Jesus and represents him.[49]

Part IV: Postscript

The problems inherent in the post-Bultmann movement have generated books and articles at an astonishing rate. In a short paper one cannot hope to cover the many aspects of the new terrain. At the same time different observers can perhaps contribute something of profit to a developing theological dialogue which raises as many problems as solutions. Some observations on two questions involved in the post-Bultmann movement may be worthwhile. We limit the notes to two subjects: the concept of theology—its objective, theoretical element and its distinction from faith—and methodology.

CONCEPT OF THEOLOGY

It is reasonably accurate to say that for Bultmann the object of theology is man; and the theme of theology is the man of faith. For Heinrich Ott theology, which proceeds by way of dialogue, is thinking in faith.[50] Theology is the task and function of the Church.[51] There is general agreement here that theology is thinking; and the man who does the thinking is no longer a subject but he is existence who exists in encounter.[52] And Raymond E. Brown, S.S., has cited with approval James M. Robinson's words about theology as *"fides quaerens intellectum,"*[53] a long accepted definition.

OBJECTIVE THOUGHT

The post-Bultmannians in general agree that theology is some sort of thinking in faith. This thinking however, breaks out of the subject-object pattern. But one may wonder if the concept of man as existing in encounter, as being constituted by the volitional, allows enough scope to objective thought as a properly theological activity. Admitting the existence of a personal, intersubjective, pre-predicative knowledge (difficult though it may be to analyze and explain), is it not true to say that even what is known about personal beings must ultimately be brought under objective scrutiny where what is experienced and understood intersubjectively in encounter must be subjected to the question, "Is it true?" At least, this writer would suggest room should be left for such a question even in forms of personal knowledge. How accurate is the statement that God can only be known as a subject? Admittedly saving knowledge comes only in the intersubjective relationship of faith in God. But is it not true to say that when God is known as an object he is also known as a subject? In any case one of the fundamental difficulties posed by those who would deny the possibility of objective knowledge about God is that such knowledge makes God one more object within nature, thus minimizing his transcendence. On the other hand it may be affirmed that objective knowledge about God is not a knowledge whereby the knower masters or dominates God. Actually, part of objective knowledge about God affirms man's inability to master God or to assert very much positively about God. If subjective knowledge about God is indeed a biblical approach, objective knowledge and the procedure involved therein seems to be a native function of the human mind. Such thought is not necessarily saving and may lead to distortions. But its consistent recurrence should make one hesitate before totally abandoning it. There are clear indications in the post-Bultmannians that more room is being given to the possibility of objective thought in theology. If there are problems with objective thinking about God, one of its assets is that such thinking enables God to be free to exist even when and where he is not acknowledged. This, too, is an aspect of transcendence.

Assuredly one of the benefits of the post-Bultmann movement is the emphasis on theological understanding; thus there are strong indications of a return to a scientific theology as such. This stress is tending to distinguish faith and theology as well as to allow scope for a more speculative theology.[54] Whatever definition of theology one chooses, it is difficult to move very far from the term "understanding." As observed earlier, there is in some of the exegetes and theologians a return to a type of understanding that could be called more scientific and objective than the subjectivism characteristic of existentialism. The need for objective modes of theological thought seems to be espoused by Amos N. Wilder in speaking about New Testament hermeneutics today. "Though our relation with God and the world is finally in terms of personal encounter and response, consent and refusal, yet we are creatures in a creation, and the structures of the creation including reason underlie the whole drama. It is not only the Greek view but also the biblical that assigns intellectual as well as moral responsibility to man."[55]

THEOLOGY AND FAITH

To clarify the distinction between theology and faith let us assert that theology is an intellectual habit in which the human reason, transformed by faith, seeks an understanding of the Word of God in the Church.[56] Some of the terms pertinent in the post-Bultmann movement need comment; others will be left unexplained. In maintaining that theology proceeds from the transformed human reason we affirm that theology is thinking in faith. But theology is a peculiar type of thinking in that it begins from belief and then proceeds to seek an understanding of that which is believed. The understanding sought will be the work of the human intellect, even though the human intellect accepts its data from faith. Thus every discipline proper to human research in a quest for intelligibility must be employed. Faith, both in the objective and subjective sense, is the beginning point. Here a distinction may be helpful. In the classic definition, *"fides quaerens intellectum,"* lurks an ambiguity—one that was successfully avoided when Anselm spoke in terms of the man of faith who seeks understanding. Faith has its own understanding in which the believer attains God (and thus has some understanding of God in the biblical sense). Such faith is evident in the strictly

religious activities of prayer, the presence of God, resignation
to God's will, abandonment of human security, and so on.
Theology, however, while beginning from belief and always
remaining closely associated with faith, is an activity of the
man who believes, now turning his mind to what he believes,
e.g., "Jesus is the Lord and Savior." The act of faith has its
own intersubjective, religious knowledge when a man sincerely
and humbly confesses, "I believe that Jesus is the Lord and
Savior." Properly theological activity would seem to be taking
place when the man asks, "What is the meaning of 'Jesus
is the Lord and Savior?'" Whatever the partial, analogous,
obscure answer be, there is some theological knowledge. This
theological knowledge is not at all necessarily the same type
of understanding as that gained in the religious act of faith.
It would, therefore, seem helpful to distinguish between the
religious act of faith with its corresponding knowledge and the
theological act of understanding with its peculiar type of
knowledge.

Assuredly the distinction between faith and theological
understanding will not always and in every instance be clear.
On the other hand one cannot adhere totally to the Kierkegaar-
dian trend that Christ can only be believed. This would be to
eliminate the human tension characteristic of Christianity
where most Christian affirmations are paradoxes as, for example, when the believer asserts that, "This man is God," or,
"The Word was made flesh." To minimize or eliminate one
aspect of the affirmation is simple, but it does injustice to the
biblical data. And the tension of the biblical data reproduces
itself in the interpreter who is both believer and thinker. The
existentialist, biblical approach common to Bultmann and his
followers has done well to restore the intersubjective, faith-
emphasis of Scripture which could be underemphasized by a
more speculative approach. Common to these men is the theory
that man is identified and individuated in his willing, in his
moral certitudes, in his choosing. This moving away from
man as pure reason or spirit preserves the religious and concrete human dimension. Stress on *geschichtlich* as opposed
to *historisch*, the concrete as opposed to the abstract, the
intersubjective and personal as opposed to the speculative and

impersonal, is necessary if theology is to retain its biblical and religious orientation. On the other hand, if theology is to be both relevant and intellectually respectable, one cannot wish to exclude the *historisch*, the abstract, the speculative and the impersonal. That there will always be some dissatisfaction with the strictly speculative and theoretical element in theology follows from the divine self-disclosure itself.[57]

If the above is reasonably true, it might be worthwhile to recall that any definition of theology will have to be aware that there are modes of understanding. Common sense and inter-subjective understanding permeate the Bible. Hence there must be room for this intersubjectivity in theology. But the question being raised today pertains to whether a scientific, objective type of understanding—found at its best in the empirical sciences—should likewise have a place in theological activity. Both the intersubjective and the objective types of understanding may be exaggerated; and the precise relation between the two modes of thought must be constantly worked out in a theological dialogue that remains in constant tension. While the proper domains of the exegete, the biblical theologian and the speculative theologian remain to be clarified, one may surely maintain that the understanding sought by an exegete examining the book of Genesis is much more on the common sense level than the work of the speculative theologian who should proceed from the works of many exegetes and biblical theologians to the world of theoretical, systematic understanding.

If it is admitted that there is room for the speculative dimension in theology, then there must be place for systematized, abstract, scientific thought which begins from the individualized specialized works of biblical interpretation. Thus one may have to admit the possibility of theoretical theological answers which transcend particular investigations. For example, an explanation of revelation will have to take into account the growth and development of consciousness in the people of God from the beginnings in Genesis to the end of the first century A.D. Whatever explanation of revelation is given will not be in the realm of intersubjectivity or common sense but in the world of the speculative and theoretical. So too the speculative theologian may not be expected to answer questions which depend upon an "imaginative reconstruction of the past."[58] The affirmation that "Jesus is Lord and Savior" does not necessarily throw light on the question of whether or not the disciples of the historical Jesus would be able to make an act of divine faith in Jesus before the resurrection. From the total biblical context and the *causae cognoscendi* one may come to the *causae essendi,* the constitutive causes explaining what it means to be Lord and Savior. Whether or not the followers of Jesus could come to the *causae essendi* is a hypothetical question which must first be answered on the common sense level of the biblical data.

METHODOLOGY

If there is a growth in reflection on the nature of theology and the relation of theological thinking to faith, no less is the reflection, both implicit and explicit, on questions of methodology arising out of the post-Bultmann dialectic. The interpreter who would seek even a fairly adequate grasp of the post-Bultmannian movement and its implications faces an immense facade of current and past data; just the primary sources themselves are diversified and involved. The hermeneutical circle where a paragraph is understood in terms of a chapter, a chapter in terms of a book, and a book in terms of a series of books, requires a growth in any interpreter and a corresponding broadening of personal horizon. No quick and easy solution is available, for data is not assimilated by a facile or automatic process. And even the most assiduous and competent interpreter runs the risk of the judgment attributed to Hegel: *"Es gab nur ein Student der mich verstanden hat; und er hat mich missverstanden."* The problem on the level of data is not simply the immensity of evidence and the historical background from which the data receive their intelligibility but the demand that the interpreter constantly revise his viewpoint and enlarge his horizon. For this there are no mechanical rules of inference.

When the interpreter has assimilated the primary sources of Bultmann, Heidegger, and the post-Bultmannians, there still remain the commentators who may modify the original authors or at least suggest further developments and modifications in the growing problematic. Among the commentators one faces the problem of inauthenticity, that is, a supposed but inauthentic interpretation. Macquarrie alludes to this problem in a review.

> Some years ago I wrote that it would be unfortunate if English-speaking theologians were to gain their impression of Heidegger only through Bultmann, since Heidegger is an important religious thinker in his own right. I am inclined to add that it would be even more unfortunate if the impression were gained through Ott.[59]

Earlier in the review Macquarrie pointed out a problem of coming to know Heidegger through commentators. Speaking of Robinson's work, Macquarrie says:

> On the whole, Robinson has done a good job. His account differs markedly from those of some other interpreters—notably, for instance, from Thomas Langan's *The Meaning of Heidegger,* with which many American readers will be familiar. But Robinson is in the main the more reliable guide, though his essay would have been better had he faced more frankly some of the ambiguities in Heidegger's thought, and had he taken time to digest more fully the mass of material to which he refers in his footnotes.[60]

Nor is the problem of the secondary sources and inauthenticity helped by the uncommitted book review where "reviewers have adopted the modern practice of a more or less uncommitted 'notice' of new publications, and have given up any concern to come to terms with a writer by a close and reasoned examination of his thought."[61] Thus those who would become acquainted with Bultmann and the discussions which he has brought about are led to use all commentators as if they were of equal weight and value. If there is one antidote, it would be found right in the post-Bultmann movement in its great emphasis on the articulation of problems and in the premium now put on understanding as such.

In addition to the problem of inauthenticity there is the inevitable tendency of problems both to multiply and diversify.

The problem of hermeneutics, for example, is but one instance of the problem of knowledge or cognitional theory. Demythologizing is a function of hermeneutics. And hermeneutics, demythologizing, and the quest for the historical Jesus are mutually interdependent issues.[62] The problem of interpretation cannot be discussed without advertence to language. Thus on all levels the interpreter is faced with the hermeneutical circle. This hermeneutical circle that appears in the approach to primary and secondary sources as well as the subsequent problems raised by the growing theological dialogue demands that the interpreter continually reflect on the data and on the intellectual procedure of the authors as well as on his own procedure. Thus reflection on reflection is a required component of understanding. Unfortunately it is just possible that the professional exegete, both because of the demanding qualities of exegesis and because of the concrete nature of literary interpretation, may not be equipped for the more speculative requirements of reflection on process and procedure. At the same time, exegetes are wont to say that the non-professional exegete, the philosopher and the speculative theologian do not have the technical grasp of Scripture to advance beyond the work of the exegete.

At this moment, however, it is generally acknowledged that the exegete, the philosopher, and the speculative theologian must work together if understanding is to grow. And the functions of the three fields are more and more combined in the works of one man, as, for example, in Bultmann, Ebeling and Fuchs. There is a growing awareness that the proliferation of specialized works—of which Bultmann and his followers are one striking instance—have reached a stage where the harvest must be reaped by explicit advertence to cognitional theory and to methodology as such.[63] In confirmation one need only look at the growing number of books on hermeneutics.

If Rudolf Bultmann and post-Bultmann tendencies have raised problems to which some answers may seem disappointing or unsatisfactory, one may be grateful that the latest developments are tending to locate and isolate the more significant problems of interpretation, as well as to indicate clearly the broad basis from which both exegesis and theology must operate. The enlarged horizon must cause the exegete and theologian to reflect on the accuracy and breadth of one existentialist assertion: *"Erkennen ist Beisichsein des Seins."*

NOTES

1. Rudolf Bultmann, *Das Verhältnis der urchristlichen Christusbotschaft zum historischen Jesus* (Heidelberg: Carl Winter Universitätsverlag, 1961) 5. A bibliography is given on this same page.

Since the publication of the above work most of the pertinent journal literature has been collected into books. Among the more important collections are the following:

Ernst Fuchs, *Zum hermeneutischen Problem in der Theologie,* Gesammelte Aufsätze I (Tübingen: J. C. B. Mohr [Paul Siebeck], 1959).

Ernst Fuchs, *Zur Frage nach dem historischen Jesus,* Gesammelte Aufsätze II (Tübingen: J. C. B. Mohr [Paul Siebeck], 1960).

Gerhard Ebeling, *Wort und Glaube* (Tübingen: J. C. B. Mohr [Paul Siebeck], 1960).

Gerhard Ebeling, *Theologie und Verkündigung, Ein Gespräch mit Rudolf Bultmann,* Hermeneutische Untersuchungen zur Theologie I (Tübingen: J. C. B. Mohr [Paul Siebeck], 1962).

Eberhard Jüngel, *Paulus und Jesus, eine Untersuchung zur Präzisierung der Frage nach dem Ursprung der Christologie,* Hermeneutische Untersuchungen zur Theologie II (Tübingen: J. C. B. Mohr [Paul Siebeck], 1962).

Helmut Ristow and Karl Matthiae ed., *Der historische Jesus und der kerygmatische Christus,* Beiträge zum Christusverständnis in Forschung und Verkündigung (Berlin: Evangelische Verlagsanstalt, 1961).

Carl E. Braaten and Roy A. Harrisville ed., *Kerygma and History, A Symposium on the Theology of Rudolf Bultmann* (New York: Nashville, Abingdon Press, 1962). The most pertinent essays here are: Ernst Kinder, "Historical Criticism and Demythologizing"; Nils Alstrup Dahl, "The Problem of the Historical Jesus"; Günther Bornkamm, "Myth and Gospel: A Discussion of the Problem of Demythologizing the New Testament Message"; Hermann Diem, "The Earthly Jesus and the Christ of Faith."

Quite an adequate though not complete bibliography will be found in the popular treatment of our question done by Heinz Zahrnt, *The Historical Jesus,* tr. J. S. Bowden (New York: Harper & Row, 1963) 151-154.

One of the best works in English, of course, is that of James M. Robinson, *A New Quest of the Historical Jesus* (London: SCM Press Ltd., 1959; German translation, 1960; French translation,

1961). For the substance of an addition found in the German edition, cf. James M. Robinson, "The Formal Structure of Jesus' Message," *Current Issues in New Testament Interpretation,* ed. William Klassen and Graydon F. Snyder (New York: Harper & Brothers, 1962) 91–110.

For a brief article, cf. Frederick Herzog, "Possibilities and Limits of the New Quest," *J Rel* 43 (1963) 218–233.

2. Albert Schweitzer, *The Quest of the Historical Jesus,* tr. W. Montgomery (New York: The Macmillan Co., 1950; German ed., 1906; first English ed., 1910) 398.

3. Cf. Robinson, *New Quest of the Historical Jesus.*

4. The term "historical Jesus" may suffer some ambiguity because it is occasionally used to distinguish *geschichtlich* from *historisch.* In this paper historical, of history, and earthly are used synonymously.

5. Cf. Schweitzer, *Quest of the Historical Jesus,* 13; Joachim Jeremias, "Der gegenwärtige Stand der Debatte um das Problem des historischen Jesus," *Der historische Jesus und der kerygmatische Christus,* 13; Maurice Goguel, *The Life of Jesus,* tr. Olive Wyon (London: George Allen & Unwin Ltd., 1954; French, 1932; first English, ed., 1933) 38–42.

6. Cf. Goguel, *Life of Jesus,* 40–42.

7. "But this was the first time that a really historical mind, thoroughly conversant with the sources, had undertaken the criticism of the tradition." Schweitzer, *Quest of the Historical Jesus,* 15.

8. Quoted by Goguel, *Life of Jesus,* 56.

9. Fritz Stern ed., *The Varieties of History* (New York: Meridian Books, Inc., 1960[6]) 54.

10. *Ibid.,* 54. It is worthwhile to recall that the concept of history as a science was also influenced by the development of the empirical sciences. Here Descartes deserves credit for examining the simple definitions of history that lasted up until his own time. Cf. Isaiah Berlin, "History and Theory: The Concept of Scientific History," *History and Theory* I (1960) 1–31. Berlin quotes Buckle to the effect that history had to wait long to be acknowledged as a science simply because historians were inferior in talent to mathematicians, physicists and chemists. *Ibid.,* 4. In any case, there was an appreciation of the empirical scientific method that prepared the way for von Ranke.

11. Martin Kähler, *Der sogenannte historische Jesus und der geschichtliche, biblische Christus* (München: Chr. Kaiser Verlag, 1956; first ed., 1892; second ed., 1896; reissued in 1928). The so-called historical Jesus is the Jesus emerging from the psychologized and imaginative lives of Jesus. This Jesus, claims Kähler, is a phantom. In this essential point Bultmann agrees with Kähler though there seems to be more of a flight from history in Bultmann than in Kähler.

For a clear presentation of Kähler's part in the demythologizing debate, cf. Hans-Werner Bartsch, "The Present Stand of the Debate," *Kerygma and Myth* II, tr. Reginald H. Fuller (London: S.P.C.K., 1963) 47–57.

12. "The choice of the Greek word kerygma was due to more than a pedantic love for scientific jargon. It was rather the symbol of a whole range of new problems that came to light when the kerygmatic character of the gospels was discovered." Bartsch, "The Present Stand of the Debate," *Kerygma and Myth* II, 47.

13. Carl E. Braaten, "A Critical Introduction," *Kerygma and History*, 21.

14. Nils Alstrup Dahl, "The Problem of the Historical Jesus," *Kergyma and History*, 147.

15. To discuss the influence of Karl Barth in ending the liberal quest for the historical Jesus is beyond the scope of this paper. The basic insight of Barth was to see that theological relevance came from speaking of Christianity from within. Cf. Barth's own balanced history of "Evangelical Theology in the 19th Century," an essay in *The Humanity of God,* tr. Thomas Weiser (Richmond, Virginia: John Knox Press, 1960) 11–33.

Ott schematizes the meanings of the word kerygma: "K. kann im NT in drei Bedeutungen gebraucht werden: für den *Inhalt* der Verkündigung . . . für den *Akt* bzw. das *Ereignis* der Verkündigung, schliesslich für das *Amt* der Verkündigung.—Es ist keineswegs zufällig, dass gerade dieses Wort zum terminus technicus für die nt. Predigt (die Predigt Jesu und die Predigt von Jesus) werden konnte." Heinrich Ott, "Kerygma," *Die Religion in Geschichte und Gegenwart* III, H-Kon (Tübingen: J. C. B. Mohr [Paul Siebeck], 1959[3]) 1250.

16. Ernst Käsemann, "Das Problem des historischen Jesus," *ZTK* 51 (1954) 125–153.

17. *Ibid.,* 152.

18. "Ich würde eine solche Meinung als Miss-verständnis ablehnen. Bei einem Leben Jesu kann man schlechterdings nich auf äussere und innere Entwicklung verzichten. Von der letzen wissen wir jedoch gar nichts, von der ersten fast nichts ausser dem Wege, der von Galiläa nach Jerusalem, von der Predigt des nahen Gottes in den Hass des offiziellen Judentums und die Hinrichtung durch die Römer führte." *Ibid.,* 151.

19. *Ibid.*

20. "Denn wenn die Urchristenheit den erniedrigten mit dem erhöhten Herrn identifiziert, so bekundet sie damit zwar, dass sie nicht fähig ist, bei der Darstellung seiner Geschichte von ihrem Glauben zu abstrahieren. Gleichzeitig bekundet sie jedoch damit, dass sie nicht willens ist, einen Mythos an die Stelle der Geschichte, ein Himmelswesen an die Stelle des Nazareners treten zu lassen. . . . Offensichtlich ist sie der Meinung, dass man den irdischen Jesus nicht anders als von Ostern her und also in seiner Würde als

Herr der Gemeinde verstehen kann und dass man umgekehrt Ostern nicht adäquat zu begreifen vermag, wenn man vom irdischen Jesus absieht. Das Evangelium steht immer in einem Zweifrontenkrieg." *Ibid.,* 134.

21. "Die Frage nach dem historischen Jesus ist legitim die Frage nach der Kontinuität des Evangeliums in der Diskontinuität der Zeiten und in der Variation des Kerygmas." *Ibid.*

22. Ernst Fuchs, "Die Frage nach dem historischen Jesus," *Zur Frage nach dem historischen Jesus,* 143–167.

23. Cf. Robinson, "The Formal Structure of Jesus' Message," *Current Issues,* 96.

24. "Es ist also nicht so, dass erst die Parabel Jesu Verhalten erklärt, obwohl sich Jesus mit ihr verteidigt, sondern umgekehrt, Jesu Verhalten erklärt den Willen Gottes, mit einer an Jesu Verhalten ablesbaren Parabel." *Ibid.,* 154.

25. "Das bedeutet aber doch, dass *Jesu Verhalten* selber der eigentliche Rahmen seiner Verkündigung war!" *Ibid.,* 155.

26. Robinson, *New Quest of the Historical Jesus,* 16.

27. Günther Bornkamm, *Jesus von Nazareth* (Stuttgart: Verlag W. Kohlhammer Gmb.H., 1956[1], 1957[2], 1959[3]); English: *Jesus of Nazareth,* Irene and Fraser McLuskey with James M. Robinson (New York: Harper Bros., 1960).

28. Robinson, *New Quest of the Historical Jesus,* 16.

29. Bornkamm, *Jesus of Nazareth,* 13.

30. *Ibid.,* 15.

31. *Ibid.,* 16.

32. *Ibid.,* 17.

33. *Ibid.,* 178.

34. *Ibid.,* 172. Bornkamm clearly distinguishes between the message of Easter which is single and clear "and the ambiguity and historical problems of the Easter *narratives.*" *Ibid.,* 181.

35. Cf. Hans Conzelmann, "Eschatologie IV, im Urchristentum," *Die Religion in Geschichte und Gegenwart* II, D-G (Tübingen: J. C. B. Mohr [Paul Siebeck], 1958[3]) 665–672.

Also, Hans Conzelmann, "Zur Methode der Leben-Jesu-Forschung," *ZTK* 56 (1957) 2–13. The Evangelical Academy at Tutzing dedicated May 25 and 26, 1959, to a discussion of the status of the *Leben-Jesu-Forschung.* Papers of Ebeling and Fuchs appear in this same *Beiheft* 1.

Hans Conzelmann, "Jesus Christus," *RGG* III, H-Kon, 619–653. (Good bibliography.)

36 Ebeling, "Jesus und Glaube," *Wort und Glaube,* 207.

37. Gerhard Ebeling, *The Nature of Faith,* tr. Ronald Gregor Smith (London: Collins, 1961) 56. Cf. also Jüngel, *Paulus und Jesus.*

38. Jeremias, "Der gegenwärtige Stand der Debatte um das Problem des historischen Jesus," *Der historische Jesus und der kerygmatische Christus,* 23–24.

39. Robinson, "The Formal Structure of Jesus' Message," *Current Issues*, 97.

40. Robinson, *New Quest of the Historical Jesus*, 66. In his book, *Jesus*, 1926, Bultmann speaks of directing his attention to what Jesus intended or proposed. Given the nature of the sources and the context this observation is not far removed from the so-called more modern approach.

41. Robinson, *New Quest of the Historical Jesus*, 28, 67.

42. Raymond E. Brown, S.S., "After Bultmann, What?—An Introduction to the Post-Bultmannians," *CBQ* 26 (1964) 1–30.

In a review of the German edition of Robinson's *New Quest*, Fr. Zerwick feels that the work manifests an existentialist bias and is too certain of its position. Danger also exists, he says, that the Catholic will not even understand the language of his separated brethren. M. Zerwick, *VD* 39 (1961) 167–170. The "danger" can only be avoided by following the discussion closely and by some familiarity with the work of Heidegger. Without the latter it would be difficult, if not impossible, even to understand Bultmann.

43. Cf. especially Heinrich Ott, *Denken und Sein, Der Weg Martin Heideggers und der Weg der Theologie* (Zollikon: Evangelischer Verlag, 1959).

The discussion has been brought to American shores by James M. Robinson, John B. Cobb, Jr. ed., *The Later Heidegger and Theology* I, New Frontiers in Theology, Discussions among German and American Theologians (New York: Harper and Row, 1963).

Being and Time was an involved work intended as much to propose questions as to formulate a position open to modifications. Cf. James Collins, *The Existentialists* (Chicago: Henry Regnery Company, 1952) 156. Heidegger's later works, beginning with *Hölderlin und das Wesen der Dichtung* (Münich: Langen und Müller, 1937), have been called "Heidegger's answer to two decades of critical studies of *Being and Time.*" Collins, *Existentialists*, 153. Commentators agree that the later works of Heidegger are easier to understand than the earlier works. An eminent French philosopher is quoted as saying that the philosophy of the later Heidegger "is so simple." Basically the desire to "let being speak to you" is "a disciplined naïveté."

44. It is interesting to observe Bultmann's use of *Christusbotschaft, Christus-Kerygma,* and *Christus der Kerygmas* in preference to the term "kerygma" alone. Bultmann's position and terminology are one in maintaining that it is in the preaching that Jesus becomes the Christ. What follows in our text is taken from Bultmann's, *Das Verhältnis*.

45. Cf. Rudolf Bultmann, *Die Geschichte der synoptischen Tradition* (Göttingen: Vandenhoek und Ruprecht, 1957) 396. From the very nature of the documents as well as the nature of revelation there is no going behind the kerygma. "Hinter den

Gepredigten Christus zurückgehen, heisst die Predigt missverstehen. . . ." Rudolf Bultmann, *Glauben und Verstehen* III (Tübingen: J. C. B. Mohr [Paul Siebeck], 1960) 31.

46. Rudolf Bultmann, "Die Rede von Handeln Gottes," *Kerygma und Mythos* II (Hamburg-Volksdorf: Herbert Reich, 1952) 207. For calling my attention to this text I am indebted to my former student, Karl Weich. Cf. also P. Joseph Cahill, "The Scope of Demythologizing," *TS* 23 (1962) 81–82.

47. Bultmann, "Der Begriff der Offenbarung im Neuen Testament," *Glauben und Verstehen* III, 18.

48. "Die neutestamentliche *alētheia* ist nicht intellektuel zu erkennen, sie ist nur zu leben." "Das Kerygma lehrt nicht systematisch einzuordnende Begriffe, sondern es *ruft*." Günther Backhaus, *Kerygma und Mythos bei David Friedrich Strauss und Rudolf Bultmann* (Hamburg-Bergstedt: Herbert Reich Evangelischer Verlag, 1956) 81.

49. Nor is there any belief in Christ which is not at the same time a belief in the Church as the bearer of the kerygma. Hence the Church, the society of believers invisibly linked together by faith and acceptance of the kerygma, is also eschatological occurrence, not a guarantee of belief, but itself an object of belief. Therefore the Church takes the place of the Jesus of history by her kerygma so that belief in Christ is at the same time belief in the Church, that is, belief in the Holy Spirit whom the Church received as the post-Easter gift. Belief in the Church as the bearer of the kerygma is the Easter belief which consists in the belief that in the kerygma Jesus Christ is present.

Cf. a balanced criticism, Dahl, "The Problem of the Historical Jesus," *Kerygma and History*, 168: "Jesus is already in existence before and outside the proclamation and the Church; he may neither be absorbed by the existential here and now of the kerygma nor by the tradition and the Church." This criticism is fairly representative of Bultmann's opponents. Cf. also, Paul Althaus, *The So-Called Kerygma and The Historical Jesus*, tr. David Cairns (Edinburgh and London: Oliver and Boyd, 1959). For a reaffirmation of the independence of faith from history, cf. Gilbert E. Bowen, "Toward Understanding Bultmann," *McCormick Quarterly* 27 (1964) 26–39. Note especially the letters of Professors von Campenhausen and Pastor Dvoracek to Bultmann and Bultmann's answer, 34–36. The paradox of eschatological occurrence taking place in a concrete, historical individual is reasserted by Bultmann.

50. Heinrich Ott, *Dogmatik und Verkündigung* (Zürich: Evz-Verlag, 1961) 7.

51. Ott, *Denken und Sein*, 10.

52. *Ibid.*, 171, 172.

53. Brown, "After Bultmann, What?" *CBQ* 26 (1964) 20.

54. Cf. Claus Westermann, *Essays in Old Testament Hermeneutics*, English translation ed. James Luther Mays (Richmond, Virginia: John Knox Press, 1963; German, 1960) 10.

55. Wilder, "New Testament Hermeneutics Today," *Current Issues*, 52.

56. The basic elements in this definition I owe to Fr. Bernard Lonergan, S. J., and to Vatican I.

57. "Previously we saw that the meaning of theological concepts is mysterious; in fact the meaning of theological concepts is always a mystery. The same must be said of theological propositions. To be more precise, in the case of theological propositions we have mystery at the second power. This is due to the very nature of a proposition, which is composed of two elements: two concepts and a nexus. Now, in theological propositions both elements (at least one of the concepts and most certainly the nexus) are wrapped up in mystery. For instance, let's consider the proposition 'God is triune.' Here, we have a mysterious element in both concepts, and the nexus is also mysterious because we cannot see how God can at the same time be three and one. The connection between these two concepts, God and triune, cannot be verified by any human experience, but by the authority of the Revealer alone.

"If our analysis of the mysteriousness of theological language is correct, we have one more reason for saying with Aquinas that 'the highest point where our knowledge of God can arrive in this life is to acknowledge that He is higher than all that we can think,'" Battista Mondin, *The Principle of Analogy in Protestant and Catholic Theology* (The Hague: Martin Nijhoff, 1963) 187.

58. Some statements from an unpublished series of private class notes mimeographed in conjunction with a lecture series given by Fr. Bernard Lonergan, Regis College, Toronto, July, 1962. A further statement of pertinence: "Conversely, the questions arising from scientific statement and from basic context contribute nothing to commonsense understanding of the text or situation.

"E.g., the council of Ephesus defined our Lady's divine maternity. The definition is a corollary to the explication of the Christian tradition and its sources: one and the same is God and man. But the naïve are prone to ask, Did our Lady know she was Mother of God? How did she know it? How did she conceive it? How did she feel about it? How do you prove all this from scripture? Does St. Luke write with your account of our Lady's thoughts and feelings in mind?

"Such questions arise solely from a total incomprehension of the nature and possibility of serious exegesis and serious history.

"It is possible to arrive at a commonsense understanding of the texts, at a scientific statement of that commonsense understanding, at a basic context that relates in a genetico-dialectical series the scientific statements.

"But this possibility does not amount to the possibility of giving reasonable answers to an imaginative curiosity. The answers have to be theological, and theological answers do not include an imaginative reconstruction of the past." *Ibid.*, 16.

59. John Macquarrie, review of *New Frontiers in Theology* I, *Theology Today* 20 (1963) 422.

60. *Ibid.*, 420.

61. Karl Rahner, *Theological Investigations* I, tr. Cornelius Ernst (Baltimore: Helicon Press, 1961) 13.

62. Wilder, "New Testament Hermeneutics Today," *Current Issues*, 39.

63. Most of the books cited in footnote 1 are replete with instances of methodological reflections. The works of Ebeling, Fuchs and Ott manifest an especial concern with methodological problems. Quite a striking work on method appeared four years ago: Hans-Georg Gadamer, *Wahrheit und Methode* (Tübingen: J. C. B. Mohr [Paul Siebeck], 1960). And, of course, Bultmann himself has always been occupied with problems of method, especially in hermeneutics.

V

Extension of Theology

A New Trio Arises in Europe

John B. Cobb, Jr.

Who are the new young Turks in European theology? To what extent are they continuing and amplifying the work of the older generation in theology, to what extent forging ahead into unmapped territory? Will their leadership make itself felt in America as well on the Continent? Well qualified to answer such questions is John B. Cobb, Jr., who sees special significance in the work of such rising scholars as Gerhard Ebeling, Heinrich Ott, and Wolfhart Pannenberg. Dr. Cobb is Professor of Systematic Theology at Southern California School of Theology, in Claremont. He and James M. Robinson, Professor of Theology and New Testament at the same school, are editors of a new book series titled "New Frontiers in Theology," published by Harper and Row. Dr. Cobb's own writings include *Living Options in Protestant Theology* and *The Varieties of Protestantism*. His essay is from the July 2, 1964, issue of *Christian Advocate*,* a Methodist publication for pastors and church leaders.

THE THEOLOGICAL RENAISSANCE associated with Barth, Brunner, Tillich, and the Niebuhrs has largely run its course.

Many of their achievements have become part of the presuppositions of theological reflection in our day. But just for that reason these achievements are less exciting to the new generation of students who now seek the way ahead. At other points, words that rang with profound relevance in the '30s seem inappropriate in the '60s. A movement that arose as a protest against a certain type of liberalism has lost some of its force, precisely because it has largely succeeded in overcoming that type of liberalism.

* Circulation office: 201 Eighth Avenue South, Nashville, Tennessee 37203. Copyright © 1964 by The Methodist Publishing House.

Thus, the need for new leadership has become acute. Since Americans have long looked to the German-speaking world for theological direction, and since this tendency has even been intensified since World War II, it is natural that we should look again to Germany and Switzerland for the creative response to the present theological problems.

Unfortunately, when we turn to Germany, we find that the leading chairs of theology are in the hands of pupils of Karl Barth who, for the most part, have proved unable to think except in the shadow of their master. The more dynamic developments, even in theology, have passed into the hands of New Testament scholars, and specifically those who have studied with Rudolf Bultmann. Yet, for the most part, these men lack the competence in systematic theology that could lead to a position beyond alternatives that have been represented by both Barth and Bultmann.

In this situation, James Robinson and I decided in 1958 that we should attempt to discover new directions of theological work which we were convinced must be already emerging on the Continent and to bring American theologians into conversation with their leading proponents. Robinson spent the year 1959–60 on the Continent and identified three developments in theology that appeared to be of special promise. At that time, no work representative of these developments had been translated into English, and none of the leaders was well known in this country. Even in Germany not all were widely recognized. Now, five years later, the accuracy of his judgments has already been vindicated by subsequent developments. We can safely predict that the three systematic theologians he identified will be widely influential in the decades ahead.

Of the three, one belongs to the pre-war generation and is now already fully established professionally and in his international reputation. Gerhard Ebeling, a German teaching at Zurich, has taught and lectured extensively in this country in the past two years. He has brought to systematic theology an unusual richness of historical scholarship. His profound study of Luther has given him fresh perspectives on a theological scene dominated by the debates between Barthians

and Bultmannians. Also, the deep impression of his personal
association with Bonhoeffer upon his life and thought has
heightened his perception of the needs of our increasingly
secular world.

Two books by Ebeling are now available in English. *The
Nature of Faith* (Fortress, $3) is the text of a series of lectures
presented for nontheological students at the University of
Zurich. It takes faith as *the* starting point for theological reflection and interprets all other theological categories as they are
effective in faith. *Word and Faith* (Fortress, $6.25) is a
collection of Ebeling's essays. Its title correctly points to the
other pole crucial to his thought. Faith comes to man as he
receives the Word. But "Word" is not to be understood primarily as informative statement. It is an event of speaking in
which the speaker communicates himself in love. In Ebeling's
terms it is a "word-event."

Ebeling is critical of Barth's tendency to distinguish the
Word of God from the word of man as if there were literally
two quite different speakers. He sees the difference, rather, as
between authentic word-event and inauthentic speaking. When
the speaking of the word is effective, that is, when it communicates love and awakens faith, there it is the Word of God.

Ebeling shares a concern for language with Ernst Fuchs,
a Bultmannian New Testament scholar now teaching at Marburg. With him he also participates in reaffirming against
both Barth and Bultmann the importance of the historical
Jesus. Jesus' language was authentic word-event from which
the possibility of such word-event comes also to us. This
feature of the work of Ebeling and Fuchs has already become
widely influential in American circles under the heading of
"a new quest of the historical Jesus."

The equally creative work of Ebeling and Fuchs in reviving
interest in hermeneutic is just now beginning to receive the
attention it deserves in this country. Just as "the new quest" is
made possible by reconceiving history and historiography, so
also "the new hermeneutic" is made possible by reconceiving
the nature of the problem of interpretation. Hermeneutic, as
understood by Ebeling and Fuchs, is not now a matter of
discussing the rules by which exegesis of Scripture is to be

conducted. It is bringing the Word of God embodied in Scripture to bear upon our human existence in such a way that existence is itself interpreted. Hermeneutic in this sense encompasses the whole range of theological disciplines.

The other two men who give promise of important leadership in the next decades are Heinrich Ott and Wolfhart Pannenberg. When Robinson selected them in 1960 for our special consideration, they were both scarcely thirty and neither had a university chair. Now Ott has succeeded Barth in the chair of systematic theology at Basel, Switzerland. In April of 1964 he was brought to this country for the first time to play a leading role in the Second Consultation on Hermeneutics sponsored by the Graduate School of Drew University.

Pannenberg is now a professor at the University of Mainz. He has taught and lectured widely in the United States, and he has turned down an invitation to Heidelberg as first occupant of a chair in philosophy of religion.

Ott, as a Swiss high school student, mastered much of Barth's *Dogmatics* and began the study of Heidegger. Later as Barth's pupil in the university, he was assigned Bultmann as a dissertation topic. To write this dissertation, he went to live in Bultmann's home. His depth immersion in the thought of Barth, Bultmann, and Heidegger has led to his proposal of a quite new synthesis. Thus far his only works available in English are an essay in the volume edited by Robinson and myself—*The Later Heidegger and Theology* (Harper, $4.50) —and an essay in *Kerygma and Myth II* (edited by Hans Werner Bartsch, London, S.P.C.K.).

In the 1920s, Heidegger applied the phenomenological method of his teacher, Edmund Husserl, to the analysis of human existence as such. This led him to an understanding of man as capable on the one hand of being molded by impersonal forces from without (inauthentic existence) but on the other hand of living responsibly in terms of his own projects (authentic existence). Bultmann was persuaded that the contrast between inauthentic and authentic existence, philosophically articulated by Heidegger, was essentially the same as that intended by Paul in his juxtaposition of flesh and spirit. Hence, Bultmann adopted much of Heidegger's complex conceptuality as a basis for clarifying and communicating the Gospel for modern man. Of course, he emphasized that for Christianity, faith, or life in the spirit, is always known as a gift of God, and at this point he sharply differentiated Christian faith from the apparent suggestions by Heidegger that man can attain authentic existence quite autonomously.

Meanwhile, Heidegger himself turned in the 1930s to a less self-assertive understanding of authentic existence. Although he has never repudiated his earlier work and continues to emphasize the continuity of the later development with his analysis in *Being and Time* (Harper, $12.50) he came to see *man's* relation to *being* more in terms of receptivity. Rather than impose autonomous will on the world, man must be open to the "call of being." Man is authentic when he "lets being be" and himself comes into correspondence with it.

Ott became convinced that Heidegger's turn from self-assertiveness to openness toward being brought his philosophy into remarkable parallelism with Barth's theology, and he has argued that the Barthians have, after all, much to learn from philosophy. Barth taught openness to God's word in such a way that man must simply let that word be what it is and conform to it. Ott believes that this relation to God can be illuminated by Heidegger's profound reflection on the parallel relation of man to being.

Bultmann has emphasized that faith comes to man only as a gift of God, but he had so directed attention to faith and to authentic existence given in faith that he had not been open to following Heidegger's turn of intellectual attention toward openness to the giver. By following this turn in Heidegger, Ott argues that a fundamentally Barthian position is vindicated against some main features of Bultmann's thought, while in other ways the two are drawn together. Meanwhile, however, the Barthian position is itself transformed and reinvigorated by a fresh contact with creative philosophy.

Both Ebeling and Ott can be seen as coming to their fresh perspectives in relation to the dominant theology of the past decades. Wolfhart Pannenberg, however, is more radically original. He finds himself free to set aside principles that have been commonly assumed by all schools of German theology since Ritschl. His attitude toward theological problems shares the freedom of the Anglo-American scene to reconsider all assumptions and always be ready to start over again. As a result he is in a position to communicate with unusual directness and clarity to the English-speaking world, much of which still finds it difficult to understand the theological situation in the terms in which it has been shaped by European scholars. Pannenberg has already shown himself unusually receptive to the rather different currents of thought coursing through the intellectual life of America.

Several articles by Pannenberg are available in English, and a volume on his work is scheduled for publication in 1965 in the series edited by Robinson and myself. Meanwhile we anticipate publication in English of his lectures on Christology. Pannenberg has the full equipment of historical scholarship characteristic of the German theologian (often in embarrassing contrast with the American). Furthermore, he is alone in the present scene in being the leader of a self-conscious school including Old and New Testament scholars who share with him a vision of what theology should be. Jointly, this group is constructing an interpretation of biblical history that bypasses the now-established Bultmannian categories.

Pannenberg and his school strongly object to the bifurcation of history into mere facts on the one hand and human meaning on the other. Responsible historiography sees fact and meaning in indissoluble connection. Hence, faith is not an act of decision that can only be viewed as arbitrary in the light of the facts, but rather an appropriate response to the meaningful factual history of God's revelation.

History itself and in its totality is the revelation of God. The Bible is seen as expressing the progressive discovery of this unity and comprehensiveness of revelation culminating in the universalism of apocalypticism. At every stage prophecy is fulfilled in unexpected ways. Jesus, standing in the apocalyptic tradition, proclaimed the universal resurrection as the end of history. His prophecy was vindicated in his own resurrection that thus also provides the key to the meaning of all history as revelation.

The revelation, however, is never direct self-revelation of

God himself. Pannenberg shows that this understanding of revelation, despite its wide acceptance among those who appeal away from philosophy to the Bible, is in fact the legacy of Hegel. In the Bible, revelation always has definite content and occurs in historical events. God is known through his indirect revelation in history.

For Pannenberg truth is one. What is learned from science and philosophy, as well as world history, must be integrated with what is learned from Scripture and the Christ-event. All the walls erected from the time of Kant to protect the sphere of theology from other spheres of inquiry are smashed. Pannenberg is not equally versed in all fields of human knowledge, but in principle he sees their interconnectedness and mutual relevance.

No additional theological directions for Protestant theology comparable to these have appeared in continental Europe in the years since 1960. Perhaps others are even now emerging. In any case, we can take keen interest and pleasure in watching these three unfold. Almost for the first time the American may be able to play not only the role of interested observer and interpreter to his American colleagues and students, but also that of serious critic and participant. Further, the time may have come when quite new developments originating on our side of the Atlantic may gain an interested hearing in the German-speaking world. If so, the community of Protestant theology may indeed become ecumenical.

The Form of the Church in the Modern Diaspora

M. Richard Shaull

Far from lamenting the contemporary crisis in the institutional life of the church, M. Richard Shaull sees in it a call to create new forms of Christian community within the diverse precarious communities in which Christians find themselves dispersed. Secularization, says Shaull, brings new opportunities for service to the world, for involvement in the human struggle. "We must be willing to see our most cherished forms of church life die in order that the Church may live. This is what happened in and through the Jewish Dispersion; it may also happen in our time." Dr. Shaull's essay, which is reprinted from the March 1964 *Princeton Seminary Bulletin,** originally was given at his installation as Professor of Ecumenics in Princeton Seminary's Miller Chapel on December 9, 1963. He has served as a missionary and educator in Colombia and Brazil with the Board of Foreign Missions of the Presbyterian Church, U.S.A. He is the author of several works in Portuguese, and of *Encounter with Revolution* in English.

THE FIRST chair of Ecumenics to exist in any theological seminary in the world was established here in Princeton by John A. Mackay. During several decades he has been one of the most outstanding leaders in the missionary enterprise, and in some aspects of the Ecumenical Movement. For many of us who were his students, his course in Ecumenics was a turning point in our lives as he provided us with a new vision of the Gospel and of the tasks of the Church in the modern world. To attempt to continue in any way the work that Dr. John Mackay began constitutes a formidable respon-

* Princeton, New Jersey.

sibility which we undertake with much fear and trembling. On this occasion we would like to express our profound gratitude to Dr. Mackay, for his teaching and example, and also the hope that, by the grace of God, we may be able to mediate to another generation of students, something of his depth of concern for and richness of insight into the Christian world mission.

Given the missionary nature of the church, it would be natural to assume that missions should arise spontaneously out of the life of the church, and that in all missionary outreach, the church would occupy a central place. Speaking historically, however, the relationship between mission and church has been much more ambiguous. In its origin, the modern missionary enterprise was, to a large extent, a lay movement. In many instances, it took form outside the ecclesiastical structure, and even where this break did not occur, it rarely came to occupy a central place in the life of the church. This, together with the fact that Pietism, the spiritual foundation of the modern missionary movement, gave relatively little importance to the doctrine of the church, produced a situation which has been aptly described by Professor Latourette in these words:

> Of all the major features of its program, the one in which the missionary enterprise of the age just passing advanced most slowly was in bringing to birth Christian communities which would continue into the next age. In translating the Scriptures, in broadcasting the Christian message, and in pioneering in the introduction and adaptation of greatly needed features and methods of Western origin, modern Protestant missions have been phenomenally successful. In helping to build the Christian Church they have not made such rapid strides. . . . In this relative lack of emphasis upon the Church . . . Protestant missions of the era just closing have differed from anything previously known in history. Never in any period in the spread of Christianity have missionaries paid relatively so little attention to building the Christian Church (*Missions Tomorrow*, pp. 94–95).

In recent decades, all this has changed. We have been led to discover that God wills to work in the world through a people, and that by definition this people is one. We perceive that Christ takes form in the world in community, that the New Humanity comes into existence as men are related to Christ and to each other. We are confronted by the fact that the givenness of our unity in Christ constitutes the starting point of all of our relationships to each other. In the Ecumenical Movement, these discoveries have taken shape before us.

All this has had a profound influence both on the missionary enterprise and the church at large. The missionary movement today recognizes that all of its efforts are set in this context of the reality of the church; those engaged in mission give central importance to its establishment and growth. This rediscovery of the church represents a major victory in the history of Protestantism and is of the utmost importance for its future development.

At the same time, the church has rediscovered its essential missionary character. As Dr. Blauw puts it in his study of *The Missionary Nature of the Church* (p. 120):

> A remarkable development has taken place in biblical theology in the last few decades which has led to the rediscovery of the Church as a community of the Kingdom, as a witnessing and serving community in and for the world. Outside the existing missionary movement, the conviction that the Church is a missionary Church or it is no Church is accepted by the great majority. The centuries-old ecclesiology which has remained so static is now gradually being replaced by a more dynamic one which is both eschatological and missionary.

These extraordinary events, however, have created a new problem for us. Theologically speaking, the church may be a missionary community. In actual fact, however, it has become a major hindrance to the work of mission. The local congregation pulls people out of the world and absorbs their time in a religious program rather than setting them free for their mission in the world. Our ecclesiastical organizations are not the most striking examples of dynamic and flexible armies which direct their energies primarily toward witness and service to those outside. Missionary boards and organizations, in their justified desire to turn over increasing responsibility to their daughter churches, have become so bound to relatively static ecclesiastical organizations that, with rare exceptions, they have shown little possibility of thinking imaginatively about the vast new frontiers of mission or becoming engaged in new ventures on them. And the Ecumenical Movement has become so involved in inter-ecclesiastical relationships that it has little time to be concerned about the crucial issues in the human situation.

Consequently, *the renewal of the church* has become one of the most important questions in missiology at the present time. In this concern the student of missions finds himself in good company. In fact, practically everyone is concerned about renewal, and everywhere people are writing about it or working at it. The rediscovery of the concept of the *ecclesia reformata semper reformanda* indicates, for us Calvinists at least, that renewal should have a central role in the life of the church at all times. And yet, after all that has been said and done, we are haunted by a sense of frustration and immobility at this point. Karl Barth is able to suggest, in a recent article in the *Ecumenical Review* (July, 1963), that Roman Catholicism may be making more progress in this direction than we are. A few months before his death, Dietrich Bonhoeffer wrote a letter to his godson, on the day of his baptism, in which he said: "By the time you are grown up, the form of the church will have changed beyond recognition" (*Letters and Papers from Prison*, p. 160). When we contemplate the ecclesiastical developments which have taken place in West Germany or in this country in the last twenty years, these words have a strangely perturbing ring to them. What is more serious, there exists, in some circles, a deep fear of radical renewal, a sense that efforts to renew the church represent a threat to the church, its ministry and its work in the world. And even where constant efforts at renewal are being made, there is much uncertainty and frustration, and a growing feeling that no clear answers have yet appeared.

It is the task of missiology to encourage serious theological reflection on this problem. Concerned as it is with what God is doing in the world and in the Church, and the relationship between the two at a particular moment of history, missiology may have a contribution to make at the point at which it is most urgently needed at the present time. Only as we are free to perceive the radical things which God may be doing in his church for the sake of the world, can we find the right direction toward renewal and the courage to engage in it. Such an undertaking may seem highly pretentious, for none of us has a special illumination at this point. And yet, if we are to find the path of obedience we are under the obligation to reflect on what God is doing in our history in the light of His action in a special history. We can only run this risk in trust and in constant openness to the correction of the Spirit through the community of believers.

Within this context the thesis we would like to propose is this: *God has brought his church today into a new Diaspora situation. After more than a thousand years of existence as a gathered people in Christendom, Christians are once again being dispersed in a non-Christian world; and the forms of church renewal must now be the authentic forms of existence of the Christian community in this dispersion.*

I. The Dispersion—Ancient and Modern

The use of the Diaspora concept to describe the life of Christians in the modern world is by no means new in ecumenical circles. To the best of our knowledge, however, it has been used in a restricted way to refer to the scattering of Christians in the world during the week as over against their gathered life in the church on Sunday. Hans-Ruedi Weber, who, as Secretary of the Department of the Laity in the World Council of Churches, gave wide circulation to this idea, writes thus in one of his best known studies:

> It should first be emphasized that *the Church lives not only in assembly, but in dispersion too.* In the time between Christ's ascension and his second coming the Church of Christ has two forms of existence: that of the *ecclesia*, the assembly, and that of the *diaspora*, the dispersion. Pastors whose service is given mainly in the assemblies of God's people are always in danger of regarding the Church much too exclusively from the standpoint of the assembly.

. . . The true role of the laity in the Church is apparent not in its *ecclesia* form, however, but in the *diaspora* ("The Marks of an Evangelising Church," in *The Missionary Church in East and West*, pp. 109–110).

The concept is helpful as far as it goes. But it does not challenge the assumption that the gathering of God's people today should take the form of the gathered community in Western Christendom. Moreover, it fails to contemplate the possibility that the *Church* today, and not merely the individual Christian in his daily life, is in a Diaspora situation. It may therefore be profitable for us to explore further this possibility.

The people of Israel lived by memory of a great act of deliverance, by which God brought them out of bondage in Egypt, guided them through the desert and gave them a Promised Land. God had given this Chosen People a Kingdom in which they could finally settle down and be at home. As a people they shared the same racial and cultural background, and were united in common hopes and longings. The God who did these great wonders in their history was the center of their national life; the temple in which He was worshipped— and in which He was present in a special way—was the focal point of their existence. Many of their most outstanding religious leaders, moreover, had a vision of Israel's mission in the restoration of all nations. With the coming of the Messianic Kingdom, Jerusalem would be the center of the world and all nations would flow unto it.

Eventually a severe crisis appeared in the life of the nation; and in the midst of it, there arose a strange group of prophets who announced that the same God who had gathered them into this unique nation was now about to scatter them across the face of the earth. This announcement was completely incredible. It could only be the product of a negative and warped mind, and the Israelites did their best to dispose of such people, who threatened their whole existence as the People of God. But the dispersion came. The vast majority of the Israelites, under compulsion or eventually by choice, were scattered among the pagan nations of the world, and obliged to live among peoples of different races and

cultures, of other religious and moral ideas. They lost their
identity as a Kingdom. The Temple was destroyed, and they
had to find new forms of worship in the midst of their
dispersion, among those who knew not Yahweh. No longer
could they await the gathering of all nations around Jerusalem.
Though this hope lingered on, many of them discovered that
God had called them to the more painful and arduous task
of making Him known, in their weakness, as they lived among
the people around them.

Since the early Middle Ages the Church in the West has
conceived of itself more and more along these lines. God has
here gathered together a people in a most unique way. It is not
surprising that some of those who have seen most clearly the
greatness of this divine work have conceived of Christendom
as a Kingdom. Christopher Dawson can speak in glowing
terms of the "organic unity and continuity of the Christian
society", "a *life* in the full sense of the word" with its "distinct
institutional forms" (*Medieval Religion*, pp. 7, 20). Cardinal
Newman once said, "Christianity is an Imperial Power, a
Counter-Kingdom which occupies ground." Here was a culture
and a society shaped by Christianity and in which Christians
could feel at home. To a certain degree it was a homogeneous
people, united in a common loyalty and by common presuppositions about life and the world. Here too God was in the
center of life and the medieval cathedral or the Protestant
chapel in the village was the center of the community. Through
the proclamation of the Word and the ministration of the
Sacraments, all of life was related to him and confronted by
his demands. The minister, by his participation in these acts
and by his presence in society, was the representative of God
and His purposes for that people. Evangelism and mission
often came to the fore, but they usually brought people into a
church with its own peculiar life and culture formed by
Christendom.

If we are concerned to see what God is doing in our history, in the light of what he has done in the history of his
chosen people in past eras, it may be worth our while to explore the idea that a new Diaspora is our lot as a church
today. Naturally, this does not occur in the same way as in

the Sixth Century B.C. But Christendom is rapidly dissolving around us, so that even in the West the church is becoming a dispersed people. Moreover, without our going into exile, the non-Christian world has engulfed us as modern means of communication create one world in which we are a small minority and as the population explosion indicates that each year the percentage of Christians decreases. We are thus in a situation similar to that of the Jews of the Diaspora, scattered among people whose culture, mores and thought patterns are not like ours nor will they become so; our cathedrals and temples are no longer in the center of life nor do they bring the whole community together under God. If we hope to reach modern man, it will not be so much in terms of gathering him into the church as of going to him in the midst of our dispersion.

If this is our situation, then the church today is called to a change of perspective and direction which is scarcely less radical than that which the Jewish Diaspora demanded. In the face of what thus seems to be such an overwhelming disaster, our greatest temptation is to heed those false prophets who will heal our wounds lightly and cry "Peace, peace, when there is no peace" (Jeremiah 6:14). We will search desperately for some easy way to make our old system work and will look anxiously for some signs of success, or trust in some new spiritual technique or evangelistic movement. Or, in the midst of our shock and despair, we may take time to ask why God has visited this upon us, and the Spirit may direct us to follow his leading *in the dispersion*.

For this to happen, only an understanding of the place in the divine economy of the dispersion of God's people can be of assistance to us. Here again, perhaps the Jewish Diaspora can shed light on our situation, for according to the prophets, the Dispersion was a divine *judgment* which, in the mysteries of God's will, was also a new *call* to Israel to be His servant.

Israel was chosen by God to be His servant for the sake of the nations. In the words of Blauw, "The whole history of Israel is nothing but the continuation of God's dealing with the nations, and is only to be understood from the unsolved problem of the relation of God to the nations" (*op. cit.* p. 19).

Through her faithfulness to Him and her obedience of His commandments in all areas of her life, Israel would be used by God for this mission. "If you return, O Israel . . . and if you swear, 'As the Lord Lives' in truth, in justice and in uprightness, then nations shall bless themselves in him, and in him shall they glory" (Jer. 4:1–2). But the people of Israel departed from this path. When they settled down in the land which God had given them, they forgot the purpose of their election and began to use God for their own selfish ends, for their own profit and security. On this road, they soon turned to idols that were much more useful for that purpose, and forgot justice as they oppressed and exploited the poor, the fatherless and the widows. In this situation, judgment meant dispersion, for only the total shattering of the very order which God himself had built up could open the way for Israel to participate again in the divine purposes. "Because they . . . have not obeyed my voice, or walked in accord with it, but have stubbornly followed their own hearts and have gone after the Baals . . . Behold . . . I will scatter them among the nations whom neither they nor their fathers have known" (Jer. 9:13–16).

Does not Jeremiah's insight into the meaning of events in his time speak in a rather disturbing way to our situation? In his study of the missionary thrust of the New Testament Church, Blaauw remarks: "The route of the Gospel is the road from Jerusalem, the centre of Israel, to Rome, the centre of the world" (*op. cit.* p. 94). The early Christians tended to abandon the Jewish concept of a people, because of its static connotations, and to speak of themselves as the *ecclesia*, those brought forth by the call of God for service. They became a pilgrim people living in the world and moving across the world. In fact, they saw themselves as living in a new Diaspora (I Peter 1:1, James 1:2). They soon arrived in Rome and conquered it, and God gave them the possibility of once again becoming a gathered people, with their own nation, ordered by the influences of the Gospel. Across the centuries Christians built a society in which this God was the center and source of its life and hope. But gradually Rome became another Jerusalem and the gathered people of God have not avoided the errors of those gathered around Jerusalem centuries earlier. For whatever the greatness of the accomplishments of this gathering in Christendom, it has now reached a point where the perspectives, patterns and structures that have been central in it are no longer adequate. To the degree that we live by it, Christianity is so identified with culture that it can neither reveal its inner crises nor offer new possibilities. The program of the local church has become a means by which Christians are pulled out of their involvements in the world where God is at work to be part of a religious institution. As our church buildings, staffs and programs expand, our imprisonment becomes even greater. In the midst of a dynamic world we are so bound to an institutionalization of our faith that the world moves away from us and we are more and more absent from those places where the real issues of life and death for modern man and for our society are being fought out. Thus we spend our time and energy trying to get our people, whose understanding of the faith is basically unrelated to these issues, to be a little less out of date, a task which, to say the least, is not very exciting or productive. The modern scientist works fearfully and precariously on the frontiers where the issues of human destiny are being met. Rather than being with him there, we spend our energies trying to convince our members that science and religion may not be incompatible. Although some of our leaders, mostly clergy, have distinguished themselves on the racial frontier, we are doing very little to lead our members into the midst of that struggle, perhaps the most decisive one for our nation at this time. Much of our effort is spent in trying to do something so that the Church will not continue to be the most segregated institution in America. And if perchance we should succeed at this task, by that time the racial frontier will have moved far beyond that point, and we will remain just as far behind. In this situation, dispersion as judgment, in which the Lord tears down what He has built up and scatters His people in a non-Christian world, may not be too wide of the mark as a clue to events in the Church today.

In the mysteries of divine Providence, this Diaspora also became a means by which Israel was led to reinterpret her existence and mission and to participate in God's purpose for the world in a way that would not have been possible otherwise. Those who were driven into exile probably saw nothing of this; they were too overwhelmed by the disaster that befell them. But by the time of Deutero-Isaiah a striking reinterpretation has begun. In chapter 43, the prophet speaks lyrically of the "new thing" (v. 19) which God is doing, as he gathers his people together from afar:

> I will bring your offspring from the east,
>   and from the west I will gather you;
> I will say to the north, Give up,
>   and to the south, Do not withhold;
> Bring my sons from afar
>   and my daughters from the end
>   of the earth (vs. 5–6).

Yet this is not to the self-centered, gathered existence of former times, but a convocation to a great assembly of the nations in which the people of Israel shall be God's witnesses and declare His praise. The climax of this reinterpretation comes in the Servant Songs, where the prophet, out of the tremendous suffering of the Dispersion, is led to see Israel's role in the divine purpose as that of a suffering servant.

As a matter of fact, it was the Diaspora which prepared the way for the spread of the Gospel throughout the Graeco-Roman world, though not quite in the way that the Jewish people had hoped. According to Harnack's estimate, more than four million Jews were scattered throughout the Empire, where the basic tenets of their religion became known and a good number of proselytes were won. Because of the Diaspora, the Old Testament was translated into Greek and a new institution, the synagogue, developed.

As the crisis in the institutional life of the gathered people of Christendom becomes more acute, many of us will probably follow the example of the exiles in Babylon and "hang our harps on the willows." Yet if it means anything to us to see our history in the light of a special history, we may be free to discern the call and the opportunity which comes to us in the Diaspora. We may catch a vision of the relevance of the Gospel to the human situation and of new forms of Christian community, which could not come otherwise. In one of his last letters, Dietrich Bonhoeffer speaks of the revolution which Luther brought about when he left the monastery and moved out into the world as the place where he had to serve God. He sees this as the "fiercest attack and assault to be launched against the world since primitive Christianity." This attack very soon bogged down in modern Protestantism, and it is only now, in the modern Diaspora, that we have no choice but to live out the consequences of it, as we discover that the place not only of the Christian life but of the *life of the Church* is not some religious sphere but the concrete orders of worldly life. As a consequence of the process of secularization, God has freed modern man of all those sacral orders which have imprisoned him. He is now free to work out his own destiny in the fullness of historical existence and to shape his own future. At the precise moment when modern man contemplates this incredible opportunity to destroy human existence or to create a new humanity, God has brought us, in our dispersion, to the point where we have no choice but to participate fully in this venture in the name of Christ.

II. New Forms of Church Life for a New Situation

In the life of the church, *essence* and *form* are inseparably related. The Christ who is present in and among His people is the incarnate Christ; the church, as "Christ existing in community" (Bonhoeffer), can only exist in concreteness. Thus when we deal with the essence of the church, this includes of necessity the specific institutional forms which it takes; when we are concerned primarily with these forms, we are also dealing inevitably with the question of the nature of the church. Yet we cannot avoid concentration at one point or the other, depending upon our objective. In the present instance, we are taking for granted that the presence of Christ expresses itself in Word, Sacrament and the life of the *koinonia*. Our specific concern is not with these elements in themselves, but rather with the changing shape of the church as it strives to give authentic expression to these realities in the new situation of dispersion in which it finds itself today. This is as far as we can go in this study. It is quite likely that as new forms of church life develop, questions about the redefinition of the *nature* of the church will arise. In this paper, we can do nothing more than hint at some of them.

It is quite likely that in this new situation, many of our traditional forms of institutional life will not survive. We are free, however, to see their collapse as the pre-condition for the coming of the new. "A grain of wheat remains a solitary grain unless it falls into the ground and dies; but if it dies, it bears a rich harvest" (John 12:24). When this happens, our central concern must be: What are the authentic forms of existence of the church in this dispersion? We should not yet expect to have any clear answers, but we may find some sense of direction and the freedom to engage in constant experimentation. There are several areas which seem to us to demand attention at the present time:

1. *The nuclear Christian community (congregation) should now take form within the diverse precarious communities in which Christians are dispersed today.*

In our efforts at the renewal of parish life, most of us tend to be preoccupied mainly with the present patterns and try to discover how certain changes, major or minor, can be made in them. If God has visited us with a new Diaspora, then a different approach is demanded. For the sake of the congregational life of the church, we must ask ourselves: What forms of Christian community are called for in the dispersion and how can they be developed realistically? For it is only as such new forms appear in our midst that the congregational life as we now know it will be transformed.

This type of Christian community is demanded by the very nature of the Gospel and of the Church. The Church is not primarily a religious organization but the first fruits of a new humanity in Christ. It is the Body of Christ, the New Man, who took form in the midst of the concreteness of human existence in Palestine at a specific point in time.

The new life is a matter of growth to maturity in interrelatedness (Eph. 4) as Jesus Christ forgives us and reconciles us to each other in the midst of the concrete world in which we live. Only as faith illumines and transforms these relationships do we receive Christ's benefits; only thus can he become visible and real for us and before the world.

In the world in which you and I are living today this new life in Christ can only take shape in the wide diversity of communities in which men live their lives: in factory, office or other professional associations; in community and political organizations; in the family and in *ad hoc* groups which come together for a specific task. It is in these fragmented and precarious communities that human lives intersect, relationships develop, and decisions are made which determine the life of the individual and of society. As a German sociologist writes,

> While nobody will be able fully to understand man standing within all his relationships, we nevertheless believe that we can meet him in each of his roles to a certain extent as a total human being; we can meet him in the depth of his being and the Word of God can confront him principally in such concrete situations.

The logical conclusion from this would be to transfer the locus of much of our congregational life from the church building to these smaller communities, and carry on within these house churches, *koinonia* groups, etc., more or less the same type of program we now have in the local church. Necessary as it may be to change the center of parish activity, this in itself is not enough. Its most likely result would be the transferral of the Christian "ghetto" from a church building to these other communities. For Christ to take form in interrelatedness in the world means that Christians must be fully *involved* in the communities in which they are dispersed; that is, they must have serious personal relationships with other people there and share with them in concern for the real human issues which there arise. Christian community in such dispersion is authentic only as it takes shape among people so involved, and helps them to relate the Gospel to the concrete issues which demand decisions.

Perhaps an example will illustrate what we mean. For some decades, the churches have been aware of the fact that the university represents one of these communities. At first, we tried to minister to it through our traditional church program carried on near the campus, or in some cases, on it. It soon became clear that this was inadequate, for the university represents one of those special worlds of our time to which we can minister only if we are inside of its life and concerns. So the churches proceeded to this by setting people aside to carry on a religious program in the university. These chaplains gave themselves to organizing study groups, teaching, counselling and, in some cases, preaching. They were kept very busy, but often very little happened. The number of "church-related" students who became interested was proportionately very small, to say nothing of those outside. Now, however, we are beginning to discern another possibility. We can focus our attention on the involvement of Christians at some point in the life of the university. This may happen as people relate to each other in a coffee shop; as a small group comes together to discuss the relationship between one discipline and another, or the relationship of a particular discipline to Christian faith; as students become concerned about some aspect of the life of the university, or as a group gets involved in the struggle for racial integration or some other major problem in our society. At any of these points, Christian students are thus present where Christ is giving new form to human life, and discover how to participate in a community relationship which frees them for this task.

As the Christian community lives on these frontiers of the modern world, we may find ourselves in a situation in which eventually new spiritual vitality will develop and the means of grace will take on new significance for us. This has frequently happened in the history of the church, as those engaged in efforts at renewal were led by the spirit to the discovery of authentic forms of community *for their particular situation*. This was certainly the case in the Reformation of the Sixteenth Century. In an article on "Calvin's Conception of the 'Communio Sanctorum'" (*Church History*, September, 1936, p. 232), Ray C. Petry shows how the type of community which Calvin developed for his time, centering in the preaching and teaching of the Word, in prayer, sacrament and discipline, had a profound impact on the total life of believers. He writes: "From the resultant corporate action proceeded a new incentive to intellectual progress, the regimentation of fundamental activities, the surveillance of morals, the encouragement of stalwart living, and the attack upon socially pathological conditions."

This is what is not happening often enough today and it is not likely to happen with the present patterns of the gathered church. Our programs of Christian education as well as our other efforts at nurture will continue in crisis until we discover how the Christian community can become a reality in the midst of modern man's involvements in the world, and there take new forms which will communicate the benefits of Christ to him there.

As yet we have no clear picture of the nature of these Christian communities of the modern Diaspora. We are convinced however, that new forms will be given to us as Christians relate to each other in their involvements in the dispersion as families, as groups in the same profession or work, or as participants in some social, community or political activity. Their program will certainly be very flexible and open, adjusted to the rhythm of life in an industrial society. The members may come together rather infrequently, in the midst of their responsibilities, but they will know a relationship which will make the Gospel more meaningful to them. If this seems quite indefinite, let us remember that we are called to be a pilgrim people and that as we live a pilgrim existence we are given a new vision of God and a new experience of His power in our lives.

As such communities come into existence in the dispersion, we will be prepared to work out their significance for the development of new forms of parish and ecclesiastical life. It is only when we are confronted by the reality of these new communities, that we can discover how they should be related to each other, how the gathering of the whole people of God for liturgical and sacramental life can best take place, or how our irrelevant denominational structure can be changed. The important thing at the moment is for each of us to discover his calling and opportunity to engage in this venture. Each pastor can try to find one or more groups of laymen in his church who are interested in experimentation along these lines. Where a church has several workers on its staff, it might set one of them aside for this task. Each Presbytery can re-examine its total mission to the total area for which it is responsible, and support new ventures of this type.

In spite of the rigidity of its ecclesiastical structures, the Roman Catholic Church has been able to renew its life across the centuries because it always makes room for new monastic communities and other similar groups which are free to move to the frontiers on which the church is not fully present. Unless we are able to develop a Protestant equivalent to this, we will be confronted with a most desperate situation in the coming decades. As has happened before, new sects will probably arise to meet the challenge and further splinter the church, or groups of laymen will take the responsibility into their own hands and attempt to find new ways.

2. *In the modern dispersion, the service of the Church to the world should take the form of solidarity with man in his struggle to make and keep human life human.*

In Western Christendom, Christianity for centuries made a decisive difference in the lives of men and of society. Society was basically stable and relatively static; its goals were defined in terms of values and principles which possessed a certain sacral character. In family life, for example, the ideal was clearly defined; all citizens were exhorted to strive toward it, and deviations from the norm were punished either by law or by social ostracism. In such a society, the church played a leading role. The preaching of the Word, the pronouncements of the church and the pastor's presence in society all helped to maintain this ideal and encourage people to move as close to it as possible.

All this, however, is changing very rapidly. The revolt of contemporary man against the paternalism inherent in this approach has occurred at a time when the church has also lost the authority to speak in some of these areas. To the degree that Christians are scattered in a non-Christian or post-Christian world, they have little opportunity to act in this way. More important is the change which has taken place in the nature of our society. In the dynamic world in which we live, all orders and institutions are losing their sacral character. Man has discovered that he is free to shape his existence within history and determine his own future. And he can see that his future will be determined by the decisions which are made for or against man's humanity by men and groups in their day-to-day involvement in the complex structures of modern life. In this situation, the affirmation of values or principles is of little avail. What counts is full and constant participation in the structure of power where concrete decisions are made daily.

If the church insists on functioning in the same old way, we will soon arrive at the place where its presence will make very little difference, indeed. At this moment, in certain areas, pronouncements by the church or the presence of a number of ministers wearing their clerical collars may change the image of the church in the minds of the community and perhaps help to bring about needed changes in society. But in the long run, the presence of Christianity will depend upon the full and constant participation of laymen on the many frontiers of the human struggle. In these spheres, the Christian soon discovers that he has no solutions to propose or impose, but that a contribution of quite another type is demanded of him. He may find that his faith in Christ gives him a certain freedom from the rigidity of ideological thinking so that he can see reality more clearly and deal with it more pragmatically. He may perceive the tendency of any movement to fall victim of sclerosis, and thus be able to help keep it open and on the move. As men become aware of the terrible freedom and power over human life which they possess, the Christian may find in Christ the foundation of an attitude of confidence and trust toward history and toward the future which makes it possible for him to act with calmness and confidence and find meaning in his efforts. To the degree that he lives the reality of his faith, the Christian will be sensitive to the fact that in each decision in any area of life, the central issue is the wellbeing of man.

For this task the traditional institutional forms of the

church will not suffice. To draw people out of these crucial areas of life into a religious program and then arm them with principles which they cannot apply is an act of irresponsibility. The withdrawal of so many of our churches from the heart of the city where the population is concentrated and where the decisive battles for the future of the metropolis are being fought, to the relative isolation of suburbia, is the most tragic proof of the inability of our present structures to cope with our responsibility in the world. Only as we are free to give form to Christian community in these areas of our modern dispersion, and there take the form of the servant, can this presence be a faithful expression of our obedience to Christ.

It was in the midst of the Jewish Diaspora that a new vision of Israel, as the suffering servant of Yahweh, appeared. This was later taken by Jesus Christ and re-interpreted as the clue to His own person and work in the world. It may be that in the modern Diaspora a new vision will be given to the Church of its calling to be a servant people, participating in God's suffering for the world. We find ourselves on the threshold of a new era, the shape of which we cannot clearly perceive. What changes it will bring in the life of our church, no one would yet try to predict. But a direction is indicated for us of full solidarity with our neighbor in his loneliness and fear, his lack of a clear orientation and of meaning in his existence, as he faces the incredible and terrifying task before him to determine his life and destiny. In this solidarity, we run the risk of losing our faith; we also have the possibility of finding new meaning in it. We will discover that we live among men constantly threatened by movements and institutions which try to transform them into objects to be used for the specific purposes of a particular group. In such a situation, we are challenged to provide a form of church life which leads to full identification with people without ulterior motives as regards the ecclesiastical organization. We will find ourselves among men and women for whom any metaphysical understanding of transcendence is meaningless, and who thus are becoming more and more bound by the limitations of radical immanentism. In our encounter with this secularism, we too may succumb. But it may also happen that, as we share Christ's sufferings for the world, we will enter into a new realm of transcendence in which the Christ existing for others meets us in the Thou whom we serve, and gives us a new knowledge of Himself as we "throw ourselves utterly into the arms of God and participate in his sufferings in the world and watch with Christ in Gethsemane." (Bonhoeffer, *Letters and Papers from Prison*, letter of July 21, 1944.)

3. *There is a third and final question—which we can present here only as a question—regarding the adequacy, in a Diaspora situation, of the understanding of the church as a "fellowship of believers" that was developed at the time of the Reformation.*

Reading over again the first chapters of the Fourth Book of the *Institutes*, I was impressed by the power of this conception of the *communio sanctorum*. Here men and women are incorporated into the realm of grace, where they hear and respond to the Word, receive the sacraments, and live a disciplined and godly life as members of a community. When the Church later awoke to its responsibility toward the growing number of unbelievers around it, the natural result was to reach out to these people and draw them in to this community. As we have been confronted with an increasing number of biblical studies which stress the missionary character of the church, we have been satisfied to ask ourselves how this "fellowship of believers" as now constituted, can be so renewed and revitalized that it becomes a missionary community. Perhaps we should conclude that this transformation is not likely to take place, and that we should rather attempt a reformulation of our doctrine of the church at this point. Several reasons, to my mind, call for this:

a. In a world in which Christianity has had such a strong impact, and in which the self-invalidation of Christianity has also gone very far, the traditional distinction between believer and unbeliever, insider and outsider, has lost much of its significance, and now stands as an obstacle to our work of evangelism. Suffice it here to cite a few sentences from the *Life* of the English theologian, F. D. Maurice, written long before this problem became as acute as it now is:

I have not ventured . . . to draw a line between one class of men and another, to call those on this side of the line righteous and believers, those on the other side of the line unrighteous and unbelievers. . . . I must take my portion with the unrighteous and unbelievers; for I am conscious of an unrighteousness and an unbelief in myself which I cannot be conscious of in another. (quoted in Munby, D. L., *The Idea of a Secular Society*, pp. 75–76).

Today we might say the same thing of the *Church* in relation to those outside it.

b. The community of believers, as now conceived, tends to stand in the way of full concern for all men for whom the Gospel is intended. As Christoph Blumhardt put it in a letter to his son-in-law: In his baptism, "Christ in the Spirit bound himself to sinners; in church baptism, we in the Spirit separate ourselves from sinners." We are inclined to look for the operation of grace only within the Church, rather than point men to its presence in the world; and by and large our life in the *communio sanctorum* does not produce that intensity of concern for the carrying of the Gospel into all the world, and its proclamation to all races, classes and groups in our society, which is inherent in the Gospel itself.

c. I have a certain suspicion that this conception of the Church, with all its richness and power, does not do justice to the New Testament witness regarding the nature of the Church. It is by no means self-evident that the community of believers in the New Testament and the community of believers as it has existed for so long in Christendom are by any means identical. Jesus himself seemed to make no special effort to form a fellowship of those who, as a result of his ministry, received forgiveness or believed in him. In his parables of the Kingdom, I find no clear stress on the immediate gathering of people into the New Israel but a decided emphasis upon the children of the Kingdom being scattered over the world like seed in the earth, leaven in the dough, or the light of a lamp in a room. And the central thrust of the Great Commission seems to me to be in this same direction:

Go forth therefore and make all nations my disciples; baptize men everywhere in the name of the Father and the Son and the Holy Spirit, and teach them to observe all that I have commanded you. And be assured, I am with you always, to the end of time (Matt. 28:19-20).

When we come to the Apostle Paul, I recognize that his thought is more complex. He does give a great deal of attention to the building up of the community of believers. But the Church is also the Body of Christ who is the New Adam. It is the first-fruits of the New Humanity. Those who were without God have now been made nigh by the blood of Christ (Eph. 2:12-13). God's redemption has changed the human situation and its ultimate intention is the reconcilation of all things in Christ (Eph. 1:10). As Blauw says: "Paul's apostleship became possible when the walls that separated Israel and the nations fell. In Christ the fullness of the times began and that means the unity of everything, in heaven and earth, under His dominion" (op. cit., p. 97). God's grace is abroad *in the world*. Christians are called to make it visible and point to it.

If these two diverging lines of thought exist in the New Testament, how are they to be reconciled? That task is for the biblical theologians. As regards the mission of the Church, we might at least provisionally raise the question: Should we not, in the modern Diaspora, place less emphasis upon the gathering of *professed believers* into a religious community, and concentrate more on the formation of *smaller communities of witnesses,* dedicated to this task of witnessing to the reality of God's grace in the world and calling men to receive it and live by it? This does not exclude a concern about the ultimate gathering of the people of God, but puts it in a more eschatological context, which may be more faithful to the New Testament.

Speaking concretely: American teenage culture presents a special problem and opportunity for the Church in America today, as peer groups and gangs come to play the role that in an earlier period, community, church and family played. Our efforts to draw individual teenagers from their groups into a religious program in church have accomplished very little. Some attempts by denominations and other groups to work in closer contact with this culture have given more hopeful results up to a certain point. But if we are really concerned about a witness to Christ in the center of the life of American teenagers, should not our primary emphasis be upon recruiting young adults who would accept full responsibility for relating themselves with these groups and helping them to see how Christ can transform life in the midst of their day-to-day decisions? Or as regards our ministry in the university: Does not the special situation in which we find ourselves there offer us an unusual opportunity to focus our efforts on the training and sustaining of those who are willing to live as Christ's servants at one point or another in the life of the university. Formidable objections can be raised to this thesis. If we do not place sufficient emphasis upon the gathered community of believers, from whence do we recruit new witnesses? This question must be faced in all honesty. Much evidence would indicate, I believe, that the fellowship of believers as now constituted is a very ineffective means of recruiting witnesses and tends often to interest the type of believer who is least concerned about or prepared for such life in the world. It is just possible that the change of emphasis here proposed would open interesting possibilities of involving a different type of person and developing a style of Christian life which would be much more adequate for a secular world.

A more difficult question has to do with the way in which grace is appropriated. We seem to have assumed that the only possibility lies in the continuation of the *communio sanctorum* of Christendom. And yet in some parts of the world at least, the exodus of so many young people and others from the church and the superficiality of the religious life of large numbers of those who remain in it are a clear sign that the means of grace are becoming less and less efficacious.

If the Church gives more attention to the community of witnesses involved in the heart of the human struggle today, something new and even exciting may happen. For those thus involved, the traditional means of grace may take new forms;

they may also become the very staff of life. Moreover, as we come to see that "grace is everywhere," we will be free to step out into the fresh air of the modern world and there find those forms which will make Jesus Christ more visible in a secular society.

Some of the suggestions made here may be quite wide of the mark. In the situation in which we find ourselves to-day, no one can speak with much confidence about the path we should follow. If our analysis has any validity, however, we will be able to know whether these or other paths are the correct ones only as we are free from the dominance of the past and open to constant experimentation. We must be willing to see our most cherished forms of church life die in order that the Church may live. This is what happened in and through the Jewish Dispersion; it may also happen in our time. And since it is the Lord of the Church who works in and through it in that way, we need not be unduly upset if we discover that he is calling us to serve *him* in a new Diaspora.

Through Dooms of Love

William Stringfellow

Writing about the Negro revolution, William Stringfellow, a lawyer and an Episcopal layman, gives counsel that even many will not want to hear. The revolution, he says, has passed beyond the "good cause" stage for whites and, perhaps, beyond all chance for them to influence it. If a Day of Wrath should come, the cross offers a way for white Christians to meet violence. "When the knife is at the belly, let the white Christian not protest. . . . Let him love in the face of his own death." Mr. Stringfellow's most recent book is *My People Is the Enemy,* an "autobiographical polemic" drawing on his six years' experience living and practicing law in the slums of New York city's Harlem. His article, from the July 1964 issue of *Fellowship,** is adapted from his address before the church assembly on civil rights, which met in May 1964 in Washington to institute a prayer vigil at the Capitol.

I AM SICK AND TIRED of the racial crisis in America.

God knows how Negroes must feel, but I am now almost overwhelmed with the feeling that I do not want to hear anything more about it, or see anything more of it, or do anything more in it. I wish it could be somehow escaped or evaded or avoided.

There was another great crisis, which this nation endured, within my own recollection, about which I felt somewhat the same. During the Korean War, I was in the military service, though, mercifully, I was not stationed in Korea or called into combat, but nevertheless I remember—as many others also must—an acute fatigue in which I did not want to hear or see or do anything more about that war. I

---

* Fellowship of Reconciliation, Box 271, Nyack, New York.

wanted it to somehow evaporate and make no more demands upon me. Yet I am pretty sure that this sentiment which I suffered during that war did not alleviate or abbreviate it in any way, but, on the contrary, contributed to the aggravation and prolongation of that crisis.

A similar thing is true of the racial crisis. I wish it would end without my being any longer or any more deeply involved. I would rather escape from what now happens to this nation. Yet I am certain both in my mind and in my guts that this exhaustion will not hasten the resolution —much less reconciliation—of the racial crisis: it can only frustrate and compound it.

A Matter of Survival

There is no one in the land who is not now involved in the racial crisis. If there ever was an option about that, which I doubt, it has expired. The only issue that remains is *how* one is involved: obstinately, stupidly, irrationally, or with concern, intelligence and compassion. On that matter, let the white people in America at last face some simple truths:

(1) The racial crisis is not a "good cause" in the sense of the conventional charities—cancer research or alms for the indigent or aid for victims of disaster. Let white folks renounce and forget the romantics of good works and the preposterous condescension of liberalism and confess that no white man is doing any favor for any Negro citizen by now advocating the ordinary rights of citizenship for the American Negro. The favor which is done by such involvement is as much for their own self-interest as for any Negro citizen.

(2) The dimensions of the Negro Revolution are such that the very survival of the nation is at issue, and, therefore, the life and livelihood of *every citizen* is also at stake. I suppose this nation can survive and continue to exclude from the mainstream of its political and economic life, for one example, the American Indian. Such exclusion will not disrupt politics or threaten the

economy in a way quickly noticed by most citizens, however damaging such an exclusion may be for the country morally and psychologically. The exile from American society of the Indian is hardly noticed, but the segregation of 22,000,000 Negro citizens from decent housing, educational opportunity, gainful employment, political responsibility, and free access to public accommodations is bound to threaten the survival of the nation for everybody. The exclusion of *that* many citizens from society jeopardizes the political freedom, economic solvency, psychological stability and moral integrity of those who are not excluded just as much as those who are. In other words, let white people be involved now in this crisis because they finally wake to the fact that their own welfare is quite as much at issue as that of the Negro. Let the profound self-interest of white people in the nation's survival finally end the paternalism of white men for black men in America.

(3) The Negro Revolution must be considered within the context of the traditions of American social revolution. The nation came into being through the Boston Tea Party and other protests which matured into the American Revolution. Thereafter was the crisis over the Articles of Confederation and, then, the abolitionist movement and, eventually, the Civil War. Soon the nation suffered the occupation of the South and the Reconstruction crisis. Later, with some time out for foreign conquest and war, was the movement for women's suffrage, the Labor Revolution, and the veterans' rebellion during the depression, and, now, the Negro Revolution. There is no great novelty to social revolution in America, and if the present revolt is seen as part of this history, an astonishing fact emerges: these revolts have been characterized by the ethics and tactics of violence until the Negro Revolution, with the possible exception of the women's suffrage movement (the women were apparently non violent in their demonstrations in the streets, but who knows what happened when they returned home to their husbands?). Considering the

vast numbers of citizens involved in the present revolution and the depth of their provocation, it is incredible that—so far—the Negro Revolution has been dominated by the ethics and tactics of nonviolence. The forbearance of Negroes during these years of open protest has surely saved the blood of many whites—indeed the best friend, not excepting George Washington, the American white man has *ever* had turns out to be Martin Luther King.

A Dilemma in Ethics

It is now about seven years since the Negro Revolution has been notorious and has had organization and direction. There have been all these years of peaceful protest: sit-ins and Freedom Rides and picketing and prayer vigils and marches. In that time, thousands of citizens have been arrested, hundreds have lost their jobs, scores have suffered abuse and humiliation in the churches, in schools, in the courts, in hotels and parks and other public places, even in their own homes, in the pursuit of their rights as citizens.

The question now seriously and urgently arises as to whether the tactics and ethics of nonviolence are vindicated in results. What does the American Negro citizen have to show for these long years of unparalleled dignity and humanity and restraint?

- They have to show the body of Medgar Evers—rotting in its grave at Arlington National Cemetery. *That's what they have to show.*
- They have to show the bodies of children in their graves in Birmingham. *That's what they have to show.*
- There is token integration now in many universities of the South. There is the same at most colleges and universities of the North. *But that is all there is.*
- And there are still the children of Harlem—and the other Negro ghettos—who every night risk being devoured by rats that infest the tenements in which their families are consigned to live. *That's what they have to show.*

- Hundreds of citizens can show you the scars on their bodies where they have been branded by cattle prods or bruised by police clubs or bitten by dogs. *That's what they have to show*.
- There is voluntarism in the churches, as well as tokenism in many businesses and public places, but virtually the only unsegregated premises in the nation are those in communities with no Negro residents at all. *That's what they have to show*.

In other words, the ethics and tactics of nonviolence have not yet yielded significant changes in the practical day-to-day lives and livelihoods of the ordinary Negro citizens, while only *that* sort of change can possibly sustain the incumbent nonviolent Negro leadership in the revolution.

A Crisis in Tactics

The kind of social change which has impact upon the practical lives of the multitudes of Negro citizens has not been launched by these years of peaceful protest, nor is there much evidence that *that* kind of change has either bothered the conscience or entered the contemplation of white citizens. And, thus, the spirit of revenge is loose to prey upon the frustration and despair which American Negroes have inherited from three centuries of slavery and segregation. The mood becomes more militant and aggressive and explosive as each moment passes. The passion is that it is better not to live than to be a Negro in American society—either in the South or the North—so what is there to be lost by turning to violent assault upon white society and white property and white people?

The watershed of the tactics of peaceful protest was reached in the March on Washington last summer. In the winter and spring that have followed, brushfires of violence have erupted in dozens of cities: in Cleveland thirty-five hundred people rioted for two days; in Manhattan a "Blood Brotherhood" of Negro youths roams the city seeking white stores to loot and white men to rob or maim or murder;

white merchants in the ghettos live in fear of their own customers; hate and the alleged futility of nonviolence is preached every night from the streetcorners of the slums; the police become a virtual occupation army in Negro neighborhoods.

There probably was a time—eight or nine months ago—when enactment of the Civil Rights Bill would have insured that the revolution remain nonviolent. Prompt passage of the Bill, following the March on Washington, would have demonstrated that the ethics and tactics of nonviolence can secure tangible results. But *that* advantage of the Bill has been daily dissipated by filibuster, compromise, and the acute myopia from which the Senate manifestly suffers.

About the only recognition of the now pathetic urgency of this crisis that I have observed in present debate on the Bill is the complaint of Senators that they will not legislate under pressure. Do Senators think all citizens are fools? When, in modern times, has the Congress acted on any legislation of significance except under pressure of one sort or another?

I for one would not expect the Senate to act out of compassion for those who have been exiled from the main stream of American life for three centuries just because they are Negroes. The Senate should act out of concern for the vindication of the ordinary rights of American citizenship. But if the Senate did not act for that cause, will the Senate at least act to forestall the anarchy and bloodletting that looms ahead? The cynical performance which took place in the Senate chamber invites a day of wrath for all of us —black men and white men—in the nation.

A Day of Wrath

As the day of wrath dawns—let it come as no surprise, especially to white men, either Senators or common citizens. After all, what is involved is not merely the frustration of these past several years of peaceful protest, nor just the insensibility of the Senate, but the inheritance of the past three centuries of slavery and segregation.

No Negro child born in this land who has a responsible

parent is not taken aside, at a tender age—at 4 or 5—when the child first goes to school, and told by his parent what it means to be a Negro in America and hears recited the whole saga of the Negro's exile from American society. And then and thereafter, for that child, it is not just his own experience and endurance of discrimination or rejection which are his cause, but now he is an heir to the suffering and travail of his whole people . . . just as each Jewish child who is born becomes an heir to the exile of the Jews from the Biblical times right up to the present time in Nazi Germany, in the Soviet Union, and, alas, also in many parts of the United States.

The exile of the Jews is as much an inheritance of the Egyptians and, now, the Germans. Both captive and captor have the same inheritance. The exile of the American Negro is as much an inheritance of white men in America. But white parents have not been wise enough to tell their children so. Why should it be surprising, then, that white men—confronted with the present crisis—respond ineptly, fearfully, vainly, stupidly, hysterically?

As the day of wrath comes, let white men in America at last confess that captors are always just as much prisoners as captives and that the emancipation of those in bondage will also free those who have kept them in bondage.

As the day of wrath begins, let it be realized that the real recalcitrant in the American racial crisis is not the so-called die-hard segregationist of the South—least of all is it the pathological segregationist whose rationality has been destroyed by racism. Let neither the die-hard nor the pathological segregationists have any comfort: they are not either so many or so important. The *real* recalcitrants—who are very many and very important—are the nice, white liberals in the North and in the South. They include multitudes of church members. They are respectable, sane, sincere, benevolent, earnest folk. They do not despise or hate Negroes, but they also do not know that paternalism and condescension are forms of alienation as much as enmity. They are the white people who, right now, are asking the question "What does the Negro want?" and think that by asking such a question progress has been made in race relations. They are the white people who are asking the question "What does the Negro want?" and fail to understand that this very question assumes that it is *their* prerogative to dispense to the Negro what the Negro will get. And, my friends, *that* assumption is the very essence of white supremacy. And it is *that* mentality—which most white Americans suffer—which must be exorcised if there is to be reconciliation between black men and white men in America.

On the day of wrath, however, as things stand now, the prospect is not reconciliation: the prospect is that Negro violence will be met by overwhelming counterviolence by the police—perhaps the Army—which the white establishment of America has at its command. If that day comes, the frightful peril for all Americans is that this nation will take an irrevocable step into a police state—and the possibility of freedom for all citizens (which is the true aspiration of this revolution) will be aborted. That is the most ominous danger that the nation confronts.

In the day of wrath, what could save the nation from such a calamity is the recognition by white people that any hostility or assault by Negroes against whites and against white society originated in the long, terrible decades of exclusion and rejection of Negroes by white men. Negro violence now is the offspring of white supremacy. The sins of the fathers are indeed visited upon their sons.

A Hope for Absolution

Now if it comes to pass that nonviolence is forsaken in the Negro Revolution, then there is, I believe, a most specific witness to which white Christians in America are summoned. And I gladly commend that witness to my fellow white men who are Christians.

The witness of the white Christian, on that day, must surely be the same as the witness already, during these long years of protest and agony, exampled by so many Negro Christians: the witness of the Cross.

The Cross is not at all a religious symbol—it is profaned when it becomes that in the minds of men. Nor is the Cross just some reference to an event which took place once upon a time but which has no reality and correspondence in the present day. Rather the Cross means the invincible power of God's love for the world even though all the world betrays, denies, fears or opposes the gift of His love for the world. The Cross means voluntary love which is unfazed by any hostility or hatred or violence or assault. The Cross means voluntary love which is not threatened by death. The Cross means voluntary love which perseveres no matter what. The Cross means the gift of love even to one's own enemy—even to the one who would take one's life.

If it comes to pass that white men who are Christians are attacked by Negroes or endure ridicule or humiliation or interference or taunting or torture, if it comes to pass that white Christians are exposed to the loss of their possessions, or status, or jobs, or property, or homes, or even families, if one's own life itself is at issue, then, let the witness of the white Christian, for himself, for all white men, and, in fact for all men everywhere, be the witness of the Cross.

When the knife is at the belly, let the white Christian not protest. Let him receive the assault without prudence, without resistance, without rationalization, without extenuation, without a murmur. Let him love in the face of his own death.

I suppose that is calling for and expecting a lot from white American Christians. I suppose my white American church members have long since forgotten and forsaken the Cross.

But God has neither forgotten nor forsaken the Cross.

And so there is *no other way* that this enormous, desperate, grotesque accumulation of guilt, enmity, estrangement, and terror can be absolved. There has never been—for any man anywhere at any time—any other way.

In the work of God in our midst in reconciling black men and white men there is no escape from the Cross.

Christ and the Christ Figure in American Fiction

Robert Detweiler

In the opinion of Robert Detweiler, the role of the Christ figure in contemporary fiction has been widely misunderstood. Assuming that the Christ figure of fiction is one with the Christ of faith, readers have accused the novelist of irreverence, of overstepping his bounds, of attempting too much. But the Christ figure is neither Jesus the man nor Christ the redeemer. "The novelist, in shaping the Christ figure with the traits of Christ but in the image of man, has effected a secondary incarnation of his own. It is not a substitution for nor a pirated duplication of the incarnation of Christ in Jesus but, as befits its artistic nature, a symbolic operation that has as its model the Christian incarnation." Dr. Detweiler, a member of the English Department at the University of Florida, Gainesville, is the author of *Four Spiritual Crises in Mid-Century American Fiction*. His essay is from the Summer 1964 issue of *The Christian Scholar*.*

THE CONFUSION inherent in contemporary American attitudes toward religion in its relation to culture is reflected in that growing literary vogue, the discovery and interpretation of Christ figures in fiction. Basic to most of the studies is the feeling that the Christ figure, in its ideal form, should be finally identical with the historical, Biblical, doctrinal Christ and should exist in fiction at all only as an imaginatively translated literary version of the Christ of Christian faith. That premise is unfair to fiction and ultimately detrimental to the religious endeavor guiding much

* Circulation office: 475 Riverside Drive, New York, New York 10027.

of the current interest in the Christ figure. The Christ figure is not Jesus the man nor Christ the Christian redeemer; the novelist bears no direct responsibility to the church nor to his Christian heritage to present a figure sympathetic to the Christian dogma; the critic who attempts to interpret the figure in terms of faith and doctrine does so at his own risk.

The Christ Figure: Misinterpretation and Definition

The bulk of the criticism directed at the presentations of Christ figures in our novels and short stories, however, rests on the assumption that the Christ figure of fiction is one with the Christ of the believer. The usual charges are three: that the novelist who employs the figure is in serious danger of committing irreverence, that he is overstepping his literary boundaries, and that in any case he is attempting more than he can hope to handle. A representative expression of the prevalent critical sentiment is the opinion of R. W. B. Lewis. As early as 1951, Lewis was "insisting that the life of Christ is not under any circumstances a subject for fiction," even while defending the Christ-likeness of Ike McCaslin in Faulkner's *The Bear* as within the bounds of literary and theological propriety. In his later study of *The Picaresque Saint,* he stated his position more clearly. Maintaining that the creation of the literary Christ figure is too simple and at once too difficult for the artist, Lewis asserted that

> To create a fictional character is to effect an incarnation; when the character is himself God incarnate, the writer's job has been done for him in advance—which is what I meant by saying it would be too easy. And the writer must try to persuade us that the figure is a man, too: which is what I meant by saying it would be impossible. When, within the limits of literature there appears the figure of Christ or even that of the truly sanctified, we have either the soft sentimentality of *The Passing of the Third Floor Back* or the stiff abstractions of *A Fable:* both—one at a vulgar and the other at a magnificent extreme—betrayals of art by their false transcendence of man.[1]

To that one must answer, "not necessarily," and on three counts. First, the incarnation of God in Christ, an article of Christian faith, is a far cry from the novelist's creation out of the imagination. There is nothing immediately exclusive about the literary origin of the Christ figure. The characters of any writer are pre-existent in the sense that he gets his models from life; whether the model is a man or a god-man does not, for the moment, make any difference. Second—and this is the main fallacy—the novelist is not obliged to persuade that his Christ figure is a man as well as a god (or the God), for seen from the literary perspective, the humanity of the figure should be taken for granted. It is the critic who muddies the issue by reading divinity into the figure in the first place. Third, the implication that the Christ figure must be at the least a sanctified person is misleading and stems also from the false conviction that the figure represents the Christ of faith.

If the Christ figure is not the Christ of faith, then who or what is it? The excess of symbolic dust may have obscured the simple fact that it is the fictional presentation of a human being, a person who is made to experience, who communicates with us as readers, with whom we come into relation as with any literary character. Instead of immediately second-guessing the author on what he might be trying to signify, one should first observe what he has done. In instances of the Christ figure, that means accepting the literary creation seriously as a literary creation and evaluating its impact on the basis of literary criteria: the multidimensionality of personality and actions, the coherence and integration of dialogue and description, the ultimate believability not by comparison with actual persons but through the reader's esthetic-emotional encounter with the character. Through the confrontation with the character one then becomes aware of its further significance, of its representational value. Imaginative literature is forever transcending itself, continually pointing beyond itself, so that through an appreciation of the being of the figure one gains hints of its meaning in a larger context and earns the right to speculate upon that meaning. The Christ figure stimulates that speculation and establishes a relationship beyond the ordinary literary boundaries by reminding one in some manner of the Christ of faith. But the suggestion of the Christ of faith does not imply identification with him. Rather, the Christ of faith and the traditional Christ story supply the best known, most viable body of material for the expression of meaning in Western culture. Whereas hardly more than a century ago there was still a near-complete correlation between Christ and meaning since, in our Christian civilization, Christ provided the focus of meaning, the advent of secularization has introduced a dichotomy between Christ and meaning. Now the object of meaning is whatever the secular mind holds it to be (provided it acknowledges the existence of meaning at all) while Christ has become objectified as the symbol of the passing Christian era. As belief dies out, in other words, the Christ of faith becomes the Christ of culture, and it is the Christ of culture that imaginative literature draws upon and refers to, even while it exploits the still prevalent emotive connotations of the Christ of faith. The confusion surrounding the creation and interpretation of the Christ figure reflects the confusion in modern attitudes regarding Christ himself.

The Christ Figure: Its Literary Structure

A fair assessment of the Christ figure, then, must begin with an interpretation of its literary nature. Four basic structural avenues are open to the writer, each of which determines to a great degree the meaning he attaches to his creation. He can work with sign, with myth, with symbol, and with allegory. The next portion of this study will be concerned with an exploration of each of these possibilities.

THE DISGUISED BIBLICAL CHRIST

The artist who chooses to deal in terms of sign is committed to the most suspect and least promising structural vehicle, since the sign carries little connotative quality in itself and is dependent almost entirely upon the pre-established meaning of the object signified. It is usually the Christian propagandist, the writer of religious fiction, who inadvertently uses the sign when he thinks he is working with symbol. His Christ figure is not a figure at all—he is a transparent character who has no substance in himself but who resembles the Biblical or doctrinal Christ at every turn. Here the critical complaints directed against Christ figures in general specifically apply. It is practically impossible to improve upon plot, characterization, or solution; there is no chance of rendering the complexity of Christ's life and mission; there develops an involuntary profanation through the failure to present adequately his divinity.

Fortunately, few writers have attempted to depict the Christ in modern dress; those concerned with Christian persuasion through literature usually stick to historical fiction or conversion stories, lacking the acumen for anything resembling symbolic writing. Where it has been tried, the results are usually disastrous. The classic American example is Elizabeth Stuart Phelps Ward's *A Singular Life,* written around the turn of the century in the fever of social-gospel Jesus-imitation. The young New England preacher in her novel lives a nineteenth-century life that is identical in most respects to Christ's; the writer's ingenuity exhausts itself in the semi-subtle disguises of the parallels. Once the similarity is established (and that occurs within the first half-dozen pages), there is nothing left for the book to do. It can only repeat the Christ story in a new setting, which, because of its inability to duplicate the universality of the New Testament context, limits rather than interprets Christ for the present. As champion of the anti-alcohol movement, Mrs. Ward's Emanuel is markedly less impressive than the Christ he imitates.

Upton Sinclair's *They Call Me Carpenter* (1926) is scarcely better in its conception and final effect, even if the writing itself is less pretentious. Of an altogether different nature but in the same category is Nathanael West's *Miss Lonelyhearts.* West's protagonist is a Christ figure who is not a symbol but an example of a man possessed of a Christ complex. The structural vehicle is thus also the sign, even though the object signified is not the Christ of faith but a precisely-defined and well-known pathological condition. The story is successful because West's external orientation is not the subjectively-experienced God-man but the objectively-construed phenomenon, about which he can write and which he can employ to reflect the modern spiritual condition without inviting the historical-doctrinal comparisons of Christianity.[2]

THE CHRIST FIGURE AS MYTHOLOGICAL ARCHETYPE

The novelist who employs myth as his framework utilizes the cultural significance of Christ without becoming involved in matters of religious belief or biographical reconstruction. The essence of myth in imaginative literature is its revelation of archetypal persons or situations as embodiments of eternal patterns of existence. Christ as myth takes his place among other heroes as an archetypal figure representing some verity or recurring action of life. The possibilities for his use in this context are obviously many. Apart from its bearing upon religious faith, the Christ story is certainly the most familiar, most pervasive narrative in Western civilization, whether in the form of the New Testament accounts, of the apocryphal additions, or of the later legends accruing to the original body of material; all of these taken together influence what can properly be called the Christian mythos: the total cultural reflection of its values, interests, fears and hopes in imaginative form. The modern writer who employs myth can work with interpretations of Christ or facets of the Christ story in the assurance that his frame of reference will be comprehended, while retaining the freedom finally to mean whatever truth or pattern of life he wishes to emphasize through his particular treatment of the figure.

Christ as mythological archetype can be made to serve any number of functions. He can be understood as the embodiment of the good and moral man who suffers for his goodness or as the misguided idealist who cannot survive in a materialistic world; he can be the redeemer on the supernatural level who mediates between God and man or the culture-bringer on the natural level who introduces his people to a better life; he can be the servant of humanity who suffers so that others are taught through him.

Most of the notably successful Christ figures in American fiction are cast in the Christian mythological setting and display archetypal significance.[3] Two examples are William Faulkner's Ike McCaslin and John Steinbeck's Jim Casy. In Faulkner's *The Bear,* Ike McCaslin emerges as the archetype of the saint, although he is not saintly according to Christian ideals of sanctification but according to his own self-imposed code of moral and material values. The Judeo-Christian mythic framework of the story is insinuated not only by the obvious Christ parallels (Ike's fundamental innocence, as a boy and as an adult; Ike as a carpenter, in conscious emulation of "the Nazarene") but particularly by the Old Testament-like allusions to the land, the inheritance, and the curse, here translated into terms of racial injustice. Ike's saintliness develops through two steps: the learning of integrity in its most natural form through his youthful wilderness training in the code of the hunt and the sustaining of that integrity in later life in the social situation, resulting in his renunciation of the tainted inheritance in favor of a life of poverty. It does not matter that the curse upon land and people continues, for Ike is not the redeemer, only the saint; he saves himself through moral aloofness while the others suffer the tragedies of involvement. Although Ike is without religion (he refers to the God of the Old Testament who still "umpires" humanity but never professes to understand him), he is an example of the prototype of the good man who is true to the nature outside and within him and who can thereby remain whole in a broken world.

Jim Casy, the ex-preacher in Steinbeck's *The Grapes of Wrath,* answers exactly to the classification of the suffering servant archetype. Here again one finds the context of Judeo-Christian myth and the Christ parallels in the personage of Jim, and here again they possess absolutely no Christian significance and are in fact not directed to supernatural orientation at all. The Okies, epitomized by the Joad family, suggest a modern parallel to the Biblical account of the Israelite wanderings: a marked instead of a chosen people, dispossessed of their rented land by the overlords, the Okies wander across America searching for the promised land; they arrive but are confined to the "Babylonian captivity" of the government camp, then subjected to the natural catastrophes of flood, starvation, and disease. The intense desire to retain the solidarity of the family (as of the Israelite nation) must finally be sacrificed in order for the individual spirit of the Okies to succeed. Jim Casy, accompanying the Joads, underscores the Christian mythic basis of the novel and its rejection of Christian doctrine through his background as an evangelist who has turned away from orthodoxy in favor of a tentative humanitarianism and nature religion. Jim as a Christ figure provides the answer to the plight of the Okies as drawn in the Old Testament similarities. He shows that if there is to be any semblance of a utopia (a promised land) for humanity, it will be found not in a particular geographical location but in a common attitude of brotherhood among men. His Christ-like death is an example of sacrifice for that fraternity; he makes at least one disciple in Tom Joad, and his compassionate understanding of desperate men forms the positive counterpart to the angry tone of social protest that dominates the novel.

Other examples might be the mulatto Joe Christmas in Faulkner's *Light in August,* as the type of the individual cursed by a double nature, and the fisherman Santiago in Hemingway's *The Old Man and the Sea,* as the archetypal nature hero. In each of these, as in the foregoing explications, one observes the Christian mythos as the foundation of experience while the Christian faith itself is ignored. In both instances the protagonist or a significant character remind one of Christ without ever becoming Christ or a direct reflection of him. Rather, the suggestion of Christ leads one further to the recognition of any one of the archetypal possibilities, all of which Christ has symbolized for the West and which the Christ figures of the novels represent according to specific modern attempts at meaning.

THE CHRIST FIGURE AS SYMBOL

The Christ figure presented as symbol is usually a minor character who does not constitute the center of interest but whose function is to stress some particular facet of meaning as an integral part of the story. It is a symbol among other symbols, a part of the whole connotative context instead of the key to it or the foundation of it; the scope of its symbolic meaning is correspondingly limited to one aspect of the Christian mythological body. The Christ symbol concentrates upon the central significance of Christ for the Christian faith—his redemptive role—transferred to the secular realm. In American fiction a variety of Christ figures possess that symbolic meaning: through suffering or even death they sacrifice themselves for an ideal. Their redemptive role lends to the story an optimism otherwise lacking and serves as a testimony to a faith in man's heroic potential where other values have disappeared.

One of the earliest Christ symbols in American fiction is Jim Conklin in Stephen Crane's *The Red Badge of Courage*. Although the specific resemblances are sparing, there are enough of them and the role itself is sufficiently delineated to permit a legitimate designation of Jim as a Christ figure employed symbolically. The initials of the name, the location of the wound in the side, the reference to "the passion of his wounds" are obvious indications of Jim's similarity to Christ. In Crane's naturalistic universe, Jim's suffering and death contribute to Henry Fleming's training in the struggle for survival. The war itself is a dramatic epitome of that struggle; Henry's participation in it is an education from which he will either emerge as a man fit to exist in a remorseless world or go under from the weight of fear and cowardice upon him. Three of Henry's most important lessons derive from Jim Conklin's death. First, in watching Jim's agony, Henry comes as close as he can to knowing the full horror of death without experiencing it himself. He has seen corpses before but never the slow dying of a mortally wounded man. Having viewed death at its worst, Henry receives some understanding of it, of its limitations, and thus loses a proportionate amount of his fear. Second, Crane emphasizes the ritual aspect of Jim's death. There is a mysteriousness about it all which seems based on a pre-set pattern. Jim knows instinctively where to die and how to die; his body performs of its own accord the movements preceding death. It is no wonder that Henry feels himself an initiate at "a solemn ceremony." From it he gains some insight into the orderliness of natural existence, which impels one to do the proper thing at the proper time; applied to himself it gives him a confidence that makes him act heroically and, as it turns out, wisely for his survival later on. That heroism itself is the third lesson Henry learns from Jim's death. Crane makes a point of the courage with which Jim meets his end. "Well, he was a re'lar jim-dandy fer nerve, wa'nt he," says the tattered soldier who watches with Henry. That example, coupled with the shame of his previous cowardice, challenges young Fleming to display a courage of his own on the battlefield that inspires his comrades and finally makes him a mature soldier. It would be going too far to say that Jim, in the naturalistic world, like Christ in the spiritual realm, is the instrument of Henry's salvation. However, like Christ he interprets death and renders it less potent, thereby helping the protagonist to save himself. Without determining the setting or philosophic framework of the story, Crane's Christ symbol acts nonetheless as the vehicle for introducing a pivotal point of the novel.

Other Christ symbols for consideration would be Seymour Glass, appearing in or behind much of J. D. Salinger's fiction, and the mysterious Boo Radley of Harper Lee's *To Kill a Mockingbird*. In each of these one discovers along with the overt parallels to the traditional Christ a redemptive role for the character in a context that is neither religiously committed nor completely dependent upon the backgrounds of the Christian mythos. That role lends to the respective story a dimension of hope and faith, seldom supernaturally based, that mitigates the otherwise dominant pessimistic tone. Although each of the stories could exist without the symbol, it would be inestimably poorer as a result.

THE CHRIST FIGURE IN ALLEGORY

Allegory, the fourth possible structural vehicle for the presentation of the Christ figure, has fallen into disrepute in modern fiction as a literary form, perhaps because of its overuse as a purveyor of religious or political propaganda. Nevertheless, in a certain sense it is uniquely fitted for expression of the Christ figure, since its nature necessitates a treatment of the symbolic potential of Christ through attention to the biographical or doctrinal details of the Christ story, yet without implying commitment to the Christian faith. Unlike the writer who works with the Christ symbol, the novelist who employs allegory is not limited to the suggestion of a Christ through an occasional nuance; unlike the artist who draws Christ as a mythic archetype, he does not become involved in the problem of adapting Christ to a cultural pattern and thus forfeiting the immediate impact of the Christ of traditional religious faith. For while the Christ symbol and the Christ of myth take religious disbelief or at least suspension of belief for granted, the Christ allegory skirts the difficulty by presenting a figure who is so manifestly *a figure* that the doctrinal implications of Christ remain untouched. The very proximity to the doctrinal Christ combined with the alien setting reveal immediately the imaginative quality of the figure and render it innocent of the suspicion of "remaking" Christ. Whereas in myth the meaning grows out of the pattern of action, in allegory the action is the embodiment of some preconceived abstraction: the myth contains and encompasses meaning, but the allegory points directly to a meaning beyond and apart from its existence. In the admitted artificiality of allegory as an instrument rather than a creator of meaning lies its particular relevance as a vehicle for the Christ figure. The author who deals with the Christ allegory is free to follow closely the particulars of the Christ story disguised through the surface narrative and to rely upon the reader's familiarity with them to provide continuity and organization to the fundamental idea that enlivens the work.

Prominent use of the Christ figure in allegory appears in Melville's *Billy Budd* and in Faulkner's *A Fable*. Whether

Billy Budd is a full-fledged allegory or whether Billy himself is actually a Christ figure is open to argument, as the enormous diversity of interpretation testifies, but enough of the allegorical elements and sufficient parallels to the Christ story are present to at least open it for consideration from that standpoint. First, the abstraction that is to be dramatized through the allegory receives a prominent introduction in the short preface often ignored by critics. There Melville states his theme: in broadest terms it is the ultimate victory of good over evil, a belief that Melville was not yet willing to accept in *Moby Dick*. More specifically, it is that human cruelty and injustice are gradually conquered through the courageous protest and suffering of the underdog, even when the protest itself is corrupted by the excesses of the oppressed. He offers first the example of the French Revolution, then mentions the Great Mutiny within the English navy as a smaller action with an analogous effect. Finally the story of Billy Budd is the particular illustration of the theme. Through the Christ parallel, the attention to correspondences between Billy's tragic career and the Passion experiences of Jesus, the theme of victory over injustice through suffering is exemplified. The symbolism of names, Billy's fatal innocence, the symbolic characters (Claggart as evil, as the betrayer, as Judas; Vere as authority, as the judge bound by law, as Pilate), the trial and hanging reminiscent of Jesus' lead to the Christian allegorical version of the theme: Billy, like Christ, dies under the law to destroy the law; through his suffering and sacrifice, human justice, which has become the license for injustice, is tempered by mercy and grace.

A Fable contains a much more intricate allegorical design and execution. There is no doubt that the pacifist corporal is a World War I version of Christ. His background, the cast of characters around him, the sequence of events leading to his insubordination, trial, and death match point for point the career of Christ. Yet Faulkner's purpose is not simply, as he remarked, to show that if Christ appeared a second time he would be crucified a second time. *A Fable* contains in dialogue much of Faulkner's Nobel Prize speech, and the central theme of that address forms the text that the allegory illustrates:

man's inhumanity, individual and collective, is the greatest
threat to his survival, and his single hope is to oppose and
overcome the innate cruelty through a conscious exercise of
his capacity for compassion and sacrifice. Faulkner has pursued that theme throughout his career. It has been expressed
through the curse of slavery upon the southern Faulknerland;
it is behind the emergence of the inhuman Snopeses, who
have become that way through exploitation by a harsh aristoc-
racy; it informs the stories of individual passions, like those
of Temple Drake, Bayard Sartoris, and Dr. Wilbourne. In
A Fable, as in *Soldier's Pay* and some of the short stories,
Faulkner sets the theme in the context of war. There the
inhumanity assumes the form of organized but senseless killing.
The corporal as Christ protests, offering the alternative of
brotherhood instead. He is shot for his rebellion against
authority, but the martyrdom impresses its share of individuals
and the grave of the Unknown Soldier comes for a few to be
an ironic memorial of an individual's fraternal love instead of
a tribute to the corporate heroism of war. The Christ parallel
provides continuous reinforcement of the theme, reminding
one not particularly of the theological facets of the dichotomy
of the human spirit but of the fact that the struggle repeats
itself in history and that other men, like Christ, will have to
give themselves in the name of goodness.

The four possible modes of existence for the Christ figure
in fiction—as sign, myth, symbol, and allegory—demonstrate
what the figure is and is not. The Christ figure, apart from
the confused utilization of it as a sign by evangelical writers,
is never intended to supplant or even modify historical or
doctrinal views of Christ. The good writer of fiction is interested in the representational, in the metaphorical qualities of
Christ; he utilizes the accumulated connotative—not the
denotative—potential of the Christ story to reflect his own
values. Implicit in the work, and especially in the choice of
structural vehicle, may be a rejection or acceptance of Christianity, but the one or the other has no *direct* bearing upon
the substance of the figure. The writer must be granted the
right to treat the Christ with complete artistic and spiritual
independence. He may appropriate from the traditional Christ

the mythos at the most and a few characteristic traits at the least, depending upon the form his fiction takes, but he should never merely copy the Christ of the Christian faith.

The Christ Figure: Theological Possibilities

It would be foolish, at the same time, to ignore the obvious concern with faith and reality that any Western artist who chooses the Christ figure as his medium will reveal. The fact that the novelist who presents a Christ figure divorces himself from theological interpretations of Christ does not mean that he is free or wants to be free from contemplating Christ in terms of the absolute. As long as belief exists as it does, as long as the residue of Christian faith forms and supports, however unconsciously, Western values, the artist like any other individual will have to take a stand. He can never be simply indifferent to the Christian understanding of Christ; he must consider it as a possibility for interpreting his own existence. He is obliged to embody his values in his art; the mere choice of the Christ figure as his vehicle of expression says something common to his attitudes of personal belief and his objective portrayal of reality. Out of his work a general attitude appears that indicates whether or not he is inclined to believe at all. The novelist, choosing the Christ figure to represent his view of reality at a time when Christian faith is on the wane, indicates that he is most strongly interested in the contemporary problem of belief even though he cannot endorse the old orthodoxy through his art.

The writer who works with the figure is acutely aware of its emotive power. He must realize that the figure as he presents it will be misunderstood, will be confused with the Christ of faith or, at the other extreme, will elude recognition as a Christ figure altogether. That he persists in employing it in spite of those difficulties testifies to the seriousness of his search for meaning and his willingness to consider the way of Christ as the possible answer. Charles Glicksberg points to Kierkegaard and Dostoevski as examples of the seeking yet heretical creative personality, men wishing to affirm a positive reality but unable to do so by any means other than through

Laocoön: the representative of "tolerable hopelessness."[6] Why Laocoön? one asks. Why not Christ as the much more natural and fitting symbol of the contemporary situation, especially now that the fetish of lostness has disappeared and only the hardly-bearable fact of dislocation remains, begging for a new wholeness? Granted, it is not the orthodox Christ who will fill the role but Christ in his ambiguity, with whom man identifies himself both in his sin and in his hopes. It is not the slick Christ of Sallman's portrait, one is tempted to say, but the broken Christ of the paintings of Nolde and Rouault. Certainly that is a heretical view, but for modern man, who has lost his sense of the sacred, it may be the only view that possesses ultimate validity and a promise of salvation. The Christ figure which is not only to reflect the values of an optimistic secularism (that really exists only as a wistful, already outmoded dream), but is also to direct the way out of the secular trap, must embody both the depth and height of man. But more than that, it must substitute, in a manner something akin to the theological function of Christ himself, for man who has become too small even to be tragic anymore. Whether or not man in his desperation is ready to consider the possibility of Christ's unique mission and nature, and whether or not the artist can ever depict that uniqueness as a vital part of his fiction, the Christ figure as the image of man transcending his own worst character, losing his shadow through standing in a stronger light, can be considered as an alternative to the studied despair of the present.

THE CHRIST FIGURE AND THE NEW BEING

For the novelist who chooses to lean on his Christian heritage, the new interest in the Christ figure is a belated confirmation of what he has believed all along. He has understood the ascendency of faith in human reason over faith in a divine being as a temporary development and has observed the ensuing disenchantment with reason, the loss of faith in man, as the inevitable next step. The problem for the novelist is to rechannel the stream of the old Christian consciousness, which, as Amos Wilder remarks, has "gone underground," in order to concentrate its force upon the predominant attitude of alienation from meaning and being, upon the prevailing ontology of nothingness. Here the Christ figure can come to his aid as the image of what Paul Tillich, for example, has called the New Being.[7] In the New Being is the theological articulation of what certain writers have no doubt been striving toward, however blindly, in their fiction. For Tillich, symbol and reality are united in the New Being as Christ in a manner stimulating to the novelist's method and concern. The good writer has learned to avoid dramatizing faith because faith is not a category of the imagination. Similarly his Christ figures, which at their most significant lead up to the question of faith, can go no further and in fact always turn back to a representation of man. Tillich's New Being suggests one further step the novelist can take without trespassing the boundaries of fiction. Tillich's Christ as "essential manhood in existence" is not just another way of asserting the divine-human nature of Christ that cannot be fictionalized; it is a means of allowing man to view himself beyond the confines of his creatureliness. Christ as the New Being encompasses man's range of possibility, from the threat of non-being on the one hand to the promise and fulfillment of being on the other. If the modern novelist has been concerned with anything, it has been precisely the fear of nothingness (the threat of non-being) and the quest for a mode of being. If he can create, as the substance of his Christ figure, the individual who simply accepts the challenge to be, who decides for being in whatever situation, instead of languishing in neurotic despair or self-pity, instead of endlessly wavering between projected alternatives, he will have at least depicted man once again capable of experiencing the tragic and thereby able to think and act in a framework of ultimate values, even if they are the ones he develops through his own decisions. The novelist will not, in the process, sidestep the problem of faith, just as in his Christ figure he will not complete the equation of symbol and reality that Tillich accomplishes through his identification of Christ with the New Being. But he will have presented a figure which demands consideration of belief as the reader's response beyond the confines of the novel.

Nathan Scott, speaking of the responsibility of the Christian critic, has said that "it is in the athleticism of Christ's penetration of the finite that the literary imagination may find its most instructive norm."[8] The statement may hold as well for the novelist who considers himself open to the Christian interpretation of life. "Christ's penetration of the finite" is, of course, another way of explaining his incarnation. The novelist, unable to dramatize the incarnation, becomes aware of its significance all the more, so that in one sense the Christ figure can lead back to the central theme of Christian theology. The novelist, in shaping the Christ figure with the traits of Christ but in the image of man, has effected a secondary incarnation of his own. It is not a substitution for nor a pirated duplication of the incarnation of Christ in Jesus but, as befits its artistic nature, a symbolic operation that has as its model the Christian incarnation. The Christ figure at its most effective depicts man in his fallen state but at the same time with a nature and actions disturbing enough, reminiscent enough, of the paradox of Christ to cause one to rethink existence in terms of God and the designs that God may have upon one's life.

NOTES

1. Lewis' 1951 study, "The Hero in the New World," appeared in *Kenyon Review*, Vol. XIII (Autumn), 641–60. The quotation is from p. 660. The quotation from *The Picaresque Saint* (Philadelphia and New York, 1959) is on p. 215. Other significant studies on the Christ figure are: Alan Paton and Liston Pope, "The Novelist and Christ," *The Saturday Review of Literature*, Vol. XXXVII (December 4, 1954), 15–16, 56–59; Charles T. Dougherty, "The Christ-Figure in the Grapes of Wrath," *College English*, Vol. 24 (December, 1962), 224–226; and W. H. Auden's analysis of *Billy Budd* in *The Enchafèd Flood* (New York, 1950), pp. 144–154.

2. For a more thorough study of Christ and the Christ figure in the popular religious novels cf. my "Christ in American Religious Fiction," *The Journal of Bible and Religion*, Vol. XXXII (January, 1964), 8–14.

3. Studies dealing critically with the Christ figure according to various archetypal patterns are: Amos N. Wilder, *Theology and Modern Literature* (Cambridge, Mass., 1958); F. W. Dillistone, *The Novelist and the Passion Story* (London, 1960); Carlos Baker,

"The Place of the Bible in American Fiction," in *Religious Perspectives in American Culture*, James Ward Smith and A. Leland Jamison, eds. (Princeton, 1961), pp. 243–272; and Edwin M. Moseley, *Pseudonyms of Christ in the Modern Novel* (Pittsburgh, 1962).

4. Charles I. Glicksberg, *Literature and Religion* (Dallas, 1960), p. 56.

5. F. W. Dillistone, *The Novelist and the Passion Story*, p. 19.

6. R. W. B. Lewis, *The American Adam* (Chicago, 1955), p. 195.

7. Paul Tillich, *Systematic Theology*, Vol. II (Chicago, 1957), 118ff.

8. Nathan A. Scott, Jr., *Modern Literature and the Religious Frontier* (New York, 1958), p. 63.